JEWS AND THE GOSPEL
AT THE END OF HISTORY

Moishe Rosen in midlife. Pictures of Moishe in other stages
of life appear on part and chapter title pages throughout the book.

JEWS AND THE GOSPEL
AT THE END OF HISTORY

A Tribute to Moishe Rosen

JIM CONGDON

EDITOR

Kregel
Academic & Professional

CONTENTS

Part 3: Eschatology

TRIBUTE TO MOISHE ROSEN

Moishe Rosen's biography reads like a movie script or perhaps a page out of the Book of Acts. In any case, it is certainly not boring! It is an action-filled drama of faith, triumph, pain, and joy.

In 1950, when they were both eighteen, Moishe married his high school sweetheart, Ceil, who is also Jewish. Three years later, Ceil came to know Jesus and was instrumental in leading her husband to the Lord. And so, at the age of twenty-one, Moishe, the son of Jewish immigrants from Eastern Europe, gathered his family together to tell them the news: "I've been studying the Bible lately and I've decided that Jesus is really the Messiah. We've all been wrong and I wanted you to know that I'm going to believe in him and follow him and give my life to him."

The response that came from his father after hearing that somewhat abrasive announcement was equally jarring: "You can just get out of my house and don't come back until you've given up this Jesus business!"

I recall Moishe once telling me that his father went so far as to tell him that if for some reason they found themselves walking down the same street in Denver, where they both resided, he would expect Moishe to cross over to the other side so that he would not have to acknowledge his son's presence.

The estrangement from his family hurt; however, it didn't deter him from following his destiny. If anything, it brought him closer to his Messiah, who was "despised and rejected" by so many. Moishe immersed himself in the Scriptures, and never wavered from being a forthright teller of the truth of the gospel. He actually came to discover that he loved to tell others about Y'shua. He not only loved sharing his faith, he was truly gifted at witnessing.

In that first year, as he was devouring the Book of Acts for the second time, he read the words "I have declared to both Jews and Greeks that they must turn to God in repentance and have faith in our Lord Jesus" (Acts 20:21) and he knew that it was God's personal call to him, a message "more real than if I had audibly perceived His voice that God was speaking to me, calling me, telling me, that I was to be a witness to Jews and Gentiles."

Knowing he needed training to fulfill that call, in 1954 he applied and was enrolled at Northeastern Bible College in New Jersey, where he trained for the ministry. After graduation in 1957, he was ordained as a Conservative Baptist.

Moishe served for seventeen years with the American Board of Missions to the Jews. For ten of those years he carried out his missionary assignment in Los Angeles, heading up their work there. It was a fruitful ministry, and he was promoted to the position of director of recruiting and training, which brought him to their New York City headquarters. Though an apparently successful mission executive (it's been speculated that he was in line to lead that historic Jewish mission), he recognized that he was too far removed from the people he was called to reach. He got out from behind his desk and resolved to "make myself more vulnerable. Make myself visible. Go where the people were. And tell the message in terms people could understand."

It was 1969 and God was doing something unusual to reach Jewish people in the United States. And he was about to use Moishe Rosen in some unique ways. Moishe started spending time on the campuses of New York, listening and learning what was on the hearts of young Jewish people and how he might find ways to connect to their spiritual hunger. He even found the anti-war activists to be instructive with the communications methods they used to get their issue heard. It was then that Moishe developed broadside gospel tracts (tens of millions have been distributed) and traded in his black suit and tie for more friendly garb.

But it was in San Francisco, where there were rumblings of a movement of young Jewish people coming to Christ, that he came to see how God was indeed going to use him to impact a whole generation. Moishe visited the Bay Area in 1970 and through a set of circumstances found himself early one morning on a hill overlooking the city. When the fog lifted and the sun came up, it was, as he described it, "as though the buildings of San Francisco were in the sky, above clouds. And because of the reflection of the fog on the buildings, they were illuminated by the sun and completely golden." He heard from God through that incredible sight and had himself transferred (and demoted) from the New York headquarters to minister to the Jews of the San Francisco Bay Area.

Three years later, the Jews for Jesus organization was born. The story of Jews for Jesus has been documented in two books, *Jews for Jesus* by Moishe Rosen with Bill Proctor (1974) and *Not Ashamed: The Story of Jews for Jesus* by Ruth Tucker (1999).

Moishe Rosen's career as a missionary to the Jewish people and mentor to many has been characterized as cutting edge, creative, controversial, and consequential in shaping a whole generation of Jewish missionaries who have led tens of thousands of Jews to faith in the Jewish Messiah Y'shua. His vision for Jewish missions has always been larger than just the organization he founded. Moishe Rosen is an innovator of methods and strategies in Jewish evangelism and an appreciator and empowerer whose gifts have been used to lift the Lord high.

For the thirty-seven years I've been privileged to know him, I have seen him encourage the development of Jewish gospel music and the use of drama, art, and poetry in evangelism. When the Internet was barely being noticed, he was championing the development of a cybermissionary Jewish evangelism force. Moishe Rosen has instituted educational scholarships for Jewish believers in Jesus, spearheaded graduate education opportunities for missionaries on the field, helped to enable other Jewish ministries, advised countless Messianic leaders, and labored tirelessly to see a unified movement proclaiming the light of Messiah to the lost sheep of the house of Israel.

In 1986 Western Conservative Baptist Seminary in Portland, Oregon, recognized his achievements by granting him a Doctor of Divinity degree.

In 1996, at the age of sixty-four, Moishe stepped down as executive director of Jews for Jesus, making way for a younger generation to take the lead. He continues to serve faithfully on the staff of Jews for Jesus as well as on the organization's board of directors. In 1997, he was named "Hero of the Faith" by the denomination that ordained him forty years earlier.

A prolific writer, Moishe has written numerous evangelistic and teaching articles and more than fifty broadsides or gospel pamphlets. He is the author of *Sayings of Chairman Moishe* (1972), *Jews for Jesus* (1974), *Share the New Life with a Jew* (1976), *Christ in the*

Passover (1977), *Y'shua: The Jewish Way to Say Jesus* (1982), *Overture to Armageddon* (1990), *The Universe Is Broken: Who On Earth Can Fix It?* (1991), *Demystifying Personal Evangelism* (1992), *Witnessing to Jews* (1998), and a revised and expanded *Christ in the Passover* (2006).

Those of us who have served with Moishe Rosen are so pleased that this volume has been produced in his honor. It stems from deep respect, gratitude, and love for a man who has given much to see our Jewish people come to know our Jewish Messiah.

—Susan Perlman

PREFACE

Jewish people. The land of Israel. Evangelism. All three are dear to God and to his people. But all are under siege at the end of the first decade of the twenty-first century. Those who hate Israel and the Jews speak longingly of "the end of Jewish history." Even some who love Israel and the Jews oppose evangelism that would win them to Yeshua.

But Christians who read their Bibles know that when the end of history arrives, the Jews will be there. At that time they will look on him whom they pierced, repent, and be restored (Zech. 12:10). And until that day, those who truly love "the apple of God's eye" will want to introduce them to God's Messiah.

Some of today's leading scholars and theologians address issues of evangelism, ethics, and eschatology in this tribute to an elder statesman of Jewish evangelism, Jews for Jesus founder Moishe Rosen.

J. I. Packer argues from the book of Romans that we should glorify God, for the Jewish unbelief we witness today is simply the tragic but temporary part of God's wonderful plan that will eventuate in Jew-Gentile unity.

Also from Romans, the late Harold Hoehner demonstrates that if we wish to imitate the example of the apostle Paul, we will share his suffering due to a conviction that Jewish people need to acquire God's righteousness by faith.

Ruth Tucker compares Moishe Rosen with other colorful and lonely prophets God has used—Moses, Paul, St. Francis, Luther, Fox, Cartwright, Moody, and Norris—unconventional eccentrics all, whose contagious message won the day.

Steve Cohen completes the four chapters on Jewish evangelism by reminding us of a principle that has held true since the days of the first-century Jewish evangelists—that opposition brings opportunities for the gospel for those who are obedient to the Great Commission.

The second of Moishe Rosen's "favorite topics" is ethics in mission work. Kai Kjaer-Hansen suggests that we reassess how we judge the success and failure of a Jewish missionary, as illustrated by the example of Melchior Tschoudy.

From recent events in his country, John Reid of Australia argues that we must reject three modern ideas: that the gospel promises material prosperity; that Jewish people can be saved apart from Jesus; and that "tolerance enforcement" legislation is an acceptable limitation to gospel proclamation.

Tuvya Zaretsky concludes from his exhaustive research into Jewish-Gentile intermarriage that it presents a unique opportunity for evangelism, but requires a multidimensional, cross-cultural approach that stays faithful to the marital ethics of Scripture.

In an award-winning paper, young scholar Richard Harvey surveys the current state of Messianic Jewish thought, concluding that it is developing its own distinct expressions of the plural nature of God, the deity of Yeshua, and the place of Torah in messianic Jewish life.

The ethics section concludes with a short argument by Jim Congdon, based on the use of the enigmatic word *fulfill* by Jesus and Paul, that Torah-centered living is permissible but not required in this eschatological age of Christ.

Walter Kaiser's biblical study of Ezekiel 37 is the first of five chapters on the end times. Kaiser demonstrates that God's Promise-plan includes a future restoration of the nation Israel to her land.

Arnold Fruchtenbaum draws from all parts of Scripture to make his point that the Second Coming of the Messiah is preconditioned upon Israel confessing its rejection of him (the "unpardonable sin"), and pleading with him to return.

We must not divorce evangelism from eschatology, says Barry Horner, because the only fruitful motive for Jewish evangelism is the Pauline motive, which affirms rather than denies the Jewish national identity and destiny.

David Larsen joyfully notes that Jewish evangelization and conversion today foreshadow a glorious time of Jewish evangelization and conversion during the tribulation period at the end of this age.

David Brickner, Moishe Rosen's successor as executive director of Jews for Jesus, closes with the challenge that we must watch for and proclaim the return of Christ, for it is our blessed hope and the hope of the world.

CONTRIBUTORS

David Brickner (M.A., Fuller Theological Seminary) succeeded Moishe Rosen as the executive director of Jews for Jesus, and has served in the field of Jewish missions for more than thirty years. His books include *Future Hope: A Jewish Christian Look at the End of the World* and *Christ in the Feast of Tabernacles*.

Steve Cohen (M.A., Fuller Theological Seminary) served as a missionary with Jews for Jesus before establishing the Apple of His Eye Mission Society, a work he currently directs for the Lutheran Church–Missouri Synod. He is the author of *Win-Some Witnessing 101* and *Disowned*.

Jim Congdon (D. Min., Trinity Evangelical Divinity School) has served as senior pastor of Topeka Bible Church for the last thirty-one years and is chair of the U.S. board of directors of Jews for Jesus. He served as editor for this volume.

Arnold G. Fruchtenbaum (Ph.D., New York University) is founder and director of Ariel Ministries, which is dedicated to evangelism of Jewish people and discipleship of Jewish and Gentile believers. He has authored many books, including *The Footsteps of the Messiah* and *Messianic Christology*.

Richard Harvey (Ph.D., University of Wales) is tutor and director of training at All Nations Christian College. He is a member of the Lausanne Consultation on Jewish Evangelism and the European board of directors of Jews for Jesus. His writings include *A Jewish Approach to the Trinity* and *Mapping Messianic Jewish Theology: A Constructive Approach*.

Harold W. Hoehner (Th.D., Ph.D., Cambridge University) was Distinguished Professor of New Testament Studies at Dallas Theological Seminary and the author of *Chronological Aspects of the Life of Christ* and the definitive work, *Ephesians: An Exegetical Commentary*. He graduated to glory in 2009.

Barry E. Horner (D. Min., Westminster Theological Seminary) is pastor of Christ's New Covenant Church in Sahuarita, Arizona. His books include *Future Israel: Why Christian Anti-Judaism Must Be Challenged* and several works on the seventeenth-century Puritan, John Bunyan.

Walter C. Kaiser Jr. (Ph.D., Brandeis University) is the Colman M. Mockler distinguished professor of Old Testament and president emeritus of Gordon-Conwell Theological Seminary. His numerous books include *Hard Sayings of the Old Testament, A History of Israel,* and *The Messiah in the Old Testament.*

Kai Kjaer-Hansen (D.D., Lund University) is the international coordinator of the Lausanne Consultation on Jewish Evangelism, an umbrella agency for Jewish mission societies around the world. He edits the journal *Mishkan: A Forum on the Gospel and Jewish People.* He authored *Joseph Rabinowitz and the Messianic Movement: The Herzl of Jewish Christianity.*

David L. Larsen (D.D., Trinity College) is professor emeritus of preaching at Trinity Evangelical Divinity School. A pastor for thirty-two years, he has authored seventeen books, including *Jews, Gentiles, and the Church* and *Biblical Spirituality.*

J. I. Packer (D. Phil., Oxford University) was the Professor of Theology for thirty years at Regent College in Vancouver, British Columbia. He is one of the most important theologians and church historians of the modern era. A prolific writer, his books include *Knowing God* and *Evangelism and the Sovereignty of God.*

John R. Reid (B.A., University of Melbourne) before his retirement was Anglican bishop of South Sydney, NSW; Australia International Chairman of Interserve; Chairman of the Evangelical Fellowship of the Anglican Communion; and Chairman of the Lausanne Committee. He is the author of *Modern, Postmodern, and Christian* and *Marcus L. Loane: A Biography.*

Ruth Tucker (Ph.D., Northern Illinois University) was Associate Professor of Missions at Calvin Theological Seminary and has authored more than a dozen books, including *Not Ashamed: The Story of Jews for Jesus* and *From Jerusalem to Irian Jaya: A Biographical History of Christian Missions.*

Tuvya Zaretsky (D. Miss., Western Seminary) has served as a missionary with Jews for Jesus for thirty-five years and is their director of staff development. He also serves as president of the Lausanne Consultation on Jewish Evangelism. He has written *Jewish-Gentile Couples: Trends, Challenges and Hopes.*

PART 1
EVANGELISM

1

JEW AND GENTILE IN PAUL'S LETTER TO THE ROMANS

J. I. PACKER

R hetorical criticism, or receptor criticism as some call it, is a fairly recent addition to the armory of academic disciplines. Scholars deploy such criticism for exegesis of biblical documents, and it is in principle valuable. Rhetorical criticism applied to the Bible pursues two questions: Whom precisely does a writer have in mind as his readership? How did the effect that the writer wanted to produce on his audience influence his selection and presentation of material? This is legitimate, necessary, basic, and common-sense enquiry, for all serious writers whose purpose is to persuade have to think through these questions before they start composing, just as serious preachers have to keep their listeners in mind as they prepare their sermons. Indeed, all of us, when we have difficult and sensitive letters to write, have to think in these terms.

These questions thus lead us to the topic at hand—a consideration of Paul's letter to the Romans. This epistle has always been acknowledged as the nearest thing to a treatise on gospel faith and life that the apostle Paul ever wrote. In it, he addresses a church that did not know him, wishing to pave the way for an extended visit to them and for them in due course to support him in his projected mission to Spain. Further, he knew that in these churches he was seen as a highly controversial figure—a sort of maverick—for his fiercely anti-Judaizing theology. It is evident, therefore, that he planned to lay out before his Roman readers a detailed account of what he really taught in his evangelizing and discipling ministry, and to warn them in advance against errant alternatives. (See Rom. 1:10–15; 15:16–24; 16:17–20, 25–27.) Thus he aimed to clear the ground for fruitful fellowship with them in what he hoped would be the near future.

How to do it, however, called for careful and detailed planning. In broad terms, to be sure, the basic perspectival decisions were already made; they were established as fixed points for all of Paul's apostolic pastoral letters. He would write as a commissioned servant, indeed a bond slave, of Jesus Christ, a servant with spiritual authority in that he was under the double authority of God's reigning Son and God's revealed truth. He would write *Christocentrically*, displaying the exalted Jesus as Savior and Lord, the fulfillment of Old Testament promises and hopes; the reconciling mediator between God the Father and mankind; the rescuer of his people from sin's guilt and penalty by his atoning sacrifice, from sin's grip and power by his domination and fellowship through the Holy Spirit, and from sin's destiny of death by endless future joy with himself in his love.

Thus, Paul would also write *soteriologically*, exhibiting God's gift of grace as salvation from the past, in the present, and for the future, in and through Jesus Christ. Thus, too, Paul would write *eschatologically*, placing his readers' personal stories within God's ongoing story as he moves everything forward toward its preordained goal, and highlighting the hope of glorification that is guaranteed to every believer.

And he would write *doxologically*, making the glory of God—that is, adoring acknowledgment of God's glorious grace in the gospel—appear as the final goal. In style, he would be both *diatribal* (argumentative, analytical, didactic) as he expounded gospel truth, and *celebratory* as he contemplated it. So much, we may confidently say, was fixed in Paul's mind from the start, and the letter to the Romans undeniably fulfills this pattern.

In shaping his strategy for fulfilling these requirements in this particular case, did Paul know anything about the church, or group of house churches (see 16:5, 10, 14), in Rome to which this letter would in the first instance be read aloud? From the letter itself it is evident that he did. He knew that the church(es) contained both Jewish and non-Jewish believers, and that sharp tensions existed between at least some of them on two points. First, there were non-Jews who held what we today would call a replacement theology: God, they thought, had simply ended the era in which ethnic Israel was his chosen people, and was now focusing his favor on Gentile believers as his alternative (see 11:17–21). Second, some Jewish believers thought it right to eat kosher and keep the weekly Sabbath of the Old Testament. In response, some Gentile believers felt strong, sound, and superior for not behaving this way and knowing that they need not, and aimed critical arrows at their Semitic brothers and sisters (see 14:10–19).

How Paul came to know about all this we are not told, and it is not important. Clearly, any of the more than twenty friends in Rome whom he greets in Romans 16 might have been his informant or, equally clearly, it could have been someone else. What matters is that Paul did know, and was upset. He had, after all, a passion for Jewish-Gentile unity in Christ, despite their cultural diversities; he longed that his fellow Jews would receive the gospel, no matter how hardened Israel might be against Jesus; he bore the conviction that for God simply to give up on Israel would show him up as unfaithful and untrustworthy, a promise-breaker rather than a promise-keeper.

All these beliefs and feelings made Paul resolve to deal at length in his letter with both tension points. He would deploy lines of thought that should undercut the tensions and hopefully melt them away, and he would set forth his gospel is such a way as to maximize awareness that believing Jews and Gentiles are united together as brothers and sisters in Christ, now and forever. He settled his sequence of topics accordingly, and then dictated his letter to Tertius (16:22) with weight, strength, clarity, passion, intensity, verve, and what we might call personal command, which readers still find majestic and overwhelming to the last degree.

Romans, then, is in substance a carefully thought-out presentation of the main elements in Paul's gospel, so arranged as to draw its Jewish and non-Jewish Christian readers into full mutual acceptance of one another, and to lead both together into a life of deep faith, hope, love, and doxology. All is set in an explicitly Christ-centered frame within the implicitly trinitarian structure of all Paul's thinking about God, and all is exhibited as in one way or another fulfilling the Old Testament Scriptures.

A close inspection of Romans shows that, apart from its introduction and conclusion, the letter consists of four solid sequential blocks of teaching. These blocks are intended to be pastorally cumulative as follows:

First block (1:16–5:21): Paul proclaims a relational reversal. Against the backdrop of the universal sinfulness and guilt of both Jew and Gentile, and the consequent wrath and condemnation of God, Paul announces that God in righteousness for Jesus' sake justifies ungodly people who have faith—faith that trusts Christ's atoning achievement on the cross; that trusts God's promises related to it; that trusts God's love, which the Holy Spirit brings home to the heart; and that trusts God's Son, Jesus the risen Lord, whose disciples and followers believers become. Justification, paradoxically, means full present acceptance of believers as not penally liable and indeed as righteous, and Paul heightens the paradox by affirming that in justification God shows his righteousness, so that he appears as *"just and* the justifier" (3:26, emphasis added). How can this be? The answer is, through Christ's penal substitution for us on the cross, whereby propitiation (quenching of wrath) was achieved and pardon of sin made possible (3:25). Romans 5 celebrates the greatness of God's grace in all this, and the teaching of this block is meant to produce humble gratitude and devotion.

Second block (6:1–8:39): Paul announces personal transformation within the new relationship with God. Identifying with believers as one of them, as he began to do in 3:27, he affirms union with Christ in the latter's death and resurrection as a transcendent fact realized through baptism. He then shows in detail what and how this reality of union must and will lead to: a Spirit-empowered life of righteousness and holiness; a life of assured confidence that our prayers, however feeble they feel, will be heard and answered; a life of certainty that God will preserve us and love us forever; certainty that we shall share Christ's glory to all eternity. This teaching is meant to produce awareness that salvation in Christ is a new relationship that both entails and generates a new lifestyle, and to induce eagerness and effort in living out the supernaturalized selfhood that Christ creates in each of his disciples.

Third block (9:1–11:36): Paul laments stubborn unbelief on Israel's part when confronted with the gospel. In face of this negativity, however, he affirms God's unchanging sovereignty and unbroken faithfulness to his own word, and on that basis looks ahead to a great ingathering of Jews into the believing community at some future date. And he praises God for the still unfolding wisdom of his mercy in saving first Gentiles and then Jews out of an equal state of unbelief and exclusion from blessing, by exactly parallel means—namely, by making them realize their personal need (partly out of envy at seeing what blessing others receive), and so leading them to appreciate what God is offering them in Christ. This teaching is meant to renew Christians' gratitude for grace and prompt constant praise for their own salvation.

Fourth block (12:1–15:13): Paul enforces Christian ethics. These include the ethic of ministry, of neighborliness, of citizenship, of living in hope, and of practicing fellowship together, with full forbearance over differences on secondary matters. He starts by calling on Christians to show gratitude for grace by consecrating themselves to God's service and ends by summoning both Jews and Gentiles explicitly to united and uniting celebration of God's act of bringing them together. They are to praise, rejoice, and hope as one. This teaching is meant to ensure that behavior in the church(es) will always honor Christ at all points, and that, motivationally, Christian hearts will always be in the right place.

If these blocks were labeled *through Christ, in Christ, without Christ,* and *under Christ,* respectively, their emphases and thrust would be well caught.

How, though, did Paul's purpose of bonding Jewish and non-Jewish Christians at Rome in a common life of loving mutuality, beyond inner tensions and divisions, affect his choice and presentation of the truths that he had to tell, and that he wanted to tell, as his personal introduction to them? In recognizing the teachings contained in the four blocks of Romans, as sketched out above, our task is already half done. When it comes to the details, however, more needs to be said.

The first block is foundational to the other three. In it, Paul repeatedly affirms, drumbeat-style, the togetherness of Jews and non-Jews (euphemistically called "Greeks" in 1:14,16; 2:10; 3:9, otherwise "Gentiles" [*ethne*, nations], 1:13; 2:14; 3:29) regarding everything with which God is now confronting the world: his saving power (1:16); his condemnation and future retribution, something that merely possessing and knowing Scripture and being circumcised does not affect (2:9–13; 2:24–3:4); his gracious effecting of justification through faith, as in the paradigm cases of David and Abraham (3:29–30; 4).

In Romans 5, Paul assumes that his togetherness point is accepted, and so he rounds off this block of teaching. He does so first with a description of the life of present peace, joy, and confident hope that "we"— that is, all justified believers—now enjoy (5:1–11). He then contrasts the ruin that Adam's transgression brought on all humanity with the riches that Christ's obedience has secured for all who believe, in whose lives grace now reigns (5:12–21). Each block rises to a doxological climax; here, the climax is celebration of how believers, who were once as low, as wretched, and as hopeless as anyone can imagine, are how high, privileged, and gloriously destined beyond the best that anyone can conceive. Now grace reigns "through [Christ's] righteousness leading to eternal life through Jesus Christ our Lord" (5:21)—praise God!

But why does Paul so laboriously go over this ground? Currently, debate rages about this. Some argue that Paul's primary purpose, already in this first block, is to make an ecclesiological rather than a soteriological point; that is, to insist to his Roman readers that God through Christ has brought them all into a single community of equals—saved sinners, justified by faith, given the gift of righteousness (5:17–19)—and has set aside for ever the "boundary markers," the ceremonial observances of Old Testament law, which had previously kept Jews and Gentiles separate from each other.

But this purpose, at this stage of the argument, is not yet in view, though foundations for achieving it are being solidly laid. Rather, Paul's concern so far is to declare, as vividly and weightily as he can, the astounding reality of how the holy, wrath-threatening divine judge engineered the sacrificial death of his Son so that he might pardon, accept, and eternally enrich ungodly sinners. Paul is actually proclaiming his gospel, rather than pursuing a corollary of it before he has properly stated it.

So I urge that while the phrase "works of the law" (by which none will be justified, 3:20, 28) certainly includes the boundary markers, that is, not, as has been argued, the whole or main part of its meaning. The virtually unanimous verdict of scholars from Luther till very recently was right; this phrase covers all God's requirements of motivation, desire, and performance, across the board—the comprehensive standard, that is, of which everyone falls so ruinously short.

And I do not, with some moderns, take the phrase "the righteousness of God" (1:17; 3:21; 10:3) to signify simply God fulfilling his Old Testament promise to incorporate faithful Gentiles into Israel's faithful remnant. The most natural meaning of the Greek phrase is dynamic, expressing the idea of God acting righteously, that is, doing what is recognizably right and totally praiseworthy now that he has done it. When Paul says that the righteousness of God is revealed in the gospel (1:17), he means that the acting of God that the gospel proclaims has this quality: both his future action in universal retributive righteous judgment (2:5, cf. vv. 6–16) and also, against that background, his present action of pardoning and accepting believing sinners on the basis of Christ's sacrificial death, "show his righteousness . . . that he might be just and the justifier of the one who has faith in Jesus" (3:26). Both actions display the righteousness of God. By this stunning exhibition of mercy to the undeserving, God fulfills Old Testament Scripture in several respects. One of them is bonding Jew and Gentile together in Christ as the people of God, but which is a corollary aspect of the revelation of God's righteousness and is not part of what the immediate context sets before us as the primary reference points of the phrase.

Throughout the letter, Paul assumes, reasonably enough, that his Roman readers, whose faith he has already celebrated (1:8), need no topical instruction on faith, nor does he offer any. But we can build up his idea of faith from his passing references to it. Faith is *cognitive*—recognizing and receiving revelation and responding to it (1:17). Faith is *confessional*—focusing upon and witnessing to the reality of the person, the resurrection, and present life, and lordship of Jesus Christ (10:8–13). Faith is *Christ-dependent*—totally relying on what Christ in mercy has done for us (3:25; 4:24–25). Faith is *calling*, praying constantly to Christ, honoring his lordship and invoking his love. Faith is *confident* that God through Christ will keep all the gracious promises that he has made (4:16–25). And faith is *committed* to serve Christ, according to one's discernment of his will (14:18; see the whole chapter). Such is the justifying faith that Paul has in mind throughout.

The second block delineates the Christian's new life in Christ; nothing in it touches on Jew-Gentile tensions. In the third block, however, almost everything does. Here Paul's aim is to show that, so far is God's Word from proving false and God himself appearing unfaithful and untrustworthy, God's planned future for Israel is beginning to be realized. Paul is sure that at least some of Rome's non-Jewish Christians are preening themselves, thinking, "Branches were broken off [from God's original olive tree] so that I might be grafted in" (11:19), and he wants to squelch the supposition that what this fact reveals on God's part is Gentile favoritism displacing Jewish favoritism.

Paul's reflective, corrective, self-involving, doxological discussion is complex and nuanced throughout this block. The following outline nonetheless attempts to catch the flow and thrust of his argument.

a. A *sad situation*. The Jews, to whom were given privileges and promises leading up to Christ, do not at present believe (9:1–5).

b. A *thesis*. God's word (to Israel, concerning Israel) is not hereby proved false (9:6).

c. A *reminder*. God has in the past chosen and called some Israelites to privilege and mercy from which he excluded others (9:6b–13).

d. An *assertion*. God is free to decide on whom he will have mercy and whom he will harden, and in this there is no injustice, since nobody has any claim against God in this matter (9:14–18).

e. A *denial*. No one may criticize God's condemnation of those whom he has hardened, for (1) creatures may not find fault with their Creator and (2) God has in this case been patient with the wickedness of the wicked in order to show the mercy that he now shows to the Jews and Gentiles whom he calls to faith (9:19–28).

f. An *assessment*. Gentiles have attained righteousness before God by faith; Jews have failed here through aiming at works-righteousness and not seeing Christ as the sole source of righteousness (9:30–10:4).

g. An *analysis*. The way of righteousness by works is living by doing. The way of righteousness by faith is eschewing doing and believing in Christ as risen Lord and Savior (10:5–13).

h. A *reminder*. An elect remnant of Israelites exists, as in Elijah's day (11:1–10).

j. A *mystery* (a present revelation of God's once secret plan). As Israel's fall occasioned blessing for Gentiles, so mercy to Gentiles is meant to bring blessing to Israel (11:11–32).

   i. Israel's return to God would bless the world (11:11–15).

   ii. Paul highlights his apostleship to the Gentiles to provoke Israelites to faith (11:13–14).

   iii. Israel remains God's holy people (11:16).

   iv. Gentile Christians should not despise unbelieving Jews, whose place in the church on earth (God's olive tree) these Christians now occupy, but rather should take care lest they, too, fall by unbelief (11:17–24).

   v. Gentile Christians should look forward to a restoration of Jews to faith, occasioned by envy of God's mercy to Christians (11:25–32).

k. A *doxology*. Glory to God for the unguessable wisdom that his sovereign ways have revealed in this matter of Jew-Gentile togetherness (11:33–36).

Paul's pastoral goals in these chapters are clear. First, he wants all the Roman Christians, both Jewish and non-Jewish, to see Israel's unbelief as a biblically explicable episode, tragic but temporary, in God's ongoing dealings with Abraham's national family. He calls on Jews and

Gentiles both—of the former, those who, like him, felt terrible about it, and of the latter, those who, "wise in your own conceits" (11:25 ASV; "proud about yourselves," NLT), saw it as an appropriate reversal of Israel's former claim to exclusive superiority—to learn that God's way of bringing mercy home to sinners is first to make them realize that by their disobedience they have forfeited all claim on his mercy, so that now it comes to them by free grace and that alone (11:30–31).

Second, he wants them all to see that, so far from being brought down in flames by this development now in process, the scriptural word of God, which actually patterned and foretold it, is being fulfilled by it through the sovereign faithfulness of God himself. Third, as the first two blocks led in closing to doxological celebration, so now Jewish and Gentile believers should together join Paul in celebratory doxology, glorifying God for his wisdom in what is happening (11:33–36).

In the fourth block, Paul speaks to divergences between, and doubtless also within, the Jewish and Gentile constituencies in the Roman church fellowship with regard to eating or not eating particular foodstuffs and observing or not observing particular holy days. Rather than attempting to adjudicate who is right and who is wrong, Paul insists that within the fellowship other people's convictions on secondary—that is, non-soteric—matters must be respected and their practices accepted, or their personal discipleship to Christ the Lord, which is the really important thing here, will be vitiated. Pride, too, will creep in to corrupt the hearts of those who rejoice in not needing to keep these rules and restrictions—thus, be warned! (See Rom. 14.) Jewish-Gentile unity in and under Christ—humble, grateful, joyful, faithful, and watchful—remains Paul's central concern, right to the end of his argumentation (15:1–16). The last thing he wants is that he, as God's appointed apostle to the Gentiles, should ever appear to be putting Jewish Christians down, and all through the writing of Romans he has been bending over backward to ensure that this will not happen.

We do not know whether Paul's letter succeeded in lowering tensions and advancing faith, hope, love, devotion, and doxology at Rome in the way that he wanted it to do. But my immediate hope is that the preceding survey of his pastoral strategy as he wrote it may help to produce these effects in the turbulent world of evangelical church life today. And then, to God be the glory! Amen.

2

PAUL'S PASTORAL CONCERN FOR THE JEWISH PEOPLE

HAROLD W. HOEHNER

Although the book of Romans addresses primarily a Gentile audience, Paul also directs much interest toward the Jewish people. First, within the context of judgment—after he notes in 1:18–3:20 the degradation of all mankind, which necessitated justification—Paul in 2:17–3:8 points directly to the Jews. Unlike the Gentiles, they had been privileged to have the Law and the specific sign of the covenant, that is, circumcision. They too, however, were in need of justification. Second, in the discussion of weak and strong believers (14:1–15:13), some of the weak believers addressed were most likely Jewish believers. Two specific issues are mentioned in this discussion: one concerns food—what should or should not be eaten; the other concerns special days and which, if any, should be observed (14:2–6). Third, of Jewish interest, a significant portion of the book (9:1–11:36) demonstrates how the Jewish people fit into God's overall program.

Some feel, however, that Romans 9–11 is not important or is not easily explained. Some time ago, for example, I passed a well-known evangelical church in Dallas. The announcement on the marquee indicated a study of Romans 1–8, 12–16, excluding Romans 9–11! Not only does this exclusion omit a significant portion of the book in volume and in theological content, but also it breaks the continuity of Paul's thought. The importance of this interruption in Paul's arguments can be demonstrated by referring to the last portion of Romans 8, namely, verses 31–39. There, Paul discusses the believers' security in Christ. He assures them that they are under the protective care of the Father and that no one can lay a legitimate charge against them. Nothing, in fact, can separate believers from the love of Christ, whether it be hardship, distress, persecution, famine, nakedness, peril, or sword. Paul reinforces this security by saying that neither terrestrial nor celestial powers and persons are able to separate believers from the love of God in Christ Jesus our Lord.

These declarations left on their own could cause some to question whether or not such promises can be trusted. Did God, in fact, keep his promises to Israel? Chapters 9–11 are critical to this inquiry. In Romans 9:6–29, Paul argues that while in the past God rejected Israel, he did keep his promises to her. By way of clarification Paul notes in verses 6–13 that God's promises to Israel were not to every descendant of Abraham but only to Abraham's seed, namely, those who are related to Abraham not only physically but also spiritually (not all Israel is Israel—9:6). Thus, God's promises are to only believing Jews who are called the children of promise (9:8). Paul makes the case that God is not unjust for not including every Israelite because he did extend mercy to the remnant, the promised seed (9:14–29).

Does this render God or, for that matter, Paul, merciless? Not at all, for Paul shows that Israel rejected God and his provision of a right standing before him by faith in the person and work of the Messiah. That rejection was, in fact, ongoing throughout her history (9:30–10:21). After an extended discussion of God's election of the promised seed (9:6–29) and Israel's rejection of God's provision of a right standing before him by faith apart from works (9:30–33), Paul expresses his heart's desire and prayer to God that Israel might be saved (10:1).

That expressed desire leads to an intriguing question: Why should one pray for the salvation of Israel when God's election of the promised seed within Israel has already been determined? Notably, Romans 10:1 is the one verse that indicates that believers need to pray for the salvation of unbelievers! Prayer is a means by which God chooses to accomplish his purposes.

All of the above observations are preceded by Romans 9:1–5, the passage now to be discussed, which I present in honor of a friend and colleague in the ministry. Moishe Rosen, the founder of Jews for Jesus, has a deep and abiding pastoral concern for his kinsmen, the Jewish people.

Before delving into Roman 9–11, however, a synopsis of Romans 1–8 will set the stage.

THE SETTING
Introduction (Rom. 1:1–17)

Paul begins his letter to the Romans by stating that he had heard of their testimony of faith, which was known around the world, and that he had long intended to come to Rome, where he desired to use his spiritual gift to strengthen them in their faith. In turn, he hoped that they, too, would share their gift(s) for the purpose of mutual growth. He was convinced that he was a debtor both to Greeks and barbarians and was therefore eager (ready, willing) to proclaim unashamedly the gospel to them because (*gar*) it is God's power for salvation to everyone who believes, to the Jew first and also to the Greek because (*gar*) the righteousness of God is revealed in the gospel. That righteousness is obtained by faith, for it was designed for faith—not for works (*ek pisteoœs eis pistin*)—just as it is written "the just shall live by . . . faith" (Hab. 2:4 KJV).

The Need of Righteousness (Rom. 1:18–3:20)

Paul develops the argument that all mankind is in need of obtaining righteousness for a right standing before God. He demonstrates that the unrighteous fall far short of God's righteousness (1:18–32). Even the moralist who thinks that he is better than the unrighteous falls short of God's righteous standard (2:1–16). The Jews, however (2:17–3:8), considered themselves better than both the unrighteous and the moralist and claimed that they were acceptable to God on the basis that they alone had God's law (Mosaic Law). Nevertheless, while indeed having the Law, they had dishonored God by transgressing it and thus were unacceptable to him. More importantly the Jews felt that they were acceptable to God because around 590 years before the giving of the Law, the rite of circumcision had been introduced as the sign of God's covenant with his people. Paul was quick to point out that their circumcision had become only external and not an inward reality, this also rendering them unacceptable to God. He concludes that all are under the domain or power of sin—both Gentiles and Jews—and hence unacceptable in light of God's righteous standard.

Justification by Faith (Rom. 3:21–5:21)

With great detail and logic, Paul next discusses justification or a right standing before God. First, he explains justification as an act of God whereby he declares the sinner righteous on the basis of grace by means of faith in God (3:21–31). Justification was accomplished as a result of God's satisfaction (propitiation) with Christ's payment for sin (redemption) at the cross. Hence, one can obtain righteousness by simply believing in what God accomplished in the person and work of Christ at the cross. Paul uses the lives of Abraham and David to illustrate that simple faith in God's provision of justification predated the cross (4:1–25). He then develops the argument that justification by faith alone—explained in 3:21–31 and illustrated in 4:1–25—is sufficient to carry believers through the turmoil of earthly life as well as save them from eternal wrath, accomplished by Christ's life of intercession and advocacy, namely, reconciliation (5:1–11). Moreover, believers will be ushered into eternal life because they are identified with the correct head, not Adam but Christ (5:12–21).

Sanctification by Faith (Rom. 6:1–8:39)

Sanctification inexorably follows justification. Although distinguishable, they are inseparable, just as a head and torso are distinguishable but inseparable. If a person shows no evidence of sanctification there is reason to doubt that the person has undergone justification. Romans 6 points out that the believer has died to sin, although sin itself has not died and desires to control the believer. Romans 7 declares that the believer has died to the Mosaic Law and thus is not to use the Law as a means to sanctification. It makes clear that one cannot, even though a believer in Christ, sanctify himself or herself by the flesh. Romans 8 emphasizes that the believer can be sanctified only by means of the Holy Spirit. In the concluding portion of this chapter, verses 31–39, Paul demonstrates that the believer's security is in Christ alone. Nothing shall separate us from the love of God in Christ whether it be celestial or terrestrial powers, things of the present or future times, or anything else in creation.

As I mentioned earlier, some might question these assertions, claiming that God had not kept his covenants with Israel. The specific promises God made in the Abrahamic covenant were a promised land, seed, and blessing (Gen. 12:1–4; 15:1–7; 17:1–8). The promise of land is further developed in Genesis 13:14–18. The seed aspect, namely, the Messiah, is further extrapolated in the Davidic covenant (2 Sam. 7:12–16; 23:5; 2 Chron. 17:12–14; Pss. 89:3–4; 27–37, 49; 132:11–12; Isa. 9:6–7; Jer. 23:5–6; 33:14–17, 20–21; Ezek. 36:23–36; Hos. 3:4–5). The blessing aspect is elaborated on in the new covenant, particularly the forgiveness of sin, regeneration, and the outpouring of the Holy Spirit (Jer. 31:31–34; Ezek. 37:21–28).

If God has not kept his promises to Israel, then can we be sure that he will keep his promise that we will never be separated from the love of God in Christ? This is why Paul stops at the end of Romans 8 and does not continue immediately with the application given in Romans 12:1–15:13. Paul explains in Romans 9–11 that God has not failed to keep his promises to Israel. As already noted, Paul expresses his concern for the Jewish people in Romans 9:1–5, the central passage for this present discussion.

PAUL'S PASTORAL CONCERN
Paul's Grief over Israel's Rejection of God's Righteousness (Rom. 9:1–5)
STATEMENT OF HIS SORROW (ROM. 9:1–2)

Paul states, "I speak the truth in Christ—I am not lying; my conscience bears me witness in the Holy Spirit—that I have great sorrow and unceasing anguish in my heart" (ESV). As mentioned above, Paul concludes Romans 8:31–39 with the promise that no believer will ever be separated from the love of God in Christ. He begins this section by expressing his grief for Israel's unbelief. This is not parenthetical, but instead anticipates the possible suggestion that God has failed to keep his promises to the nation Israel. That he begins this section without a conjunction may well indicate, as Godet notes, a "lively emotion which breaks, so to speak, the logical bond; but this form attests at the same time with all the more energy the profound relation of feeling which unites this piece to the preceding."[1] Paul emphatically states, positively, that he is speaking the truth and, negatively, that he is not lying.

This claim of speaking the truth in a positive sense is not unlike that of 2 Corinthians 12:6 and also appears in classical literature, the difference from classical literature being that the claim here is made "in Christ."[2] To lie in the presence of Christ would be unthinkable.[3] The negative assertion that he is not lying is also stated in 2 Corinthians 11:31 and as well as in classical literature[4] but in the present passage, he substantiates that he is telling the truth and not lying by connecting his integrity of conscience with the Holy Spirit's[5] witness. Since one's conscience can become seared, it is imperative that it must be tempered by the Holy Spirit, the third person of the Trinity. In brief, then, he is speaking the truth in Christ propelled by his conscience and verified by the witness of the Holy Spirit.

The content of the truth is given in verse 2, namely, that (hoti) Paul was experiencing great sorrow and unceasing anguish in his heart. The depth of his concern is seen in the vocabulary utilized

---

1. F. Godet, *Commentary on St. Paul's Epistle to the Romans*, trans. A. Cusin, rev. and ed. Talbot W. Chambers (New York: Funk & Wagnalls, 1883); reprinted under the title *Commentary on the Epistle to the Romans* (Grand Rapids: Zondervan, 1956), 338.
2. Robert Jewett, assisted by Roy Kotansky, *Romans: A Commentary*, ed. Eldon Jay Epp, Hermeneia—A Critical and Historical Commentary on the Bible, ed. Helmut Koester et al. (Minneapolis: Fortress Press, 2006), 557.
3. Leon Morris, *The Epistle to the Romans* (Grand Rapids: Eerdmans, 1988), 346.
4. Jewett, *Romans*, 557.
5. In Greek it is a dative of association, see Daniel B. Wallace, *Greek Grammar Beyond the Basics: An Exegetical Syntax of the New Testament* (Grand Rapids: Zondervan, 1996), 160.

here. The first term, *lypeō,* occurs forty-seven times in the LXX (nineteen times in the canonical books), sixteen times in the New Testament, nine times in Paul's writings, only here in Romans, and denotes physical pain (Gen. 3:16–17; John 16:21) and emotional suffering, thus, "sorrow, grief" (Gen. 42:38; John 16:20, 22; 2 Cor. 2:1, 3, 7).[6] The second word, *odyneō,*[7] used sixty-eight times in the LXX, fifty-six times in the canonical books, and only twice in the New Testament (Rom. 9:2; 1 Tim. 6:10), denotes physical pain (Exod. 3:7; Ps. 31:11) and mental pain or grief, hence, "distress" (Gen. 44:31; Rom. 9:2; 1 Tim. 6:10). Not only are these two words emotively filled synonyms, but also they are reinforced by two powerfully descriptive adjectives designed to intensify Paul's expression of grief. His "great" sorrow and "unceasing, constant" anguish indicate that there was never a day that it did not weigh on him in his innermost being ("in my heart"). It was obviously not superficial or transitory but rather an abiding condition. Such anguish of the soul is typical among the Old Testament prophets (Jer. 4:19; 14:17; Dan. 9:3).[8]

Why has Paul so strongly stressed his concern for Israel? Is it, as suggested by Moo, that since he was an apostle to the Gentiles, defending freedom from the Mosaic Law, he had gained the reputation of being anti-Jewish?[9] To some extent this is suggested when the Jews allegedly accuse Paul of saying "Let us do evil so that good may come of it" (see Rom. 3:8). This probably refers to evil in a general sense, but to the Jewish person any disobedience of the Law was doing evil.

---

6. Walter Bauer, *A Greek-English Lexicon of the New Testament and Other Early Christian Literature,* rev. and ed. Frederick William Danker, 3rd ed. (Chicago: University of Chicago Press, 2000), 604–5; R. Bultmann, "λύπη, κτλ.," in *Theological Dictionary of the New Testament,* ed. Gerhard Kittel, trans. and ed. Geoffrey W. Bromiley (Grand Rapids: Eerdmans, 1967), 4:313–22; and Hermann Haarbeck and Hans-Georg Link, "Lament, Sorrow, Weep, Groan [λυπέω, λυπέομαι, λύπη]," in *The New International Dictionary of New Testament Theology,* ed. Colin Brown, trans. G. H. Boobyer et al. (Grand Rapids: Zondervan, 1976), 2:419–21.
7. Bauer, *Greek-English Lexicon,* 692; and Friedrich Hauck, "ὀδύνη, ὀδυνάομαι," in *Theological Dictionary of the New Testament,* ed. Gerhard Friedrich, trans. and ed. Geoffrey W. Bromiley (Grand Rapids: Eerdmans, 1967), 5:115.
8. James D. G. Dunn, *Romans 9–16,* Word Biblical Commentary, ed. David A. Hubbard and Glenn W. Barker; New Testament ed. Ralph P. Martin (Dallas: Word, 1988), 38B:524.
9. Douglas J. Moo, *The Epistle to the Romans,* New International Commentary on the New Testament, ed. Gordon D. Fee (Grand Rapids: Eerdmans, 1996), 556.

Some even thought that Paul had dismissed the Mosaic Law and encouraged evil.

This argument, however, does not hold. He had already clearly stated in Romans 8:2–4 that the law of the Spirit of life in Christ Jesus had made him free from the law of sin and death, and that God had sent his son to condemn sin in the flesh so that the righteous requirements of the Law might be fulfilled in us who do not walk according to the flesh but according to the Spirit. Hence, he was not anti-Jewish but very concerned for his kinsmen.

Rather, it is best to view his abiding anguish in light of chapters 9–11. His deep concern was over Israel's rejection of a right standing before God through the person and work of the Messiah Christ Jesus. That is the cause for his concern, well delineated in Romans 9:30–10:21, where he describes Israel's rejection of God's way of salvation. He begins by noting that the Gentiles, who did not pursue righteousness, did obtain (*katalambanō*) it by faith (9:30) whereas Israel pursued the law of righteousness but did not attain (*phthanō*) it (9:31–32). These two verbs are very close in meaning, but there is a subtle difference. The first verb (*katalambanō*) means "to attain definitively,"[10] thus "to obtain, seize." Though the Gentiles did not pursue righteousness, they did obtain God's righteousness because it was obtained by faith and not by self-effort. The second verb (*phthanō*) has the idea "to get to or reach a position" or particularly "to come to or arrive at a particular state" and thus "to attain."[11] In the present context, Israel pursued a law of righteousness but did not attain the Law. The "Law" is a reference to the Mosaic Law,[12] and Paul states that even though Israel pursued the law of righteousness, she failed to achieve righteousness through obedience to the Law.[13] Literally, the Greek states that Israel has not attained unto (*eis* indicates goal or direction) the Law. Why? Because Israel pursued righteousness not by faith but by works or self-effort (9:32). Paul agonizes that Israel had stumbled

---

10. G. Delling, "καταλαμβάνω," in *Theological Dictionary of the New Testament*, 4:10. Cf. Bauer, *Greek-English Lexicon*, 519–20.

11. Bauer, *Greek-English Lexicon*, 1053; Gottfried Fitzer, "φθάνω, προφθάνω," in *Theological Dictionary of the New Testament*, ed. Gerhard Friedrich, trans. and ed. Geoffrey W. Bromiley (Grand Rapids: Eerdmans, 1974), 9:90.

12. See Moo, *Romans*, 622–24.

13. Jewett, *Romans*, 610.

right over Messiah, who was planted in Zion, when all they had to do was to believe in him, thus not be put to shame (9:32–33). Ignoring God's way of righteousness obtained by faith, they continued to seek to establish their own righteousness (10:1–4).

Paul reinforces this assertion by noting that one cannot attain righteousness by one's own efforts but can obtain the righteousness of God by simply believing. All those in Israel needed to do for salvation was to confess that Jesus is Lord (not Beelzebul) and believe that God (Yahweh) had raised him from the dead and they will be saved (10:5–13). Israel must believe the message that has come to them (10:14–16). Paul then negates two possible reasons for Israel's lack of response. First, is it possible that the message had not reached them? To this he responds by declaring that the message had gone throughout the inhabited world. Or was it perhaps that Israel did not understand the message? Paul responds to this conjecture by pointing out that even Gentiles understood the message. He concludes that the Jews' refusal of the message was neither because they did not hear nor that they did not understand, but because of their disobedience and stubbornness (10:17–21).

Through his grief, Paul would have been reminded of his own initial rejection of the truth. He himself had refused the message of a right standing before God through Jesus Christ. He had not only witnessed and approved the martyrdom of Stephen (Acts 7:54–8:1) but also had violently persecuted the church (Acts 9:1–2; 22:4–5; 26:9–12; 1 Cor. 15:9; Gal. 1:23) because he did not believe the claims of Christ as the Messiah. On the way to Damascus to persecute more Christians, he was intercepted by Christ, who appeared to Paul and asked him, "Why do you persecute me?" (Acts 9:5 NIV). Only then did Paul come to realize that Jesus truly was the Messiah (Acts 22:6–16; 26:13–18) and began to proclaim him (Acts 9:19–30; 26:19–20; Gal. 1:15–16). It took this remarkable traumatic event to get Paul's attention, bringing him from disobedience to obedience, becoming a slave to Christ, and as such, an apostle to the Gentiles!

Yet, though an apostle to the Gentiles, he was still deeply concerned for fellow Israelites. He saw them obstinate, as he had been obstinate, and longed for them to obtain a right standing before God through Jesus, the Messiah. In Acts 9:2; 18:25–26; 19:9, 23; 22:4, 14, the Christian movement was called the "Way,"[14] and formerly Paul had persecuted those who belonged to the Way, but upon conversion he recognized that the Way indicated the "way" to God's righteousness, in other words, to be fully accepted by God. To his great sorrow and unceasing anguish, most of the Jews rejected this way of righteousness as he had done before he came face to face with the one whom he persecuted—the way, the truth, and the life, through whom is the only way to the Father (John 14:6).

Reason for His Sorrow (Rom. 9:3–5)

Paul now gives the reason (*gar*) for his sorrow. Paul's response to his sorrow is stated in verse 3: "For I could wish [or pray] that I myself were accursed, separated from Christ for the sake of my brothers, my kinsmen according to the flesh." First, the verb "to wish" (*euchomai*) occurs eighty-four times in the LXX (sixty-two times in the canonical books), and seven times in the New Testament (Acts 26:29; 27:29; Rom. 9:3; 2 Cor. 13:7, 9; James 5:16; 3 John 1:2) and most often means "to pray."[15] Second, the noun "accursed" (*anathema* or *anatheœma*), appearing twenty-seven times in the LXX (twenty-three times in the canonical books), and seven times in the New Testament (Luke 21:5; Acts 23:14; Rom. 9:3; 1 Cor. 12:3; 16:22; Gal. 1:8–9), can mean "votive offering" (2 Macc. 2:13; Luke 21:5) but most often means "cursed, accursed" or "to be delivered up to divine destruction."[16] In this context to be accursed or cursed means to be separated or cut off from

---

14. Bauer, *Greek-English Lexicon*, 691–92; Wilhelm Michaelis, "ὁδός, κτλ.," in *Theological Dictionary of the New Testament*, 5:88–89; and Günther Ebel, "Way, Road, Highway, Way of Life [ὁδός]," in *The New International Dictionary of New Testament Theology*, ed. Colin Brown, trans. G. H. Boobyer et al. (Grand Rapids: Zondervan, 1978), 3:941–42.

15. Bauer, *Greek-English Lexicon*, 417. Heinrich Greeven and Johannes Hermann, "εὔχομαι, κτλ.," in *Theological Dictionary of the New Testament*, ed. Gerhard Kittel, trans. and ed. Geoffrey W. Bromiley (Grand Rapids: Eerdmans, 1964), 2:775–78.

16. Bauer, *Greek-English Lexicon*, 63; Johannes Behm, "ἀνάθεμα, ἀνάθημα, κατάθεμα," in *Theological Dictionary of the New Testament*, ed. Gerhard Kittel, trans. and ed. Geoffrey W. Bromiley (Grand Rapids: Eerdmans, 1964), 1:354–55; and Hugo Aust and Dietrich Müller, "Curse, Insult, Fool [ἀνάθεμα, κτλ.]," in *The New International Dictionary of New Testament Theology*, ed. Colin Brown, trans. G. H. Boobyer et al. (Grand Rapids: Zondervan, 1975), 1:414.

Christ, or "is nothing short of eternal condemnation, or in a word, hell"[17] or "to forfeit final salvation."[18]

Would Paul not know, however, that such a voluntary separation would be impossible? On closer examination it becomes clear that the use of the imperfect tense of the verb "to wish" is what grammarians call a "desiderative" imperfect,[19] used "to contemplate the desire but fail to bring oneself actually to the point of wishing."[20] Paul knew that his wish or prayer could not be achieved because in the immediate previous context of 8:35–39, he had stated that nothing will separate believers from the love of Christ or the love of God in Christ.

Nevertheless, here we see the intense pastoral concern he had for his people, demonstrated by his contemplation that it would be better for one person, himself in particular, to endure a lost eternity than for that same fate to befall countless of his fellow kinsmen. Paul may have reflected on his own past, during which he had rejected the provision of a right standing before God through the Christ, but now he had been accepted by God because he had put his faith in Christ Jesus the promised Messiah. He does not want to see his fellow kinsmen make the same mistake he had made by refusing the gracious provision of justification. In turn, this caused him to wish it would be possible for him as one Jew to be accursed of God, separated from his presence for eternity, rather than to have countless Jews be under God's curse.

Paul's concern is reminiscent of that of Moses, who when coming down from the mountain saw Israel worshipping the golden calf. The Lord proclaimed to Moses that he would destroy those people, but

---

17. Brian J. Abasciano, *Paul's Use of the Old Testament in Romans 9.1–9: An Intertextual and Theological Exegesis*, Library of New Testament Studies, ed. Mark Goodacre (London: T & T Clark, 2005), 301:96.
18. C. E. B. Cranfield, *Commentary on Romans IX–XVI and Essays*, vol. 2 of *A Critical and Exegetical Commentary on the Epistle to the Romans*, International Critical Commentary, ed. J. A. Emerton and C. E. B. Cranfield (Edinburgh: T. & T. Clark, 1979), 457.
19. C. F. D. Moule, *An Idiom Book of New Testament Greek*, 2nd ed. (Cambridge: Cambridge University Press, 1959), 9.
20. Buist M. Fanning, *Verbal Aspect in New Testament Greek*, Oxford Theological Monographs, ed. R. C. Morgan J. Barton, B. R. White, J. MacQuarrie, K. Ware, and R. D. Williams (Oxford: Clarendon Press, 1990), 251.

Moses prayed that God would forgive their sins, and if not, that his own name would be blotted out of "the book" (see Exod. 32:30–32).[21] Unlike Paul, Moses does not offer his life in return for their lives but does identify with them by requesting that he suffer their fate. And like that desire of Moses, Paul's sacrificial desire never came to pass. His Christlike compassion for his people was, however, genuine and magnanimous, the highest ideal in true pastoral care.

Paul now knew that if he had continued in his former way, he would be destined to suffer God's eternal wrath. The Damascus road experience had made him realize that he was wrong to reject the Messiah Christ and that he must turn from his stubborn unbelief to trust in Christ for salvation. He turned from persecuting the church to pursuing fellow Jews, testifying of the saving grace found in the promised Messiah. Paul realized that he had been hardened against the message of the Messiah Christ until he saw the Christ, whom he had been persecuting, at which time he turned from detesting the message of Messiah to embracing it. Acknowledging his hardened condition before his conversion, he sees his fellow kinsmen also hardened (Rom. 9:30–10:21). He so desires that they might come to faith as he had. What primarily grieved Paul was that his kinsmen were anathema, excluded from the covenant and devoted to destruction under the wrath of God.

In 9:4–5a, Paul elaborates on his fellow kinsmen. He defines his people thus: "who are Israelites, of whom belong the adoption, the glory, the covenants, the giving of the law, the service [worship], and the promises, of whom are the fathers, and from whom is the Christ." He begins verse 4 with the indefinite relative pronoun "who" (*hoitines*), which gives it a qualitative force, namely, "the very ones who." Here it probably has a causal sense, revealing the reason why Paul would want to sacrifice himself for them, namely, that he is not only connected with them nationally but also associated with

---

21. Cf. Gordon P. Wiles, *Paul's Intercessory Prayers: The Significance of the Intercessory Prayer Passages in the Letters of St. Paul*, Society for New Testament Studies Monograph Series, ed. Matthew Black (Cambridge: Cambridge University Press, 1974), 24:256; Abasciano, *Paul's Use of the Old Testament in Romans 9.1–9*, 301:45–146; and Mark A. Seifrid, "Paul, Luther, and Justification in Gal 2:15–21," *Westminster Theological Journal* 65 (Fall 2003): 639.

their special privileged position, which God had graciously granted to them. Here he uses the term "Israelites," rather than the normal term "Jews," which appears twenty-six times in his letters, eleven of which are found in Romans (1:16; 2:9, 10, 17, 28, 29; 3:1, 9, 29; 9:24; 10:12). The term "Israelite" is used nine times in the New Testament and three times by Paul (Rom. 9:4; 11:1; 2 Cor. 11:22). Similarly, in Moses' intercession for his people he reminds God to remember the covenant promises he made with Abraham, Isaac, and Israel, rather than using the more usual designation of "Jacob" (Exod. 32:13).[22] The use of "Israelite" indicates that they are "the covenant people of the one God."[23]

Continuing in verse 4, Paul describes Israel's privileges using relative clauses grammatically subordinate to "Israelites" (*hoœn . . . hoœn . . . ex hoœn*—of whom . . . of whom . . . from/out of whom). The first relative clause "of/to whom belongs" names six privileges. First mentioned is adoption (*huiothesia*). In the New Testament the term "adoption" is used only by Paul (Rom. 8:15, 23; 9:4; Gal. 4:5; Eph. 1:5) and in all instances it refers to believers' adoption as adult sons into God's family. Specifically in the present passage it denotes that Israel as a nation was adopted as full adult sons. Exodus 4:22–23 refers to Israel as "my firstborn" and Deuteronomy 14:1 (ESV) states "you are the sons of the Lord." The second privilege is "glory" (*doxa*), which most likely refers to the Shechinah glory (Exod. 16:10; 24:16; 40:34–35; 1 Kings 8:11), God's personal presence with his people.[24]

The third privilege is that of the "covenants" (*diathecœkeō*). This term occurs 346 times in the LXX (300 times in the canonical books), 33 times in the New Testament, and 9 times in Paul's writings (Rom. 9:4; 11:27; 1 Cor. 11:25; 2 Cor. 3:6, 14; Gal. 3:15, 17; 4:24; Eph. 2:12). Normally it is used in the singular, but it appears in the plural 6 times in the LXX (Ezek. 16:29; 2 Macc. 8:15; Wis. 18:22; Sir. 44:12, 18; 45:17) and 3 times in the New Testament (Rom. 9:4; Gal. 4:24; Eph. 2:12). In the LXX some of the passages refer to unconditional covenants that God made with the patriarchs (2 Macc. 8:15; Wis. 18:22;

---

22. Abasciano, *Paul's Use of the Old Testament in Romans 9.1–9*, 301:116.
23. Dunn, *Romans 9–16*, 526.
24. Thomas R. Schreiner, *Romans*, Baker Exegetical Commentary on the New Testament, ed. Moisés Silva (Grand Rapids: Baker, 1998), 6:484.

Sir. 44:12). In the New Testament, the plural is used in Galatians 4:24 to refer to two covenants, namely, the Mosaic covenant in contrast to the Abrahamic covenant. In Ephesians 2:12, Paul speaks about the covenants of promise, which refer to the Abrahamic covenant, Davidic covenant, and the new covenant.[25] In the present context the "covenants" apparently refer to those three, thus ascribing to Israel the privileges of the covenants of promise. (Immediately following these unconditional covenants there is the giving of the Law, which is the Mosaic covenant, a conditional covenant.)

The unconditional covenants that God made with the nation Israel contained promises for that nation.[26] The particular promises were land, seed, and blessing. First, from the days of Abraham until the last prophet in the Old Testament, Israel as a nation had been promised a land (Jer. 16:15; 23:3–8; Ezek. 11:17; 34:13; 36:24, 28; 39:25–29; Hos. 1:10–11; Joel 3:17–21; Amos 9:11–15; Mic. 4:4–7; Zeph. 3:14–20; Zech. 8:4–8). Second, Israel was promised a continued seed whereby the nation of Israel would continue to exist, but more particularly the seed of David would survive until it brought forth the Messiah, who would redeem and rule that nation (Ps. 89:3–4, 34–36; Isa. 9:6–7; Jer. 23:5–6; 30:8–9; 33:14–17, 20–21; Ezek. 37:24–25; Hos. 3:4–5; Amos 9:11; Zech. 14:3–9). And third, they were promised the blessing of the new covenant by which they would know God and have the Law written in their hearts rather than on tablets of stone (Jer. 31:31–34; Ezek. 11:19–20; 16:60–62; 36:24–28; 37:26–28; cf. also Isa. 59:21; 61:8–9). Gentiles did not have the covenants of promise and thus were excluded from them. These covenants were, indeed, tremendous privileges exclusive to Israel.

The fourth privilege named is the "giving of the law" (*nomothesia*), which refers to the Mosaic Law and was divine revelation (Exod.

---

25. See Dunn, *Romans 9–16*, 527. For a discussion of various views, see Calvin Roetzel, "Διαθῆκαι in Romans 9,4," *Biblica* 51, no. 3 (1970): 377–90.

26. For an up-to-date discussion on covenants, see Stanley E. Porter, "The Concept of Covenant in Paul," in *The Concept of the Covenant in the Second Temple Period*, ed. Stanley E. Porter and Jacqueline C. R. de Roo, Journal for the Study of Judaism: Supplement Series, ed. John J. Collins and Florentino García Martínez (Leiden: Brill, 2003), 71:269–85. Cf. also James D. G. Dunn, "Did Paul Have a Covenant Theology? Reflection on Romans 9.4 and 11.27," in *The Concept of the Covenant in the Second Temple Period*, 301–3.

19:16–21).[27] It was divine instruction on how the covenant nation was to live a life pleasing to God. It was legislation for every aspect of life both corporately and individually. The fifth privilege is the prerogative of "service" (*latreia*), a reference to the "worship" of God,[28] "ordained by Yahweh himself (Exod. 25–31; cf. Josh. 22:27; 1 Chron. 28;13) and distinct from the idolatrous worship of Israel's neighbors, which often included prostitution and human sacrifice."[29]

Finally, the sixth privilege listed within the first relative clause is "promises" (*epaggeliai*). The term appears eight times in the LXX, three times in the canonical books (Esther 4:7; Ps. 56:8; Amos 9:6), fifty-two times in the New Testament, twenty-six times in Paul's writings, eight times in Romans (Rom. 4:13, 14, 16, 20; 9:4, 8, 9; 15:8), and signifies the declaration to do something with the obligation of carrying out what has been stated, thus "promise, pledge."[30] Certainly there are promises in the covenants delineated above in the third privilege. Earlier in Romans, Paul alludes to the promise of a son for Abraham, which is a part of the Abrahamic covenant (Rom. 4:13, 14, 16, 20; 9:8, 9), and in 15:8 he refers to confirming the promises made to the fathers, a direct reference to the Abrahamic covenant. But since in this verse (9:4) Paul mentions promises in addition to covenants, it may well be that he is referring to particular promises, namely, the Messianic salvation fulfilled in Christ (Gen. 3:15; 49:10; Deut. 18:15).[31] Only Israel has the promise of Messiah and his deliverance.

The second relative clause, "of/to whom belongs," located in verse 5, mentions only one privilege, namely, "the fathers" (cf. Exod. 3:15). That is a reference, no doubt, primarily to Abraham (cf. Rom. 4:12, 16; Matt. 3:9; Luke 1:50, 73; 3:8; 16:24, 30; John 8:39, 53, 56; Acts 3:13) but would also include Isaac (cf. Rom. 9:10; Acts

---

27. Cranfield, *Romans*, 2:462–63.
28. Cf. H. Strathmann, "λατρεύω, λατρεία," in *Theological Dictionary of the New Testament*, 4:58–65.
29. Joseph A. Fitzmyer, *Romans: A New Translation with Introduction and Commentary*, Anchor Bible, ed. William Foxwell Albright and David Noel Freedman (New York: Doubleday, 1993), 33:547.
30. Bauer, *Greek-English Lexicon*, 355–56.
31. Julius Schniewind and Gerhard Friedrich, "ἐπαγγέλλω, ἐπαγγελλία, κτλ.," in *Theological Dictionary of the New Testament*, 2:583–84.

3:13; 7:8), Jacob (cf. John 4:12; Acts 3:13; 7:8, 32), and the twelve patriarchs, the sons of Jacob (cf. Acts 7:8–9, 12, 15; Acts 7:32).[32] The fathers Abraham, Isaac, and Jacob are named specifically in Romans 9:6–13.[33] It is to these fathers that God had promised the land, seed, and blessings expressed in the unconditional covenants, namely, the Abrahamic, Davidic, and new covenants, which were discussed previously. As Schreiner notes, the mention of "the patriarchs" is significant in the context of Paul's deep concern that Israel not reject a right standing before God by faith alone. It is connected to the future salvation of Israel mentioned in Romans 11:26–27, which is followed in verses 28–29 by "the saving of the end-time generation of Israel as a fulfillment of the promise first made to the patriarchs. Thus in Romans 9:5, the reference to 'the fathers' is a reminder of the eschatological promise of salvation that waits Israel."[34] This salvation, however, may not be limited to the future. In 11:28 Paul states that from the standpoint of the gospel they (Israel) are enemies for your (Gentiles') sake but from the standpoint of God's election they are beloved for the sake of the fathers.

It would seem that Paul's reference to an elect remnant of Israel for the sake of the fathers not only indicates the eschatological future of Israel, when it will be saved as a nation, but also points to Jewish believers in the present age—the elect remnant of Israel in Paul's day right up to the present day. In other words, the present church composed of all believers is not the fulfillment of the promise that "all Israel will be saved" (11:26). Rather, 11:28 is referring to the elect Jewish remnant in the present day, "beloved for the sake of the fathers." These Jews have obtained a right standing before God by faith alone in the promised Messiah. Hence, the designation "the fathers" is an important referent because the present Jewish remnant is related to Abraham not only physically but also spiritually in that they "walk in the footsteps of the faith of our father Abraham" (see Rom. 4:12).

The third relative clause, also found in verse 5, marking the climax of the privileges for Israel, is slightly different from the first two

---

32. Cranfield, *Romans*, 2:464.
33. Abasciano, *Paul's Use of the Old Testament in Romans 9.1–9*, 301:137.
34. Schreiner, *Romans*, 486.

clauses (*hoœn . . . hoœn . . . ex hoœn*—of whom . . . of whom . . . from/ out of whom). The first two relative clauses begin with "of/to whom belongs" while the third relative clause is preceded with a preposition (*ex*) signifying "from" or "out of whom." Rather than the Christ who *belongs to* Israel, it is the Christ who is *from* Israel. In verse 4 the privileges that belong to Israel are adoption, glory, covenants, Mosaic Law, worship, the promises. In verse 5, the privilege is that of their intimate connection to the fathers. Now Paul makes a significant change to indicate that "the Christ according to the flesh," the promised Messiah, actually comes from the people of Israel. This Messiah promised deliverance for Israel not only nationally but also individually, as those who trust in him receive salvation.

The final line of this verse has been debated since the inception of the church. The debate is not over the wording of the text but the punctuation of the text.[35] Greek manuscripts rarely contain punctuation marks and even then they are only irregular and sporadic. The line, then, could be punctuated in two basic ways: First, "out of whom is the Christ according to the flesh. God who is over all, be blessed forever. Amen." This means that God, the Father, is to be blessed forever.[36] Second, "out of whom is the Christ according to the flesh, the one who is God over all, blessed forever. Amen." This means that Christ is God over all, blessed forever.[37] The second scenario is preferred, meaning that out of Israel is the Messiah, who is God over all and is to be blessed forever. Further, the second rendering is in keeping with Romans 1:3–4, which implies that the Son of God existed before he was born in the flesh, and with 10:9–10, which states that Israel was to confess that Jesus is God. Hence, Christ, who is God, is to be blessed forever.

---

35. For a discussion of the problem, see Bruce M. Metzger, "The Punctuation of Rom. 9:5," in *Christ and Spirit in the New Testament: In Honor of Charles Francis Digby Moule*, ed. Barnabas Lindars and Stephen S. Smalley (Cambridge: Cambridge University Press, 1973), 95–112; and Murray J. Harris, *Jesus as God: The New Testament Use of Theos in Reference to Jesus* (Grand Rapids: Baker, 1992), 143–72.
36. For example, RSV, NEB, Ernst Käsemann, *Commentary on Romans*, trans. and ed. Geoffrey W. Bromiley (Grand Rapids: Eerdmans, 1980), 259–60; Dunn, *Romans 9–16*, 528–29.
37. For example, NASB, NIV, NRSV, Cranfield, *Romans*, 2:464–70; Fitzmyer, *Romans*, 548–49; Moo, *Romans*, 565–68; Schreiner, *Romans*, 486–89; and Abasciano, *Paul's Use of the Old Testament in Romans 9.1–9*, 301:139–42.

The ultimate privilege, then, is that the Christ or the Messiah is out of the people of Israel. As stated previously, Paul's anguish is for Israel to recognize their need to put their trust in him in order to have a right standing before God, just as Abraham their father had done many centuries before. Although Abraham did not know of Christ, he believed that God had imputed righteousness to his account. In the same way, it is necessary for the Jews to believe in the person and work of the Christ, the Messiah. The history of Israel right up to Paul's time was one of continual rejection of God's free salvation by faith (Rom. 9:30–10:21).

CONCLUSION

Paul had a very deep concern for his Jewish kinsmen. In his past, he had rejected the Messiah and vehemently persecuted the Christians (Acts 8:1–3; 9:1–2, 13; 22:4–5; 26:9–12, 15; 1 Cor. 15:9; Gal. 1:13–14; Phil. 3:6; 1 Tim. 1:13). However, the Damascus Road encounter with Christ forever changed Paul. Instead of persecuting the church for its belief in Christ the Messiah, Paul now proclaimed salvation through Christ and was persecuted as a result. Immediately after his conversion, he proclaimed in the synagogues in Damascus that Jesus was the Son of God (Acts 9:19–22), and for this he was persecuted (Acts 9:23–25). The persecution was repeated in Jerusalem and Judea (Acts 9:26–29; 26:20). The persecution continued in his first missionary journey (Acts 13:50; 14:2–6, 19), his second journey (Acts 16:19–24; 17:13, 32; 18:6, 12–13), his third journey, and his subsequent trips to Jerusalem and Rome (Acts 19:9, 23, 28–29; 20:3; 21:27–32; 22:22–23; 23:12–14, 21, 30; 24:5–9; 25:7, 24; 26:21).

Most of this persecution came from the Jews. Although Paul was the Apostle to the Gentiles, it was his policy to proclaim the gospel to the Jews first and then to the Greeks or Gentiles (Rom. 1:16). But as a result he was beaten with rods, stoned to the point of death, shouted at, threatened with death, confronted with false charges, and denounced as a traitor. Why was Paul willing to endure these things? It was his conviction that his Jewish people needed to have a right standing (God's righteousness) before God by means of faith alone and not by the works of the Law, just as Abraham had believed God and been credited with righteousness (Gen. 15:6). In other words, the

Jews were to be related to Abraham not only physically but also spiritually by following in the footsteps of the faith of their father (Rom. 4:12). Paul endured persecution not because he enjoyed it but because of his deep personal concern for his fellow Jews.

What I have presented here serves as an example of the experiences of Moishe Rosen, the founder of Jews for Jesus, to whom it is dedicated. Over the years he has been harassed, pelted with cigarette butts, stabbed, briefly imprisoned on more than one occasion, cursed, ridiculed, and called a traitor by his Jewish people—all because of his desire to tell them that they can be related to God by faith alone in Jesus Christ, the promised Messiah. As with Paul, Moishe does not enjoy persecution but has been willing to endure suffering because of his deep pastoral care and concern for his kinsman. Like Paul, he longs for them to believe in the promised Messiah named Y'shua

A genuine first-hand religious experience . . .
is bound to be a heterodoxy to its witnesses,
the prophet appearing as a mere lonely madman.
If his doctrine prove contagious enough to spread to any others,
it becomes a definite and labeled heresy.
But if it then still prove contagious enough to triumph over
persecution,
it becomes itself an orthodoxy;
and when a religion has become an orthodoxy,
its day of inwardness is over:
the spring is dry; the faithful live at second hand exclusively
and stone the prophets in their turn.

—William James
The Varieties of Religious Experience

3

LONELY PROPHETS

*Eccentricity and the Call
of God Through the Ages*

RUTH TUCKER

Our colorful heritage of faith spanning the centuries from the Old
Testament patriarchs to present-day street preachers is filled
with prophets—prophets who often appear as mere lonely madmen.
If the reputations of these prophets somehow survive within the
realm of orthodoxy, we are tempted to tame them to correspond
with our more refined tastes. Could any of us endure the real Moses
or Paul or St. Francis or Martin Luther? The list goes on. These
individuals, however, might not be remembered at all apart from
their sense of calling that bade them follow an often unconventional course. They echoed the words of Paul, *I am not ashamed of
the gospel*. This lack of shame and the zeal for their calling combined

to fashion colorful lives and compelling ministries. It is within this eccentric cloud of witnesses that we find Moishe Rosen.

Who is Moishe Rosen and how does he fit into this larger picture of our heritage of faith? As a household name, he does not rank with Billy Graham or even Bill Hybels and Rick Warren. Google him and you find thousands of results, but not the two million for Billy. He rates an article in Wikipedia, but not as long as the ones for Bill and Rick. Will church history texts find space for him? Probably not. But that should not surprise us. Jewish believers generally have gotten short shrift in church history texts.

The overall legacy of Moishe Rosen is an important matter that I will not attempt to tackle here. Some have sought to convey his contributions through honors and awards. In 1997 the Conservative Baptist Association, for example, named him a "Hero of the Faith." True enough. And like most such "heroes of the faith," he has had his detractors. But apart from the usual opposition that a forthright gospel message incites, Moishe has drawn hostility that at times might appear excessive. It is his response to such opposition and his response to his minority status as a Jewish believer that has set him apart. He has dared to be different. He has not tried to conceal his bent for eccentricity. Indeed, he has flaunted it. It is no exaggeration to suggest that in many respects he is a wild and crazy guy. But so also were many of the so-called heroes of the faith who merit space in our church history texts. It is this colorful aspect of our heritage of faith that I now explore.

Moishe was born Martin Mayer Rosen on April 12, 1932. His Hebrew given name was Moshe (or Moses), and Moishe is the Yiddish vernacular for Moses. So when contemplating the eccentric in our faith heritage, Moses is not a bad place to start.

MOSES: A TIMID AND TORTURED HERO

Moses is—like that designation given Moishe—a Hero of the Faith. Indeed, his story has many of the commonly identified characteristics of the universal hero: being set aside at birth or in youth, resentment from others and/or persecution, possessing identifiable character flaws or sins, driven by a divine calling or electrifying experience, undertaking a journey or task of great hardship, rescuing people in trouble, and finally leaving a legacy that stands the test of time.

The account of Moses takes many twists and turns as the universal hero characteristics unfold. His rescue at birth, after being hidden in the bulrushes, alerts us at the beginning of the story that he is being set apart to be used by God. Birth and childhood stories are critical (though not always necessary) elements in the lives of our heroes of faith. So also are stories of flaws and failures. In the case of Moses, his killing of an Egyptian serves as a metaphor for his role in standing up to the Egyptian Pharaoh, but in this case we see the flawed man for who he is. The sin was murder, plain and simple. True, he was defending a brother, a fellow Hebrew. But his violence resulted in a capital crime and its cover-up—burying the body and fleeing the scene. His flashes of temper are seen elsewhere as well.

"Moses is the most haunted and haunting figure in all the Bible," writes Jonathan Kirsch "To be sure, he is often portrayed as strong, sure, and heroic, but he is also timid and tortured with self-doubt at key moments in his life. He is a shepherd, mild and meek, but he is also a ruthless warrior who is capable of blood-shaking acts of violence." If he were required to submit to seminary psychological testing, might Moses be diagnosed as bi-polar? He "is a gentle teacher who is also a magician and a wonder-worker, a lawgiver whose code of justice is merciful except when it comes to purging and punishing those who disagree with him, an emancipator who rules his people with unforgiving authority." And if that were not enough to screen him out of the pool of ministerial candidates, the Bible shows him "to act in timid and even cowardly ways, throw temper tantrums, dabble in magic, carry out purges and inquisitions, conduct wars of extermination, and talk back to God."[1]

Who was this Moses? Are we afraid to let Scripture speak for itself? "The real Moses—the Moses no one knows—was someone far richer and stranger than we are customarily allowed to see."[2]

THE APOSTLE PAUL: A FANATIC
STRUGGLING WITH INNER DEMONS

The historian Michael Grant, in the opening lines of his biography of Paul, calls him "one of the most perpetually significant men who

---

1. Jonathan Kirsch, Moses: A Life (New York: Ballantine Books, 1998), 2.
2. Ibid.

have ever lived." It was Paul who transformed an obscure Jewish sect into a universal faith that decisively changed the course of history.

But was Paul respected in his own day? "I doubt very much whether Paul impressed sophisticated people as an appealing character," writes Peter Berger. "To say the least, he must have embarrassed them. He was obsessed with his mission, unbending and endlessly aggressive in his religious views, absolutist and authoritarian in his dealings with others. We may reconstruct the adjectives and phrases used to describe him both at the cocktail parties of the Corinthian elite . . . and in the pubs:

"fundamentalist,
"simplistic,
"compulsive,
"asking too much of sensible people,
"never listening to the other side of an argument,
"perhaps a little crazy—
in sum, something of a disagreeable fanatic."[3]

It does not require an exercise in imagination to see Paul as a first-century fanatic who was more than a little bit eccentric. His appearance probably did not draw attention. From the *Acts of Paul*, an early Christian writing, he is described as "a man of middling size, and his hair was scanty, and his legs were a little-crooked, and his knees were far apart; he had large eyes, and his eyebrows met, and his nose was somewhat long."[4]

Like Moses, Paul would not easily fit in with the other seminary seniors in the spring graduation ceremony. He would have been held back though surely not for lack of intelligence or academic preparation. Before he could even be considered for ordination, he would need to undergo a series of psychological evaluations. Today's therapists would not dismiss lightly his serious personality disorders. He would create disruptions in any ministry or profession he entered.

Such a conjecture is not merely idle speculation. Paul's letters show a man who is deeply troubled—and very openly so. Perhaps in

---

3. Peter Berger, *A Far Glory* (New York: Macmillan, 1992), 14.
4. Cited in Stephen M. Miller, "Bald, Blind & Single," *Christian History* 47 (July 1, 1995): 33.

the hope of helping his reader, he let them know about his painful struggles. For those who allow Paul's words to speak for themselves, he serves as a model not of a super-saint, but rather an honest and frail—and all too human—ordinary man.

If we were to pull phrases and paragraphs out of his letters and string them together, we would find an individual who needs help. He knows that. And he is convinced that Christ is the answer. Imagine him spilling his gut to a church college and career group. Here he is in his own words—with a contemporary interpretive slant:

I'm not saying for a moment that I'm perfect—far from it. But I do try to forget what is behind me—to just let the past and all its problems go. I've quit looking back. I'm pressing forward in my Christian life.

I still struggle. O, yeah . . . I still struggle with those same old sins—though it's sure not for lack of knowledge.

We all know that the Law is spiritual. True? Problem is, I am unspiritual. It's like I'm sold as a slave to sin. I don't even understand what I do. What I want to do I don't do, but what I hate I do. It's absurd. It's like I got OCD. I'm an obsessive compulsive mental case. I just can't stop. . . . I hate myself.

I can't understand it. Am I doing this myself, or is it sin living in me? I surely know that there's nothing good that lives in me—at least in my sinful nature. But I just can't stop myself. The honest truth is I really want to do what is good, but I cannot carry it out. I just keep screwing up my life.

When I try to stop and rationalize it, it makes no sense— though . . . though maybe there is this law at work. I don't know; I'm not sure; it's just weird. Now, stay with me here: When I want to do good, evil is right there with me. Yet deep inside I delight in God's law; but then I see another law at work in the members of my body. Is this making any sense? I see another law at work in the members of my body, waging war against the law of my mind and making me a prisoner of the law of sin at work within my members.

O, dear God, what a wretched man I am! Who will rescue me from this body of death? . . . I'm such a loser. . . . I'm helpless. . . . But, you know, there is a ray of hope. No, it's more than a ray.

Thanks be to God—through Jesus Christ our Lord! Thank you, thank you, Lord.

When we seek to clean up Paul for a nice Sunday sermon and give him a Bill Hybels makeover, we do him and Scripture a disservice. Paul was a bundle of tangled emotions. He was a first-century misfit, and we do well to let him be himself.

ST. FRANCIS: A CRAZY MAN CALLED BY GOD

How would Francis (c. 1181–1226) fare in a seminary psychological assessment? Would he be sent to perpetual group therapy? Lighten up. Chill out. These might well be the admonitions from his fellow seminarians. According to his traveling and ministry companion, Brother Leo, he disdained laughter and jesting. "Not only did he wish that he should not laugh, but that he should not even afford to others the slightest occasion for laughing."[5]

Before his conversion, Francis was a profligate youth. He was a typical spoiled rich kid growing up in the little Italian town of Assisi. According to this first biographer, "he squandered his time" and was taken up with "foolishness of every kind."[6] At age twenty, looking for adventure, he joined the military and went off to war. He was captured in the heat of battle and held as a prisoner of war until his father could negotiate his ransom a year later.

He emerged from prison a changed man. He was convinced that God was calling him to a special work. The story is familiar. He began living the life of a hermit and stealing his father's money to give to the poor. Pietro, his father, "may have been indulgent of Francis's adolescent high jinks," writes Lawrence Cunningham, "but he was absolutely livid about this new kind of life. Outraged by the squalor of his life and his prodigal generosity, his father even tried to imprison him in the cellar of the family home."[7]

Finally Pietro brought his crazy son before the bishop. Hoping his

---

5. Cited in Mark Galli, "Francis of Assisi: Did You Know?" *Christian History* 42 (April 1, 1994): 3.
6. Thomas of Celano, cited in Lawrence Cunningham, "Tattered Treasure of Assisi," *Christian History* 42 (April 1, 1994): 8.
7. Ibid., 10.

son would repent and stop steeling, Pietro was in for a surprise. Francis took off his clothes and handed them over to his father. Standing naked before the bishop, he repudiated his father with words that have since become famous: "Up to today I called you father, but I now say [only] 'Our Father who art in heaven.'"

In the years that followed, Francis ministered to the poor, particularly to lepers who had once repelled him. Now he kissed them and encouraged them to respond in kind. He permitted himself no comforts in lodging, preferring to sleep on the ground with a stone for a pillow. He denied himself all but the barest essentials of nourishment. Once when he had indulged in a small portion of chicken, he later felt such remorse that he ordered a companion to fasten a rope around his neck and pull him through the town like a common criminal, while announcing to the bewildered onlookers that this man was a glutton.

It surprises some that Francis was married—though surely not to Clare, his female counterpart and partner in monasticism. No, he was married to Poverty, the queen of virtue. He found her on a mountain top, "sitting on the throne of her neediness." She told him that "she had been with Adam in paradise, but had become a homeless wanderer after the fall until the Lord came and made her over to his elect." Since that time the number of her children increased but always there was great opposition from her enemies—greed and worldliness—particularly among the high-living monks. On hearing her story, Francis took Poverty as his bride and she, he told his followers, had come to live with him.[8]

As eccentric—and some might say insane—as he was, Francis was revered in his own day. Indeed, so much so, that after his death his followers took extreme precautions to prevent someone from stealing his body. They buried his coffin "beneath the main altar in the Basilica of Saint Francis—under a slab of granite, gravel, ten welded bands of iron, a 190–pound grill, and finally a 200–pound rock."[9] So concealed and secure was the coffin that it was not discovered until some seven centuries later.

---

8. Philip Schaff, A History of Christianity (Grand Rapids: Eerdmans, 1979), 5:398.
9. Galli, "Francis of Assisi," 3.

MARTIN LUTHER: A VULGAR AND SACRILEGIOUS SAINT

Most Protestants have never even entertained the thought that Martin Luther (1483–1546?) was anything other than a great Reformer. But to vast numbers of professing Christians in the generations following the Reformation, he was viewed as a heretic or worse. King Henry VIII pronounced him the antichrist. Johann Bullinger, a Swiss Reformer and a contemporary of Luther, was exasperated by his "muddy and swinish, vulgar and coarse teachings," and went on to lament that "it is as clear as daylight and undeniable that no one has ever written more vulgarly, more coarsely, more unbecomingly in matters of faith and Christian chastity and modesty and in all serious matters than Luther."[10]

Patrick F. O'Hare, an early twentieth-century Roman Catholic biographer of Luther, was no less virulent in his criticism: "That he was a deformer and not a reformer is the honest verdict of all who are not blind partisans."[11]

Martin Luther is, indeed, an enigma. His own best friends and strongest supporters were troubled by his often outrageous conduct, and in the centuries since his death he has not attained the realm of piety that is typically bestowed upon dead saints. He is truly the father of Protestantism, but his image is tarnished. He railed against his enemies, both Catholics and fellow Protestants, in vitriolic explosions. He threw an inkwell and cursed the Devil, who with his minions had ganged on him. He was vulgar and sacrilegious, and his philosophical injunctions were sometimes shocking—as in his controversial "Pecca fortiter" (Sin bravely). He called church loyalists, especially supporters of the pope, "papal asses," and the unlearned Catholic laity were senseless swine. The biblical interpretations of Jewish rabbis were deemed no less than "Jewish piss and shit."

Can we excuse him? Was he merely an ordinary man crawling out of the medieval backwater of pre-modern Germany? Or was he mentally disturbed? Did he suffer from a personality disorder that would thwart ministerial ordination today? He did endure a wide range of physical ailments for which there were no adequate treatments. Likewise, he

---

10. *Wahraffte Bekanntniss*, B. 1, 9, quoted in Patrick F. O'Hare, *The Facts About Luther* (New York: Frederick Pustet & Co., 1916), 350.
11. O'Hare, *The Facts About Luther*, 314, 355.

"complained of headaches, insomnia, and what he called 'night wars'—nightmares, anxiety attacks, and *Anfechtung*, meaning 'inner turmoil' or 'temptation.'"[12]

It is no wonder that Luther, the prolific writer and speaker (with students taking notes) is a psychoanalyst's dream. Freudian psychologist Hartmann Grisar diagnosed Luther as having a pathological, manic-depressive personality. The most popular of these historical analyses was *Young Man Luther* (1958) by Erik H. Erikson. Here, Luther's emotional impairments are linked directly to emotional and physical abuse as a child, causing him to rebel against his parents and even more so against the established church.

Eric Gritsch speculates that Luther may have played the part of a court jester—like those he may have seen coming to town in their outrageous attire, lampooning the authorities of the day. "The jester walked a fine line between satire and prophecy, just as the Old Testament prophets Jeremiah or Ezekiel sometimes did."[13] How do we make sense of Luther? Was he indeed a court jester, or was he merely a lonely prophet following in the footsteps of eccentric Old Testament figures, preaching repentance and throwing inkwells at the Devil?

GEORGE FOX: BIZARRE AND BAREFOOT IN LEATHER BREECHES

In many respects, George Fox (1624–1691), founder of the Society of Friends (Quakers) epitomizes the eccentric lonely prophet. In his journal he describes being set apart by God.

> I fasted much, walked abroad in solitary places many days, and often took my Bible, and sat in hollow trees and lonesome places until night came on; and frequently in the night walked mournfully about by myself; for I was a man of sorrows in the time of the first workings of the Lord in me.
>
> During all this time I was never joined in profession of religion with any, but gave up myself to the Lord, having forsaken all evil

---

12. Eric W. Gritsch, "The Unrefined Reformer," *Christian History* 39 (July 1, 1993): 35.
13. Ibid., 36.

company, taking leave of father and mother, and all other relations, and traveled up and down as a stranger on the earth, which way the Lord inclined my heart; taking a chamber to myself in the town where I came, and tarrying sometimes more, sometimes less in a place: for I durst not stay long in a place, being afraid both of professor and pro-fane, lest, being a tender young man, I should be hurt by conversing much with either. For which reason I kept much as a stranger, seeking heavenly wisdom and getting knowledge from the Lord. . . . As I had forsaken the priests, so I left the separate preachers also, and those called the most experienced people; for I saw there was none among them all that could speak to my condition. . . . When I was in the deep, under all shut up, I could not believe that I should ever overcome; my troubles, my sorrows, and my temptations were so great that I often thought I should have despaired, I was so tempted.[14]

Fox's ministry began to take shape after he encountered God through a visionary experience on Pendle Hill, an event that marked the turning point of his life. Through his outdoor preaching, he soon gained a following. Like John the Baptist and the Old Testament prophets, he called people to repentance. He walked barefoot in his homemade leather breeches, raising his hands and shouting out God's curses on the cities and towns. Walking through the crowded markets of Litchfield, he bellowed, "Woe unto Litchfield, thou bloody city! Woe unto Litchfield!" Persecution and imprisonment inevitably followed.

Wherever he went, he attracted attention. "On a Saturday in the late summer of 1655 a strange little group made its way from Arundel into Chichester," writes Michael Wooley. "The leader was a 31 year old roaming preacher . . . an eccentric and difficult man. . . . He was given to wearing a leather suit and an extremely large hat [and] his hair was unfashionably long. . . . Fox was no figure of fun though. . . . He had great presence [and a] strong personality giving him a dangerous magnetism."[15]

Like John the Baptist, his appearance set him apart as a prophet.

---

14. George Fox, *Journal* (Philadelphia, 1800), 59–60.
15. Michael Wooley, *The Quakers in Chichester, 1655–1967* (Chicester: Religious Society of Friends, Chicester Meeting, 2006, http://www.chicesterquakers.org/booklet.htm

Thomas Carlyle, a Scottish historian, rated Fox alongside Luther and captured his essence in a suit of clothes:

> The most remarkable incident in modern history perhaps is not the Diet of Worms. . . . The most remarkable incident is passed over carelessly by most historians and treated with some degree of ridicule by others—namely, George Fox's making for himself a suit of leather. No grander thing was ever done than when George Fox, stitching himself into a suit of leather, went forth determined to find truth for himself—and to do battle for it against all superstition and intolerance.[16]

PETER CARTWRIGHT: A PRANKSTER PREACHER

For Methodists who are aware of their history, Peter Cartwright (1785–1872) easily draws an amused smile. His story captures the wonderful lore of the American circuit-riding preacher. But unlike Francis Asbury, whose journals reflect the stern and somber holiness of Christian piety, Cartwright is as playful and eccentric as he is serious. For nearly sixty years he rode the circuit in Kentucky, Tennessee, Indiana, Ohio, and Illinois. In political history he merits a footnote as the congressional candidate defeated by Abraham Lincoln in 1846.

Cartwright's claim to fame rests largely on his autobiography. Here he tells stories of how he jumped into the fray and fought off rowdies who tried to disrupt his camp meetings.

> As I dismissed the assembly a man stepped up to me, and warned me to be on my guard, for he had heard the two brothers swear they would horsewhip me when meeting was out, for giving their sisters the jerks. . . . [Then] it came into my mind how I would get clear of my whipping, and, jerking out the peppermint phial, said I, "Yes; if I gave your sisters the jerks I'll give them to you." In a moment I saw he was scared. I moved towards him, he backed, I advanced, and he wheeled and ran, warning me not to come near him, or he would kill me. It raised the laugh on him, and I escaped my whipping. I

---

16. Thomas Carlyle, *Sartor Resartus* (n.p., 1834), http://www.fullbooks.com/Sartor-Resartus3.html.

had the pleasure, before the year was out, of seeing all four soundly converted to God, and I took them into the Church.[17]

At another camp meeting, a bunch of rowdies brought a keg of whisky for after-hours entertainment. Cartwright, through a stealthy scheme, appropriated the keg. When the rowdies realized it was gone, they threatened to stone the "preachers' tent" that night. Cartwright, dressed in disguise, infiltrated their group discussion: "I mixed among these rowdies, and soon got all their plans." After the evening meeting was over, he writes, "[I] slipped down to the brook, and filled the pockets of the old overcoat that I had borrowed, with little stones; and as I came up to them, they were just ready to commence operations on the preachers' tent." Cartwright, like an adolescent boy, began flinging his stones at them. "They broke at full speed, and such a running I hardly ever witnessed. I took after them, hollering. . . ."

On still another occasion, Cartwright entered a town only to learn that there would be a community dance that night. Though not a dancer himself, he recognized a potential opportunity for evangelism. A young woman, noticing the stranger in their midst, invited him to dance. He agreed but told her that he never made such a decision without consulting the Lord. As they proceeded onto the dance floor, he fell down on his knees. She tried to pull away, but he would not let her go. The music stopped, and people looked on in astonishment. Cartwright loudly prayed for God's power to fall upon them so that their souls would be saved. According to his account, fifteen people were soundly converted that very night, and in the days that followed a church of more than thirty people was formed.[18]

Cartwright was God's man for unruly frontier evangelism, a fearless, imaginative, wild preacher, often unruly himself. No conventional buttoned-down parson could have accomplished half what he did.

CRAZY MOODY: AN EARNED NICKNAME

D. L. Moody (1837–1899) "earned his famous nickname 'Crazy

---

17. Peter Cartwright, *Autobiography of Peter Cartwright: The Backwoods Preacher*, ed. W. P. Strickland (New York: Carlton Porter, 1856), 45–52.
18. Ibid., 270–72.

Moody,'" writes Kevin Miller. His unconventional style grabbed attention. "To attract poor, urban children to his Sunday school, he bought a little Indian pony and offered rides. To preach the gospel to people who resisted attending church, he held meetings in theaters, auditoriums, and sprawling circus tents."[19] His uncle may have contributed the widespread use of the *crazy* label when he quipped, "My nephew Dwight is crazy, crazy as a March hare."

The label certainly applies to Moody's early ministry when he went about building the world's largest Sunday school in Chicago. By some accounts he literally pulled children off the street into his meeting. The story is told how he spotted a girl who had been skipping class and avoiding him. "There coming down the sidewalk, was the absentee. Suddenly she stopped, reversed her direction and took off like a rabbit before a hound dog. Moody, convention to the winds, raced after her. Down the sidewalk, across the street, though an alley, down another sidewalk—the chase was on!" When she dashed into a saloon and out the back door and up the steps to her tenement flat, Moody was "breathing down her neck every inch of the way," pulling her out from under the bed. Fuming at the stranger, the girl's mother demanded an explanation. As only he could do, Moody explained his presence as perfectly normal and then "inquired as to the size of the good woman's family, and within weeks had everyone of the tribe in his mission school."[20]

While many people were amused by Moody's craziness, others were scornful. An early historian, reflecting on Moody, wrote, "There was the revivalist Moody, bearded and neckless, with his two hundred and eighty pounds of Adam's flesh, every ounce of which belonged to God."[21]

Despite all his eccentricities, Moody was dead serious. His first career had been that of a shoe salesman, a job that offered him the hope of amassing a fortune. As an evangelist he was a salesman *par excellence*, selling the gospel with more fervor than he had ever sold shoes. But he was far more than a salesman. He was the first to bring a managerial mentality to revivalism. Organization and advertising

---

19. Kevin Miller, Editorial, *Christian History* 25 (January 1, 1990): 2.
20. Richard K. Curtis, *They Called Him Mr. Moody* (Grand Rapids: Eerdmans, 1962), 66–69.
21. Cited in David Maas, "The Life and Times of D. L. Moody," *Christian History* (January 1, 1990): 5.

were key elements in his campaigns, but his keen understanding and utilization of the popular press set him apart from other evangelists before and since. During his late autumn meetings in 1876, for example, the message of "what the Lord had wrought in Chicago," writes Bruce Evensen, "had been trumpeted across the Great Northwest." An often-quoted claim was that "Never did one man reap such a harvest since the Reformation."[22]

Moody's eccentricities served him well in the media. His self-deprecating style and his quotable quips ideally suited the hungry press, eager to sell their penny-papers. His lack of education and proper etiquette, his poor grammar and pronunciation made him all the more endearing—and eccentric. When he was challenged once regarding his theology, he retorted, "My theology . . . I did not know I had any."[23] Those newspapers who ignored or belittled him did so to their peril. He was a phenomenon in his era—described at his death, only days before the turn of the twentieth century, as the most dominating force of the nineteenth century. Some suggested that he had reduced the population in hell by more than a million souls.

Whatever his legacy, he remained true to himself. Even at the height of his popularity he avoided cleaning up his act to make the gospel respectable. He was a very ordinary servant of God, carrying on in his own crazy style.

J. FRANK NORRIS: A TWO-GUN PARSON

During most of the first half of the twentieth century, John Franklyn Norris (1877–1952) was the minister of the First Baptist Church of Fort Worth. This church was known as the "home of the cattle kings" and the richest in Texas. When Norris arrived in 1909 to assume the pastorate, he described himself as a sophisticated speaker, complete with "tuxedos, swallowtail coats, a selection of 'biled' shirts." He was anything but modest, boasting that he was "the main attraction at all the gatherings of the Rotarians, Lions,

---

22. Bruce J. Evensen, *God's Man for the Gilded Age: D. L. Moody and the Rise of Modern Mass Evangelism* (New York: Oxford University Press, 2003), 158.
23. Cited in Stanley N. Gundry, "Demythologizing Moody," in *Mr. Moody and the Evangelical Tradition*, ed. by Timothy George (New York: T & T Clark, 2005), 15.

Kiwanis, Eagles." Indeed, he was "Will Rogers and Mark Twain both combined."[24]

Born into an Alabama sharecropping family, he pulled himself out of poverty through education. But he was not content in sophisticated circles. In 1911, he underwent a change that has been described as a burning bush experience: "When I came back from Owensboro, after a month's meditation on the banks of the Ohio," he later wrote, "I began to preach the gospel after the fashion of John the Baptist in the wilderness of Judea. I didn't use a pearl handle pen knife. . . . I had a broad axe and laid it at the tap root of the trees of dancing, gambling, saloons, houses of ill fame, ungodly conduct, high and low, far and near. And you talk about a bonfire—the whole woods was set on fire."[25]

The result was mixed. On the one hand, "the crowds came; large numbers were saved," but on the other hand, he made many enemies both inside and outside the church. As a shrewd wheeler-dealer who quickly took control of smaller Baptist publications, he promoted his own style of belligerent fundamentalism. He fanned the flames of the red scare and warned his audience about the evils of Catholicism and particularly against the dangers of a Catholic, Al Smith, in the White House.

When efforts to shut down a house of prostitution failed, he began advertising his Sunday evening sermons as forums for exposing the names of those who wanted to remain anonymous. Crowds overflowed the auditorium, and a tent was erected. Then Mayor Davis stepped in and ordered the tent removed. The fight was on. At one point the mayor threatened to arrest and hang the preacher. Accusations were hurled back and forth, as small fires blazed and shots were misfired. But then in February of 1912, the church was burned to the ground, and a month later the Norris home was burned. For Norris supporters, the mayor was the obvious suspect. But Norris himself was charged. He had given conflicting accounts to the investigators, and it was well known that he wanted both a new church and new house. In the trial that followed, however, the judge acquitted him.[26]

---

24. Cited in Michael Wes et. al., "John Frank Norris," http://www.higherpraise.com/preachers/norris.htm.
25. Ibid.
26. Ibid.

An even more bizarre and serious situation broke out in 1925, amid his anti-Catholic diatribes. The city council voted to purchase land from the Catholic diocese. Norris accused the mayor and council of a pro-Catholic bias. When a close associate of the mayor threatened Norris and showed up at his office, Norris pulled out his gun and fired four shots, killing the man. He claimed self-defense, and the jury agreed. He was found "not guilty."[27]

Prior to that time, he had been expelled from the Fort Worth Baptist ministerial conference and his church was removed from the local Baptist association. When he was censured by the Texas Southern Baptist leaders, Norris labeled the action a "hatefest." They in turn called him, among other things, a liar, a thief, a perjurer, reprobate, corrupt, and devilish.[28]

Such accusations did not stifle his showmanship. Will McDonald described the services as "The best show in Fort Worth." Sunday evenings were particularly popular:

> He advertised his sermon titles on a large canvas banner that stretched along the side of the church building. The provocative titles got Fort Worth's attention. . . . He treated the congregation to visual spectacles as well. Once, when a cowboy was converted, he had the horse brought into the service to witness the baptism . . . when Norris preached against evolution, he brought a monkey into the meeting. The monkey, dressed in a little suit, sat on a stool next to the pulpit. Each time Norris made a point against evolution, he turned to the monkey and asked, "Isn't that so?" Norris was quite the showman.[29]

The showmanship paid off. Circulation of his various publications reached seventy thousand, radio listeners increased, and church attendance skyrocketed. He vowed to have the largest church in the world. In 1926, the year after he had shot and killed a man, membership was listed at more than eight thousand. Several years later he started an expansion program in Detroit, and eventually the attendance for the combined

---

27. Ibid.
28. Ibid.
29. Ibid.

locations grew to some twenty-five thousand. In his later years, Norris repeatedly joined forces with other fundamentalist groups only to split soon after. He was a fighting fundamentalist in every sense of the word.

Today, as megachurch ministers ply their seeker-friendly wares, Norris is an utter anomaly. But among declining numbers of independent fundamentalist Baptists, he stands as a prophet. He was dogmatic and severe and, as Francis had done centuries earlier, he demanded followers live a lifestyle that was separated from the ways of the world. "Ungodly conduct" could not be tolerated.

MOISHE ROSEN: FERDINAND THE BULL?

In comparison with some of his eccentric predecessors, Moishe Rosen seems on the surface to be outright tame, though like Norris he certainly has had his enemies. In fact, some who once faithfully served with him in the ministry now speak out forcefully against him and the organization. On the website "Ex Jews for Jesus," Aaron, a disaffected member, blasts the organization on the matter of discipline: "We had a military model, into which we were all initiated during the military-style campaign training—the only common experience that all the Jews for Jesus staff had." Referring to Moishe, he writes, "He would scream at the staff and storm out. Sometimes he would scream at a particular person in the presence of the group." Another individual calls him a "rage-aholic" and describes the "pain training" he inflicted on staff (before the board put an end to it) as "sadistic." Still another writes in reference to the passage, By their fruit you shall know them. "Who can judge the heart of a man, but Moishe Rosen's fruit is rotten."[30] Moishe admits that in anger he sometimes threw objects "for shock value to drive home a point," and the pain training is a matter of record that in his mind served a purpose: his volunteers would be prepared for any opposition that came their way.

Who really is this rotund man I introduced several years ago in a seminary chapel service as "the only Jewish Buddha" I had ever known? He sat on stage in a large easy chair and told stories in a

---

30. "Excursus—Bondage and Discipline" http://www.exjewsforjesus.org/stories/aaron2 .html; and "Reviews of Not Ashamed: The Story of Jews for Jesus," http://www .exjewsforjesus.org/stories/nareviews.html.

barely audible voice carried over the sound system. I worried, sitting in the front row, that I might be the only one catching his drift. But my worries dissipated when the service ended. The platform and the center aisle were packed with students who wanted to greet him. I followed the rest of the students out through the extended walkway. In front of me and behind me everyone was chattering about this Jewish patriarch who was funny and self-deprecating and dead serious about his ministry.

His story on the founding of Jews for Jesus is legendary. He was speaking to a group of Christian students at Columbia University in the spring of 1969. He enjoys telling how he stole one of Ronald Reagan's wisecracks: "A hippie dresses like Tarzan, walks like Jane, and smells like Cheetah." A friend later asked him if he had ever actually smelled a hippie. How could he, he retorted, he'd never gotten that close to one. But he could not put the thought out of his mind. It was a turning point in his ministry. He could no longer be satisfied with a conventional ministry.

> He was a successful director of a Jewish mission, shielded by a receptionist, a secretary, and two assistants. His was part of a world of respectable, ambitious achievers. The hippies ambling the streets in ragged jeans and tee-shirts were losers. But his conscience was pricked: *"Nobody sees me without making an appointment well in advance. I have become more concerned with administrative procedures than with people. How can I get to know the hippies."*[31]

With the founding of Jews for Jesus, Moishe capitalized on his weaknesses with his throw-away lines: "I'm overweight, overbearing, and over forty. What am I doing leading a youth movement?" But in many respects, Moishe was in his own element. Here were young people challenging authority figures, even as he had when he left behind his Jewish religion and professed his faith in Jesus as Messiah.

Moishe likes to tell the story that before going off to Bible college in the East, his father insisted he see a psychiatrist—fearing his Jewish

---

31. Catherine Damato, "The Man Behind the Jews for Jesus," *Power for Living*, September 2, 1979, 2.

son might have truly gone over the edge in his fervor for Jesus. Moishe was not offended because "I thought there was always the possibility that I might really be insane." After two sessions (at fifty dollars an hour), the doctor sent Moishe a letter:

To whom it may concern:

Martin Rosen . . . was examined psychiatrically by the under-signed on August 2 and 3, 1954. He was found to be psychiatrically normal."

"So no matter what anyone says about my mental stability these days," Moishe insists, "I at least have a letter to prove it. Most people don't."[32]

For many people, a fifty-year-old letter proves nothing. Not that Moishe cares. He is comfortable with who he is, and if people have problems with that, so be it. When asked about his eccentricities, his answer almost seemed to speak for all those peculiar prophets who have come before him. Indeed, his words might have come from George Fox or from the court jester Martin Luther. "Eccentricity is armor that gives you an advantage," he muses. "By not letting people know what you're doing keeps them guessing. Always keep people guessing." What impact have Jews for Jesus had on the Jewish community? "Jews for Jesus is like an elephant in the room; you can't ignore us."[33]

What about the inevitable opposition that was sometimes manifested in violence? "Worse than persecution, much worse," Moishe responds without missing a beat, "is disregard." On one occasion someone shot a bullet through a window at the San Francisco head-quarters. How did he react? By issuing whistles to the staff. "Most of them didn't work, though."[34]

What about his achievements as a Christian leader? His response is matter-of-fact: "I'm not impressed with my own achievements."

---

32. Moishe Rosen with William Proctor, *Jews for Jesus* (Old Tappan, NJ: Revell, 1974), 36–37.
33. Interview with Moishe Rosen, San Francisco, November 7, 2007, November 8, 2007.
34. Ibid., November 8, 2007.

And a follow-up question: Did you sometimes feel like you were just bumbling along in the work?

> Sometimes I wasn't even bumbling. The work was at a complete standstill. . . . I'm not an over achiever. I'm like Ferdinand the bull who didn't want to charge; all he wanted to do was go out in the field with the flowers and bees. . . . I was no paragon of dedication. . . . I didn't like outdoor street preaching; I would go out with a real soapbox (used for making soap) and would carry an American flag and would pick a corner where I could be fairly certain that no one would walk by; I'd preach with only a handful of volunteers listening. . . .[35]

When Moishe reminisces about his long life of ministry, he relates it in no clear chronological order. Events decades old are easily blurred with those of recent days. Indeed, now in his seventies, he's still, figuratively speaking, preaching on a soapbox to a handful of volunteers and not always altogether liking it. He just might rather be out in the field with the flowers and bees.

• • • • •

In their own day these "prophets"—Moses, Paul, Francis, Fox, Cartwright, Moody, Norris—were viewed by most observers, as William James suggests, as mere lonely madmen. But in each case the message was contagious despite persecution. Indeed, the message triumphed and became respectably orthodox. The day of inwardness (and insanity) passed. The faithful followers would carry on but with a secondhand experience, and they would often mock the lonely prophets coming in their wake.

Is Moishe Rosen another one of these lonely prophets—unconventional and eccentric? Have he and his message triumphed over persecution only to become simply another respectable orthodoxy? Is the day of inwardness for Jews for Jesus over? Come on . . . is the spring dry? And will yet another lonely madman rise up in another time and another place to carry on what began on Mt. Sinai?

---

35. Ibid., November 9, 2007

4

OPPORTUNITY, OPPOSITION, AND OBEDIENCE

Observations on Jewish Evangelism

STEVE COHEN

I first met Moishe Rosen at the Lutheran Bible Institute in Seattle in the mid-1970s. This was the first time I had met any other Jewish believers in Jesus following my own conversion in 1973. I was unaware that there were Jews who had been faithful followers of Christ for thirty years or more.

Moishe showed slides of an early Jews for Jesus witnessing campaign in New York City. Young Jewish believers had taken to the streets with music, drama, and broadsides—homemade-style gospel tracts. I was initially opposed to street evangelism. Later I realized that my opposition was due to my failure to see it as a golden opportunity to meet Jews outside my circle of acquaintances.

Moishe invited me to visit him in Portland, Oregon. During that visit, he asked me to accompany him to the airport to make some changes in his ticket. While there, he handed me a stack of broadsides and asked me to stand in a location that would allow me to distribute them to passersby. I did so, and within a few minutes was confronted by a burly police officer, who asked me for my "permit" to hand out the literature. I had no idea what he meant, so I walked over to Moishe and informed him of the situation. He gave me two options: (1) I could stand with him and continue to distribute the broadsides, and in all likelihood we would be arrested; (2) I could stand to the side and watch as he would probably be arrested and taken away.

Because I had to be back to work the following day—and because I really did not understand the implications of being arrested, and I admit I was afraid—I chose to stand aside. Sure enough, the arrest came a few minutes later. Instead of being carted off to jail, he was given a citation to appear in court, and we left the airport within the hour.

Here was my first lesson in opportunity, opposition, and obedience. The opportunity was to reach passengers with the gospel at the airport. The opposition came from an unexpected source. The obedience to move ahead in spite of threatened opposition was the essential requirement. That incident ultimately led to a victory in the Ninth District Federal Court—*Rosen v. Port of Portland*—which was a stepping stone to the unanimous Supreme Court decision allowing literature distribution at the Los Angeles International Airport.

OUR JOURNEY BEGINS

My wife, Jan, and I joined the missionary staff of Jews for Jesus in 1976. Moishe informed us that the organization had nothing tangible to give us. They could not give us mission support or a new vehicle for transportation. One thing, however, they could offer: the opportunity to engage in ordinary conversations and convert them into extraordinary occasions for telling the gospel.

My earliest lesson was that mission work is primarily an entrepreneurial activity. In partnership with the Holy Spirit, we have the privilege of creatively declaring the gospel to both Jews and Gentiles.

Jan's and my first venture was nine months of personal deputation. We sought to win the hearts of God's people to pray, witness, and give in support of Jewish missions over and above their regular church giving. We traveled throughout most of the Midwest, seeking opportunities for a hearing for our work and inviting others to become our mission partners.

During that time, we prayed as to where we might be posted. I vividly recall praying "*Hineni* [here am I]. Send me anywhere to serve you—anywhere, that is, except New York City!" Growing up in the Pacific Northwest, I knew little of the Big Apple except what we were fed in the media—all the grime, all the crime, all the time. Afraid of the unknown, I was experiencing a form of opposition—spiritual warfare that sought to stifle our mission efforts even before we began. And the first place we were assigned? New York City. The choice for us was the same as that faced daily by all Christians: obey and join the fray, or run away. We chose to obey.

RECOGNIZING OPPORTUNITY

In 1977, I was assigned to conduct a weekly outreach at Queens College, a commuter campus with more than 20,000 Jewish students. I traveled by bicycle, as it was close to our apartment, and the butterflies would swarm in my stomach while I was still pedaling. Yet without fail, the moment I stepped onto the campus, God gave a peace that passes all understanding.

It didn't take long for the opposition to organize. Jewish students who were opposed to the gospel soon surrounded me, shouting warnings to passersby to shun the literature. I learned the lessons of frontline mission—how to manage crowds, how to engage and disengage from conversations, and how to use the opposition to further opportunities to tell the gospel.

These lessons were contrary to a lesson my father taught me: Don't rock the boat! If you want to get along with people, don't talk about politics, don't talk about sex, and don't talk about religion. Often when I speak in churches, I begin repeating this advice, and the congregation completes the last clause for me. How do we follow the biblical mandate to speak the gospel in the face of the cultural mandate to avoid controversy? The answer is to understand that sharing the gospel is not talking about religion, but talking about a person—Y'shua, the Jewish Messiah.

I spent an entire school year on the campus. Some might say that each week I generated more heat than light. Eventually the opposition of the Jewish students caught the attention of the student media, and by April 1978, all five student newspapers had featured front-page articles about Jews believing in Jesus and the opposition by the Jewish students. *Good opposition brings good opportunities to broadcast the gospel!*

It was not just the students who gave their opposition. The Catholic student leader and the Lutheran leader also claimed in newspaper letters to the editor that Jewish evangelism is offensive and should not be condoned.

As I evaluated our efforts for that year, I realized that our outreach had resulted in more than thirty articles in the student papers, seminars and workshops, Bible studies, one-on-one conversations, and hundreds of gospel tracts distributed. But to the best of my knowledge, not one Jewish person confessed Jesus as Savior during that year. But the parable of the sower and soils (Matt. 13:1–9) teaches us not just about the condition of the soil, but the attitude of the sower. He did not differentiate between the soils, nor did he evaluate the results; he simply was obedient to his calling, and he sowed his seed wherever he went. Here's the lesson I learned that year: *The hallmark of successful evangelism is obedience—being faithful to show up, fulfill one's duty, and leave the results up to God.*

As it turns out, I had sown some gospel seeds at Queens College. A few years later I was at a retreat for Jewish believers. A young lady approached me and told me that she had been a student at Queens when I was on the campus. From a distance, she had watched me face verbal hostility, yet return week after week to approach people about Jesus. She had never taken one of my broadsides but had picked up some that others discarded. After reading them, she had approached her Christian friends with questions about Jesus. They had explained the gospel to her and she had trusted Jesus and was baptized. She just wanted to thank me for being there. But I knew that I had been there because of the lessons I had learned from Moishe Rosen.

FEARING FAILURE

All of us avoid some activities because we fear failure. I've heard from countless Christians over the years that they do not engage in personal evangelism for fear that they will fail, or perhaps worse, even drive people away. The battle for effective evangelism is sometimes fought most fiercely between our two ears. But we need to be ready to move forward in the face of an enemy who breathes doubt and fear into us.

The Great Commission gives us the privilege to declare God's mighty works so that people will hear and respond in faith. Our role in personal evangelism is *not* to convert people. That is the responsibility of our sovereign God, who draws men and women to himself. Our role is simply to speak so that others can give honest consideration to the gospel. Here's another lesson I've learned: *Failure is not measured in people's rejection of our witness, but by the failure to witness at all.*

A good example of this took place in the 1980s at York University in Toronto. The campus was right across the street from our office, and university officials had declared the public university to be private property. We tried to establish a student group, but the interfaith council was populated by self-proclaimed Jewish student leaders who propagandized that Jewish evangelism was offensive and that we were being deceptive by claiming to be simultaneously Jewish and believers in Jesus. So in order to maintain peace on the campus, the council took the easy way out and denied our application.

I went onto the campus anyway and began to distribute gospel literature. The Jewish students rallied against us and lobbied the administration to have us removed. When I refused to leave, believing we had the right to be there, I was arrested and taken away in handcuffs and charged with trespassing on private property. The case went to court and focused on the rights of individuals to speak in public places. At that time, the Canadian constitution was less developed in case law in this area than in the United States, and we ended up losing.

As a result of that loss, the *Canadian Jewish News*, which previously had ignored our activities in order not to give us a platform, had a change of mind and began writing regular articles about how the Jewish community had "fought us on the campus and won." Ironically, the publicity and student opposition brought more opportunities for us to speak to those who had not already made up their minds. And a few years ago, I received a phone call from our missionary in Toronto, who had just attended a wonderful baptismal service. One of the student leaders who had so vocally and proudly opposed us at York University had studied the Scriptures, discovered that Jesus truly is the Jewish Messiah, believed, and decided to be baptized. At this baptism, affirming his faith in Jesus, he publicly asked for forgiveness for his opposition on campus. This taught me yet another valuable lesson: *We may not always see the end from the beginning, but God works for his glory even through what might initially seem failure!*

EXPECTING OPPOSITION

"I can't witness to my Jewish friend; I respect him too much and I don't want to lose his friendship." I've been sad at hearing these words many times over the years. Many leaders and laymen alike have shied away from including Jewish people in the gracious sweep of the gospel. They feared that someone might take offense and lose respect for them.

But Jesus tells us in the Sermon on the Mount, "Blessed are you when people insult you, persecute you and falsely say all kinds of evil against you because of me. Rejoice and be glad, because great is your reward in heaven, for in the same way they persecuted the prophets who were before you" (Matt. 5:11 12 NIV).

Our Lord informs us that we are blessed when we are persecuted, insulted, and spoken of falsely. How discomforting! Perhaps there should be a "ministry of discomforting" among believers today, helping people work through the fear of rejection, insults, sneers, and slanders.

In response to one of the planned outreaches by Jews for Jesus in the Washington, D.C., area, the following article appeared in the *Washington Times*:

> . . . the Baltimore-based counter missionary organization Jews for Judaism is training local Jewish leaders to prepare for what Washington Jewish Week is calling the "evangelical attack." Scott Hillman, executive director of Jews for Judaism, says . . . "These people are telling the Jewish community what it means to be Jewish," he said. "When you dress up fundamentalist evangelicals

in Jewish clothing and tell them this is Judaism, we find that problematic."

"These aggressive and deceptive tactics demonstrate a lack of religious tolerance and respect," said Rabbi David Bernstein, director of the Washington office of the American Jewish Committee. "Jews for Jesus uses what we consider deceptive practices: Jewish garb and symbols to attract Jews into a different religion."

Mr. Katz [of Jews for Jesus] responded that evangelists on the street will be wearing bright-colored T-shirts with slogans such as "Jews for Jesus," "Jews and others for Jesus" or "Jews and Gentiles for Jesus. We're accused of being deceptive, but we always identify ourselves on our shirts," he said. "It can't get more straightforward than that."

Rabbi Stuart Weinblatt of Congregation B'nai Tzedek in Potomac said some mainstream Protestant groups are sympathetic to their cause. He cited a meeting last week between local Jewish and Presbyterian leaders over a vote at the national assembly of the Presbyterian Church USA (PCUSA) that approved a Presbyterian-sponsored Messianic congregation in Philadelphia. "Our goal is to get Christian groups to condemn these practices," he said.

Several Christian denominations have issued statements criticizing evangelism of Jews, including the Evangelical Lutheran Church of America, the United Church of Christ and the PCUSA, which said in 1988 that Jews have their own covenant with God. In 1996, Pope John Paul II said Jews shouldn't be targeted for conversion.

In 1987, the Interfaith Conference of Metropolitan Washington condemned proselytizing of Jews by Christians.[1]

This one article reveals several aspects of the opposition to Jewish evangelism:

---

1. *Washington Times,* August 10, 2004, originally found at http://www.washingtontimes.com/national/20040810–123436–5028r.htm (no longer available except in archives). See "Statement on Proselytization," InterFaith Conference of Metropolitan Washington, March 16, 1987 at http://jewsforjudaism.org/index2.php?option=com_docman&task=doc_view&gid=17&Itemid=47.

- There is a denial that one can be Jewish and believe in Jesus at the same time.
- There is an accusation that, by indicating we are Jewish *and* believe in Jesus, we are being deceptive.
- There is organization to the opposition.
- Jewish leaders seek to sway Christian leaders against Jewish evangelism and are often successful.
- Some in the opposition adhere to a two-covenant theory: Jewish people are already saved by virtue of the covenant with Abraham and not in need of evangelistic efforts by the church.
- Evangelism, in and of itself, is labeled as "aggressive."

But what's new, after all, about organized opposition? The prophets faced organized opposition, the apostles faced organized opposition, Jesus faced organized opposition. Do we deserve better? What is more, I agree with Moishe, who says that opposition brings opportunity for the gospel. Jesus often confronted his opponents, not that *they* might necessarily have their minds changed, but that those who were listening in and had not made up their minds might hear and consider spiritual truths. I reiterate, opposition provides opportunities to broadcast the gospel! And let us be clear that while people may be *opponents* of the gospel, the real *enemy* is Satan (Luke 13:16).

RECOGNIZING DECEPTION

A great modern deception that has resulted in withholding the gospel from the Jewish people is called the two-covenant theory. Simply put, it claims that Jewish people, by virtue of their covenant with God, are saved already and do not need to go through Jesus for personal salvation. Therefore, there are two ways of salvation, one for Jews and the other for Gentiles.[2] Representative of this view are the words of Eric Gritsch in a publication of the Lutheran Council in the USA, distributed by the Evangelical Lutheran Church in America (ELCA):

---

2. Franz Rosenzweig, *The Star of Redemption* (Madison, WI: University of Wisconsin Press, 2005).

There really is no need for any Christian mission to the Jews. They are and remain the people of God, even if they do not accept Jesus Christ as their Messiah. Why this is so only God knows. Christians should concentrate their missionary activities on those who do not yet belong to the people of God, and they should court them with a holistic witness in word and deed rather than with polemical argument and cultural legislation. The long history of Christian anti-Semitism calls for repentance, not triumphalist claims of spiritual superiority.

The two-covenant theory of salvation that Franz Rosenzweig developed in *The Star of Redemption* states that God has established two different but equally valid covenants, one with his people Israel and the other with the Gentiles.[3] The Covenant in Moses and the Covenant in Jesus are complementary to each other. Glatzer quotes Rosenzweig on this as follows: Christianity acknowledges the God of the Jews, not as God but as "the Father of Jesus Christ." Christianity itself cleaves to the "Lord" because it knows that the Father can be reached only through him. . . . We are all wholly agreed as to what Christ and his church mean to the world: no one can reach the Father save through him. No one can reach the Father! But the situation is quite different for one who does not have to reach the Father because he is already with him. And this is true of the people of Israel (though not of individual Jews).

Concerning this Rabbi Jakob J. Petuchowski stated: "Rosenzweig conceded more than any Jew, while remaining a Jew, had conceded before him. He admitted the truth of John 14:6." This is immediately qualified, though, by the assertion that "the Jew does not have to come to the Father. He has been with the Father ever since Sinai."

The Catholic Church agrees with the two-covenant theory, as evidenced by this statement in *Reflections on Covenant and Mission*:

In a remarkable and still most pertinent study paper presented at the sixth meeting of the International Catholic-Jewish Liaison Committee in Venice twenty-five years ago, Prof. Tommaso Federici

---

3. Joe Gudel, *To the Jew First*, 3–5, at www.aohems.org.

examined the missiological implications of Nostra Aetate. He argued on historical and theological grounds that there should be in the Church no organizations of any kind dedicated to the conversion of Jews. This has over the ensuing years been the de facto practice of the Catholic Church.

More recently, Cardinal Walter Kasper, President of the Pontifical Commission for the Religious Relations with the Jews, explained this practice. In a formal statement made first at the seventeenth meeting of the International Catholic-Jewish Liaison Committee in May 2001, and repeated later in the year in Jerusalem, Cardinal Kasper spoke of "mission" in a narrow sense to mean "proclamation" or the invitation to baptism and catechesis. He showed why such initiatives are not appropriately directed at Jews: The term mission, in its proper sense, refers to conversion from false gods and idols to the true and one God, who revealed himself in the salvation history with His elected people. Thus mission, in this strict sense, cannot be used with regard to Jews, who believe in the true and one God. Therefore, and this is characteristic, there exists dialogue but there does not exist any Catholic missionary organization for Jews.

As we said previously, dialogue is not mere objective information; dialogue involves the whole person. So in dialogue Jews give witness of their faith, witness of what supported them in the dark periods of their history and their life, and Christians give account of the hope they have in Jesus Christ. In doing so, both are far away from any kind of proselytism, but both can learn from each other and enrich each other. We both want to share our deepest concerns to an often disoriented world that needs such witness and searches for it.

From the point of view of the Catholic Church, Judaism is a religion that springs from divine revelation. As Cardinal Kasper noted, "God's grace, which is the grace of Jesus Christ according to our faith, is available to all. Therefore, the Church believes that Judaism, i.e. the faithful response of the Jewish people to God's irrevocable covenant, is salvific for them, because God is faithful to his promises."

This statement about God's saving covenant is quite specific to Judaism. Though the Catholic Church respects all religious traditions and through dialogue with them can discern the workings of the Holy Spirit, and though we believe God's infinite grace is surely available to believers of other faiths, it is only about Israel's covenant that the Church can speak with the certainty of the biblical witness. This is because Israel's [s]criptures form part of our own biblical canon and they have a "perpetual value . . . that has not been canceled by the later interpretation of the New Testament."[4]

The issue is simply this: Jesus said in John 14:6 that he is the way, the truth, and the life, and that no one comes to the Father but by him. At the time, he was speaking to Jewish people who had Moses, the Law, the prophets, the festivals, the Temple, the sacrifices, the priesthood, the high priest, the land of Israel, and the promise of the Messiah. Yet Jesus did not exempt the Jewish people from the requirement of coming to the Father through him. Essentially, therefore, Jesus is either the Messiah for all or no Messiah at all. As Moishe has often said, "One of the most anti-Semitic things we could do is to withhold the gospel from the Jewish people."

What are we to do, then? Our direction is clear. *Opportunities* abound. *Opposition* will seek to make us detour from our main mission. But in *obedience* to the Great Commission, we choose to move ahead anyway. On a personal note, I thank Moishe for his influence in my life and the lives of so many over the past fifty years.

---

4. Consultation of the National Council of Synagogues and the Bishops Committee for Ecumenical and Interreligious Affairs (August 12, 2002), at http://www.jcrelations.net/en/?item=966.

PART 2

ETHICS

5

MELCHIOR TSCHOUDY: FAILURE, CROOK, OR MISSIONARY ORDINARY?

A Study of the London Jews Society's First Emissary to the Levant in the Nineteenth Century

KAI KJÆR-HANSEN

Translated from the Danish
by Birger Petterson

In 1980 Moishe Rosen was instrumental in founding the *Lausanne Consultation on Jewish Evangelism* (LCJE).[1] Since then he has invested time and strength to take part in practically all International and North American LCJE conferences. At the Seventh International Conference in Helsinki 2003, his topic was *The Fact of Failure*. Because

---

1. Cf. *Christian Witness to the Jewish People*, Lausanne Occasional Papers no. 7 (Wheaton, IL: Lausanne Committee for World Evangelization, 1980).

of illness he had to cancel his participation, but his paper was read by Tuvya Zaretsky, LCJE's president.[2]

In his Helsinki paper, Moishe Rosen mentioned, among other things, how we are fooling ourselves about our achievements when we give far too high numbers for Jews who come to faith in Jesus. "Just knowing about the exaggeration and that it is accepted as being true by my colleagues in Jewish missions makes me feel like a failure by belonging to a profession that need[s] these exaggerations. I am ashamed of us."

Moishe Rosen continued,

> We overstate our effectiveness and achievements and do many other things to avoid facing our failures.
>
> Some ministries are careful to have goals so large that nobody expects them to meet those goals, and that is their way to avoid admitting failure. When one is committed to reaching all the Jews of Paris, the task is so daunting that no one would expect success.
>
> On the other hand there are those who will announce no goals and then whatever is accomplished can be considered a success. For some, the best way to avoid failure is to not attempt anything that could result in failure.[3]

With these comments Moishe Rosen has set the stage for a critical assessment of how we, today, describe success in Jewish evangelism, our own as well as that of the past. It goes without saying that "success" and "failure" are not the only criteria to be applied when an "ordinary" missionary is to be appraised. History shows examples of how a board's expectations have had a negative influence on the appraisal of the individual.

A case in point concerns Melchior Tschoudy, in 1820 the first representative for the London Jews Society (LJS) to be sent to the Levant.[4] The man has a bad posthumous reputation, the main source dating back to 1860. But in examining historical evidence, it is not

---

2. Moishe Rosen, "The Fact of Failure," in *LCJE Helsinki 2003*, ed. Kai Kjær-Hansen (Århus, Denmark: LCJE, 2003), 297–303.
3. Ibid., 297–98.
4. In contemporary sources the name also appears with the spelling Tschudi (a form

just a question of digging up old sources, it is also a question of *assessing* them critically. In doing so I hope to give Tschoudy some sort of rehabilitation. Myths die hard, however, and only by going deeply into the historical details is it possible to challenge them.

MELCHIOR TSCHOUDY AND
HIS POSTHUMOUS REPUTATION

Little has been written about Melchior Tschoudy, and few sources from his own hand have thus far emerged from the archives. Thus, the existence of a letter written by Tschoudy himself is important. Dated December 16, 1826, the letter was written in Basel, Switzerland, and in it Tschoudy states that he was born in Schwanden in the Canton of Glarus (in Switzerland) in the year 1790.

After studying theology in Basel in 1809, he served as a minister in several places in Switzerland, after which the London Jews Society (LJS) employed him to be a "preacher" in Jerusalem in "Canaan."[5]

W. T. Gidney, LJS's historian, wrote this about Tschoudy in 1908:

Anxious to ascertain the state of the Jews in Palestine and other countries bordering on the Levant, the Committee in the year 1820 secured the service of a Swiss pastor, the Rev. Melchior Tschoudy, who had some experience of the East. He was sent out to Palestine, and called at Malta on his way, where he received valuable information from the Rev. W. Jowett and Dr. Naudi, representatives of the C.M.S. in the island. Tschoudy's labours do not appear to have been successful, judging from certain remarks of Dr. Wolff, who, however, states that [Tschoudy] baptized two Jews at Beyrout.[6]

---

he used himself in German), Tschudy or Tschoudi. In this chapter the sources are quoted with their own name forms.

5. The letter is in the Basel Mission Archive, which has kindly provided me with a copy. I got on the track of the letter through Yaron Perry, *British Mission to the Jews in Nineteenth-Century Palestine* (London; Portland, OR: Frank Cass, 2003), 16–17.

6. W. T. Gidney, *The History of the London Society for Promoting Christianity Amongst the Jews, from 1809 to 1908* (London: LJS, 1908), 118. Gidney refers to Joseph Wolff, *Travels and Adventures of the Rev. Joseph Wolff* (London: Saunders, Otley, 1860), 1:173, 227. Anyone who wants to study LJS's earliest history will greatly benefit from Gidney's historical work. But in order to get to the core of this history it is necessary to reappraise the sources.

Recently Dr. Yaron Perry, director of the Gottlieb Schumacher Institute for the Research of Christian Activities in Nineteenth-Century Palestine, has argued—with support in sources from the nineteenth century—that choosing Tschoudy "was a bad bargain" for LJS. Writes Perry,

> Tschudy left Alexandria for Palestine at the beginning of 1821, and during the course of his journey managed to convert a few Jews. However, it soon became clear that choosing him was a bad bargain, as he turned out to be a crook, and that among his other double dealings he had offered his service to the Turkish governor as a military strategist.[7]

So to Gidney, Tschoudy is "not successful"; to Perry, Tschoudy is "a crook." I intend to put some question marks against both views *without*, however, declaring Tschoudy an absolute "success."

CONSIDERING THE EVIDENCE

London, February 8, 1820. LJS's Sub Committees for Missions and Correspondence held a meeting.[8] There were some encouraging issues on the agenda, since the committee was considering individuals from abroad who were willing to be employed as missionaries in LJS's service. For some years, LJS had experienced difficulty finding British people for this task.

Letters were presented in which LJS was offered two students as missionaries from Johann (John) Jänicke's Missionary College at Berlin.[9]

Next the committee looked at letters from Paris of January 12 and 28, 1820, from John Bayford, who was ardently engaged in the spiritual welfare of the Jewish people and who, in several periods, was a member of LJS's committee.

One cannot help feeling frustrated that these letters presumably have been lost. From LJS's minutes and resolutions, it is nevertheless possible to see that the letters concerned "a Mr. Melchior Tschudy, a

---

7. Perry, *British Mission to the Jews*, 17.
8. The minute books are kept in the archives of LJS at Bodleian Library, Oxford under the heading CMJ (The Church's Ministry Among Jewish people).
9. Bodleian, CMJ, d.12, no. 37.

German by birth, lately officiating at Geneva, whom [Mr. Bayford] proposes to be employed by the Society."[10]

The minutes read, "Resolved that Mr. Bayford be requested to send over Mr. Melchior Tschudy for the examination of this Sub Committee." The committee was, as usual, willing to pay for travel and maintenance—but not more—"while [Mr. Tschudy] remains in England awaiting the decision of the Committee."[11]

In other words, no one—no one—was employed by LJS without the committee's personal "examination" of the candidate. The committee took their responsibility very seriously. Thus, before LJS sent an invitation to Tschoudy, they tried to procure opinions about him from others.

London, February 21, 1820. The subcommittee resolved that letters be sent to Paris and Switzerland to make enquiries respecting Tschoudy's "former situation and character."[12] It was decided that the members of the committee who knew French "be requested to converse with Mr. Tschudy on the subject of his Religion and general View, and Character, and that Mr. Tschudi be requested to state his opinions in writing with respect to his General Religion Views and the Jewish Question in particular."[13]

London, March 28, 1820. A letter was in hand from "Mr. Blumhart of Basel, respecting Mr. M. Tschudy." The general committee read the letter, which must have been a positive one for it was resolved that the subcommittee would now write directly to Tschoudy, (implied) to invite him to negotiations in England.[14] In April of 1820, then, Tschoudy presents himself in London, accompanied by his wife, to meet with the London Jews Society.

London, April 24, 1820. In regard to the subcommittee's negotiations with Tschoudy, the interview with him was "very satisfactory." Therefore it was "resolved that it be recommended to the General

---

10. It is not quite correct that Tschoudy was "a German by birth"; he was a Swiss with German as "his native language"; cf. *Jewish Expositor* (London: Ogle, Duncan, & Co., 1821), 22; he also spoke French.
11. Bodleian, CMJ, d.12, no. 38.
12. Ibid., d.12, no. 50. "Paris" presumably stands for John Bayford and "Basel" for C. G. Blumhardt, who was then director of the Missions Institute in Basel, established in 1815.
13. Ibid., d.12, no. 51.
14. Ibid., c.9, no. 413.

Committee to employ Mr. Melchior Tschudy to take a Voyage and Journey through the Mediterranean and parts adjacent (more especially Palestine) for the purpose of conversing with the Jews, collecting information respecting them and distributing Testaments and Tracts."[15]

London, April 25, 1820. The general committee recommended that the subcommittee be entrusted "to make the necessary arrangements for Mr. and Mrs. Tschudy proceeding on their Voyage without delay" and negotiate with Tschudy about the salary.[16] At this same meeting the general committee granted £2,2,0 per week for food and lodging and a further £15 to provide the Tschoudys with clothes.[17]

So far the process had gone well, and from now on it gathers speed.

London, May 10, 1821. Committee member Joseph Gibbs Barker informed the committee that a vessel "named the Juno is on the point of sailing to Malta, and the Captain would take Mr. Tschudy and his Wife for £42." The boat was leaving "next Monday" (May 15); the next boat would not leave until four or six weeks later. It was resolved that the couple leave "without delay," and it was noted that Mr. Tschudy "be allowed a Salary for one year of £150– to commence from the 15th Inst. [May 1820] to provide himself and Mrs. Tschudy in Food, Raiment and all personal wants." Travel expenses were not included in this but were, as usual, paid as per account by the Society.[18]

London, May 23, 1820. It was entered into the minutes that Tschoudy had set out on his journey.[19] The general committee also approved a grant, with retrospective effect, to Tschoudy "to purchase presents."[20]

The committee, then, had done what was expected of a responsible committee: after a thorough examination of the candidate they have determined the length of the employment and the size of the salary. And Tschoudy lived up to LJS's expectations to leave without delay.

The task for Tschoudy to perform was tripartite: (1) converse with the Jews; (2) collect information; (3) distribute Testaments and Tracts. Note that these three tasks do not seem to have been listed in

---

15. Ibid., d.12, no. 82.
16. Ibid., c. 9, no. 418.
17. Ibid., c.9, no. 420.
18. Ibid., c.9, no. 448.
19. Ibid., c.9, no. 461.
20. Ibid., c.9, no. 469.

prioritized order. The committee gave no precise instructions about details, but neither did they leave Tschoudy to his own devices. When he arrived in Malta, Tschoudy was to be advised about the future proceedings by Jowett and Naudi. This does not mean that the committee disclaimed responsibility for Tschoudy but that they acknowledged that people in the Levant were better qualified to give advice than they were back in London. It was a very sensible attitude.

Before Tschoudy left London, LJS held its twelfth anniversary meeting at the beginning of May 1820. It is uncertain whether Mr. and Mrs. Tschoudy were present at that meeting, but the report of that meeting includes these words:

> [The committee] has already succeeded in engaging a Swiss Protestant minister of whose piety and talents, after much enquiry, they have reason to think well; as he has already travelled in the East, and is acquainted with the languages necessary for such an undertaking, it is intended that he shall direct his course without delay to the shores of the Mediterranean, to labour amongst the numerous Jews in those parts, and largely to circulate amongst them the words of eternal life.[21]

What precisely was meant with the words that Tschoudy had already "travelled in the East" and had language skills was not spelled out. It is noteworthy that to the friends of the mission it was stressed that Tschoudy was expected to involve himself in *direct* missionary work among Jewish people and not also to collect information, that is, be a researcher.

In the June 1820 issue of the *Jewish Expositor* appears a short announcement that Tschoudy "has sailed for Malta since the [LJS] Anniversary, with letters of introduction to Mr. Jowett, and Dr. Naudi, from whence he will proceed (as they shall advise) either to Egypt or Palestine."[22]

The committee in London had thereby placed the planning of Tschoudy's future mission into the hands of the experts in Malta. The

---

21. *Jewish Expositor*, June 1820, 224.
22. Ibid., 228.

Malta committee, however, made some adjustment to the London committee's agreement with Tscoudy.

Malta, July 26, 1820. The committee received letters from Jowett and Naudi—and also one from Tschoudy—"announcing the safe arrival of the latter." These letters had reached the general committee on September 26.[23] Note that four and a half months of Tschoudy's twelve-month employment period had now passed.

The Malta committee to advise Tschoudy consisted of Jowett and Naudi.[24] In the beginning of September it was expanded with Joseph Greaves as treasurer; he had been sent out by the London Missionary Society.

Immediately on Tschoudy's arrival in Malta, the parties began discussing his future, and it was "determined that the latter should confine his route at present to Syria." Comprehensive notes confirm three more meetings held July 28, August 4, and September 5, 1820.[25]

Malta, July 28, 1820. Tschoudy suggested that he should first go to Baghdad. The Malta committee did not completely reject Mr. Tschoudy's suggestion. The Malta committee would make a route and a schedule so Tschoudy would be in Jerusalem at Easter 1821, although the schedule would be tight. Further, "It is impossible to travel according to calendar and map." The importance of "know[ing] the modern state of Syria, relative to the Jews" is to be given the highest priority and, we say that it "is better to begin with what is near [Syria] than with what is far off."

The Malta committee pointed out that the journey to Syria is best undertaken via Alexandria, Egypt, and, what was more important, not until Tschoudy reached Alexandria would his twelve-month employment for his mission begin, which meant an extra five months, approximately, compared with the agreement in London. Further, the Malta committee suggested that the LJS in London would have to decide for themselves

---

23. Bodleian, CMJ, c.9, no. 604.
24. William Jowett, who had arrived in Malta in 1815, published his findings in two copious volumes: *Christian Researches in the Mediterranean, From MDCCCXV to MDCCCXX.* (London: Church Missionary Society, 1822); and *Christian Researches in Syria and the Holy Land* (London: Church Missionary Society, 1825). Dr. Cleardo Naudi, who was a Roman Catholic, was of great help both for the British and Foreign Bible Society and the LJS; his efforts might be worth studying.
25. *Jewish Expositor* 1821, 16–23.

whether or not Tschoudy through his journals had provided the committee with the necessary information and therefore could return to Europe.

It was mentioned that Tschoudy on his arrival in Malta manifested "a wish to remain in the Levant." This wish entered into the negotiations. The possibility of a further extension of his employment must have been, seen from Malta, an open question for LJS in London. Maybe the LJS in London wanted him, after the twelve months, to wait in the Levant "for the arrival of the other Gentleman expected." And back in London they had to calculate with unforeseen causes—want of ships, plague, disturbances, etc.—so it was recommended that LJS allow Tschoudy "a discretionary power of three months additional; the reasons for using which, he will of course specify in his communications with the Society." No precise date was given for Tschoudy's departure from Malta.[26]

Malta, August 4, 1820. It was resolved to postpone Mr. and Mrs. Tschoudy's departure from Malta.

Tschoudy's departure did not happen "without delay," as the journey from London did. The reason for this is given by Yaron Perry in the following way: "An outbreak of malaria in the East resulting in the temporary closure of the Mediterranean ports forced Tschudy to spend a few more months in Malta."[27]

But this is not quite what the sources say. Rather, the postponement is on grounds of principle and is not based on knowledge of an actual outbreak of malaria. The *season*, as such, was too dangerous, which the LJS in London had not taken into consideration, but in Malta they did not want to risk Tschoudy's life. Experience—not to mention *research*—has shown that malaria prevails "almost universally in the ports of the Levant in the months of Autumn." Jowett was earlier warned by Mr. Barker, consul at Aleppo, "not to approach the coast of Syria and Cyprus in the Autumn."

Christoph Burckhardt's "melancholy" death was used as a warning. This Bible-man was buried in Aleppo on August 14, 1818. Perhaps Jowett was still haunted by the memory that he was the architect behind Burckhardt's journey to Syria.[28] Now Jowett does not want to be

---

26. Ibid., 16–17.
27. Perry, *British Mission to the Jews*, 16.
28. See *Mishkan*, no. 42 (2005): 57–67.

responsible for a similar fate for Tschoudy because of bad planning. "It was therefore considered that for about six weeks Mr. Tschoudy might profitably employ his time in some preparatory studies, and enquiring into the state of the few Jews in Malta."[29]

Malta, September 5, 1820. Exact dates for the future communication between Tschoudy and LJS in London had now been decided upon my the Malta committee. "Mr. Tschoudy must aim at sending from Syria by the safest hand he can procure, under date of Feb. 1, 1821, a full account of his proceedings up to that period, by which the Committee in London may form their determination." The committee in London was then to commit itself to answering Tschoudy with a letter to reach him by June 30 in Aleppo with "Instructions from London." The Malta committee was aware that the postal service might be delayed, for they allow for the possibility that Tschoudy "may remain there [in Aleppo] even till August, should the Instructions not come sooner."

Just so there was no doubt that the London committee was kept apprised, "Considering the extreme uncertainty of opportunities of post or courier in the Levant, Mr. Tschoudy is directed to have a letter (whether longer or shorter) ready-closed every fortnight, to dispatch as opportunities may offer; in every letter mentioning letters sent."

Finally, the Malta committee "after much consideration" determined "to furnish Mr. Tschoudy with £200 partly in cash, partly in credit, to be in his actual possession on arriving at Alexandria, from which point his mission begins."[30]

After the matter of Tscoudy's allowance, came his "Instructions" in three points: (1) *To qualify himself* "by learning languages"; (2) *To examine into the State of the People,* "that is, *Research*, in reference to the future plans of the Society"; (3) *Measures of Improvement of the Jews*—"the distribution of the Hebrew New Testament must not be done with violence to the feelings of the ignorant Levantines, but according as they are able to bear it,—'if any man will.' . . ."[31]

While Tschoudy during the negotiations in London had accepted an assignment in three points (conversing with the Jews, collecting

29. *Jewish Expositor,* 1821, 17–18.
30. Ibid., 18.
31. Ibid., 19–21; followed by Miscellaneous: *The Consuls* and *The Jews,* 21–23.

information respecting them, and distributing Testaments and tracts), a significant *prioritization* of these was made during the talks in Malta. It was emphasized in the instructions that future "Preachers cannot go forth with the best effect, till many things are first enquired into." Research, then, had to be the first priority in Tschoudy's mission, and details were not unimportant: "such an apparently trivial thing as the *date* of a voyage or journey, may perhaps be the saving of the lives, or the expediting of the plans, of a future Missionary-party." The prioritization in Tschoudy's mission was expressed in the following words: "As appears by the tenor of the present Instructions, nearly all that is intended by [Tschoudy's] Mission is Research: though the distribution of Hebrew Scriptures is also included."

But the expectations were great:

> The topics of *Research* in the *Instructions* are numerous and highly important. The main thing is not to take them in the letter merely, but also in the spirit. Invent new topics. Imagine this case:—that in the year 1825, five persons will proceed on a Mission to the Jews in Syria. Mr. Tschoudy is to be their *Pilot and Guide*. Either personally, or by his papers, he ought to be.[32]

During the negotiations in Malta it may have become clear that Tschoudy's knowledge of English was not the best. It was suggested to the London Committee that they should let Tschoudy write his journals "in his native language, German." Translation would cost LJS only a few pounds![33]

Tschoudy and his wife could now leave Malta, and from then on his wife disappeared from the picture. Tschoudy had clear instructions

---

32. *Jewish Expositor,* 1821, 20.
33. That the experts in Malta have Tschoudy's and his mission's interests at heart appears from the following: "As it is to be hoped that Mr. Tschoudy will send to England very full journals, and as these, whether he survives or not, will be for the present the most valuable fruit of his Mission, we recommend him to write his journals and letters in his native language, German. The translation of them will cost the Society at home a few pounds; the saving will be, Mr. Tschoudy's time and health, which would be greatly interrupted, if in the midst of his arduous and various pursuits, he had to write in a strange tongue; in which, moreover, he could never adequately express his genuine feelings and opinions." *Jewish Expositor,* 1821, 22.

about what was expected of him. His primary task was to be that of re-searcher and, what was more, the Malta committee's agreement with Tschoudy implied that LJS in London from then on was to consider him as such.

Without casting the Malta committee, headed by Jowett, in the part of villain, it may be said that Tschoudy was now about to fulfill Jowett's (good) ambitions of research for the sake of the gospel in the Levant. It is easy, in the clear light of hindsight, to question if it was wise to *narrow* Tschoudy's task compared with the tripartite task he was given in London. While the Malta committee had the main responsibility for this narrowing, Tschoudy did accept, and LJS did not object.

Once Tschoudy left Malta, what was his itinerary? With basis in Tschoudy's (few) letters to LJS, it is possible to make a qualified guess. It is certain that Tschoudy was in Alexandria in the middle of November 1820, and that he did not leave Egypt before January 5, 1821, and that it was his plan to sail to Beirut.[34] It is certain that he was in Beirut and/or Acre, either before or after he went to Jerusalem. It is certain that he was in Nazareth on March 27 and 28 and in Jerusalem on April 6 and 7, and that he intended to continue to Aleppo. It is relatively certain that he was in Aleppo in the end of October 1821. Finally it is certain that Tschoudy was in Malta on February 10, 1822.

On this background it is fairly safe to assume the following itin-erary: *Malta*; *Alexandria*; *Beirut* (and hereafter perhaps Acre, Safet, Tiberias); *Nazareth* (and then probably Nablus); *Jerusalem* (and maybe then Jaffo, Beirut, Damascus); *Aleppo* (and then presumably Beirut and then either Alexandria or Cyprus); *Malta*.

Details other than Tschoudy's general location, however, are sketchy. The sources leave no doubt that the number of letters sent by Tschoudy were few and insufficient and did not live up to LJS's expec-tations. The committee in London experienced, in fact, a disturbing lack of reports. And the dates of these reports are not irrelevant. The clock was ticking in London. Did they get value for their money?

London, February 22, 1821. The first letter from Mr. Tschoudy was received by LJS in London, which means that nine months out of his original twelve-month employment period had now passed.

---

34. *Missionary Register* (London: L. B. Seely 1822), 39.

To make matters worse, Tschoudy *did* write a letter earlier but it had been a long time underway and arrived after the one that LJS received first. So the letter that was written first chronologically was considered later, not until March 22, 1821, which Tschoudy naturally cannot be blamed for.

London, February 22, 1821. The subcommittee read Mr. Tschoudy's letter from Alexandria dated January 5, 1821. Mr. Tschoudy informed the committee in this letter that he had drawn £100. We do not know what else was mentioned in the letter. There were also letters from Jowett, who was on leave in Cambridge. Presumably these letters answered to the committee's request for an explanation for this money.

London committee member Joseph Gibbs Barker drew attention to the fact "that the 100£ drawn was on account of the credit given to the Rev. M. Tschudy by the Rev. Mr. Jowett." The money transaction was approved.[35] Further, it was "resolved that the consideration of the Rev. M. Tschudy's future employment be postponed until the next Meeting of this Sub Committee."[36]

With the scanty reports from Tschoudy in mind, a money transaction like this did not help to create understanding for his lack of reports.

London, February 27, 1821. The general committee approved the postponement and resolved that letters be sent to Tschoudy to meet with the British consul, John Barker, in Aleppo.[37]

London, March 22, 1821. The subcommittee read the letter from Mr. Tschoudy, dated Alexandria, November 16, 1820.[38] More than four months had passed from the time the letter was sent until it reading, when it was considered in the committee. More than ten months had passed since Mr. Tschoudy left London. The committee wondered why they had not received Mr. Tschoudy's report, which, according to the instructions, he was supposed to send by February 1.

London, March 27, 1821. The general committee felt it must chastise Mr. Tschoudy and resolved "that the Rev. M. Tschudy be informed

---

35. Bodleian, CMJ, d.12, no. 278.
36. Ibid., d.12, no. 279.
37. Ibid., c.9, no. 750.
38. Ibid., d.12, no. 291.

that the Letters hitherto received from him, are not by any means satisfactory to the Committee."[39]

What they could not know in London on March 27 was that Tschoudy on that very same day, and the next, wrote letters from Nazareth. These were not read in London until July 23, 1821. We do not know the content of them—perhaps he mentioned a few baptisms in Beirut (see below). But by that time the committee had lost patience with him.

London, May 21, 1821. The subcommittee decided to send a letter to Consul Barker in Aleppo about Tschoudy's engagement with the society.[40]

London, May 22, 1821. The general committee entered the following with reference to the above resolution:

> Resolved that a Letter be written to Mr. Tschudy informing him that this Committee has not received any Letter from him subsequent of his leaving Alexandria and that he be desired immediately to send a Copy of all his Letters and his Journal subsequent 1st Jan. of 1821 to this Committee, and to wait at Aleppo for further direction.[41]

The thirteenth anniversary of the LJS was held in the beginning of May 1821. Thus, the preceding resolution was entered about three weeks after the anniversary. What did the committee tell the friends of the mission? They were informed, with reference to last year's 1820 anniversary, that Mr. Tschudy had left for "the Eastern shores of the Mediterranean, for the purpose of making enquiry into

---

39. Ibid., c.9, no. 786.
40. The resolution from the subcommittee, May 21, 1821, reads, "Resolved that a Letter be written to Mr. Barker the Consul of Aleppo stating the circumstances of the Rev. M. Tschudy's engagement with this Society and that he had taken the Sum of £100 with him from Malta, and had drawn for another £100 at Alexandria, and requesting Mr. Barker on Mr. Tschudy's arrival at Aleppo to advance him such Money as shall be due to him after the rate of £150 Pr. Annum from the 3rd Oct. 1820 to 3rd Oct. 1821, allowing for Travelling Expenses according to the original agreement (the account of which the Committee will thank Mr. Barker to ascertain the correctness of,) deducting the Sum of the £200 already received, and further request that Mr. Barker will have the goodness to give the Committee his opinion of Mr. Tschudy's past, and present operations, as well as any future ones he may contemplate, sending a Copy of such communication to Mr. Josh Greaves at Malta." Bodleian, CMJ, d.12, no. 320.
41. Ibid., c.10, no. 39.

the state of the Jews in those parts." The change in the definition of his assignment—from Bible-man to researcher—had been made in accordance with the adjustments that were made in Malta. Profuse thanks were extended to Jowett and Naudi for the instructions they had provided to Tschoudy.

After this comes a digression about the Jewish immigration to Palestine, which removes attention from the concluding words: "No intelligence has been received from Mr. Tschoudy since he left Alexandria."[42]

In this way LJS publicly gave expression to a hope that dates back to Malta, August 1820, even though the committee, in May 1821, was frustrated and disillusioned with Tschoudy. It took a lot for LJS to publicly expose a missionary.

THE LJS COMMITTEE'S DISMISSAL OF TSCHOUDY

London, June 26, 1821. The general committee resolved that a letter "be written to the Rev. M. Tschudy to be at Malta by the beginning of September."[43]

The committee's great frustrations showed through, for the time frame was quite unrealistic. Probably they sent the letter to several contacts, for they did not know exactly where Tschoudy was or when he would receive it.

London, July 23, 1821. The committee at last received two letters from Tschoudy, dated Nazareth, March 27 and 28, 1821. These letters may have contained encouraging information about Tschoudy's having distributed Scriptures and even baptized some Jews in Beirut. But the committee in London was so frustrated at the lack of reports, all they could think of was how to get him back to Europe.

---

42. I wonder what considerations have gone before the formulation of this paragraph from the anniversary in 1821: "For these services the most cordial thanks of the Society are due to those truly Christian friends, and they [the Committee] trust that the judicious advice they afforded Mr. Tschoudy will be serviceable to many future missionaries to the countries bordering on the Levant; which will become, every year, more interesting scenes of missionary labour, in connection with the Society, if it be true, as stated in advices from Odessa, that Jewish emigrants continue to embark at the port for Palestine, in expectation of the approaching advent of their Messiah. No intelligence has been received from Mr. Tschoudy since he left Alexandria." *Jewish Expositor,* 1821, 234.
43. Bodleian, CMJ, c.10, no. 63.

The committee "resolve[d] that a Letter be written to the Rev. Dr. Naudi and Joseph Greaves at Malta requesting them to settle accounts with Mr. Tschudy on his arrival at Malta, paying him such balance as may be due to him for one Year's Salary and travelling expenses to the 3rd of October next [1821], the day on which his engagement with the Society terminates, and also to allow him such a sum of Money as will convey him either to Marseilles, or Switzerland, according as he may prefer; and if it shall turn out that he has expended his whole Salary in his support, that they give him an additional £20– for his immediate necessities when he arrives at either of the above places."[44]

The committee furthermore made allowance for the possibility that they might have treated Tschoudy unfairly. Therefore, it was further "resolved that if upon investigation it shall appear to the Rev. Dr. Naudi and Mr. Greaves that the services of Mr. Tschudy in Palestine have been more efficient than they appear to the Committee to have been, a discretionary power be left to them, of delaying the discharge of Mr. Tschudy until they have communicated their opinion to the Committee.[45]

London, July 24, 1821. The general committee confirmed "the dismissal of the Rev. M. Tschudy on his arrival at Malta."[46]

London, October 23, 1821. Through a letter from Greaves in Malta, dated August 15, the general committee was informed that the former "had no information from, or of Mr. Tschoudy since he left Egypt."[47]

In other words, in Malta, where they were supposed to forward letters from London to Tschoudy, they did not know how to reach him.

London, November 27, 1821. The committee treated four letters with reference to Tschoudy, presumably answers to the Committee's requests for information about him.[48]

London, January 14, 1822. The committee read a letter from Mr. Barker "dated Aleppo 23rd Oct. 1821 respecting the Rev. Tschoudy." It is most likely, however, that at the time when the letter was written,

---

44. Ibid., d.12, no. 348.
45. Ibid., d.12, no. 349.
46. Ibid., c.10, no. 87.
47. Ibid., c.10, no. 209.
48. It is a pity we do not know the content of the letters from Wolff, dated Alexandria, September 4 (even if he does not arrive there until September 6); from Greaves, Malta, September 22; from Consul Barker, Aleppo, September 10; from Levi Parsons, Jerusalem, May 5, 1821. Bodleian, CMJ, c.10, no. 262.

Tschoudy was still in, or had just left, Aleppo.[49] On his arrival in Malta in the beginning of 1822, Tschoudy got busy writing letters, doubtless after he had received letters with the information that he had been fired.

London, March 26, 1822. At long last the committee received a letter from Mr. Tschoudy, dated Malta, February 10, 1822. It was "resolved that Mr. M. Tschudy be informed that the engagement of this Society with him, having been specifically for one Year only, and that period having expired, this Committee can only confirm their former Resolution."[50]

London, April 23, 1822. The committee treated four additional letters from Mr. Tschoudy, written in Malta on February 13, 15, 19, and 25, 1822. In addition, the committee received a letter from Mr. Joseph Greaves dated Malta, February 19. But as far as the committee was concerned, nothing more was left to negotiate. Therefore it was "resolved that the arrangement adopted by the Malta Committee respecting the Rev. M. Tschudy be approved."[51]

As to details in this "arrangement" one will have to guess on the basis of the above-mentioned correspondence. One thing is certain: LJS did not prolong Tschoudy's employment. Judged by the Fourteenth Report of the London Society, which was read early in May 1822, the committee chose to say absolutely nothing about Tschoudy. When mission in the Mediterranean is mentioned in the report, they ignore Tschoudy and focus instead on Joseph Wolff and his emerging mission in the Levant.[52]

But this does not mean that friends of LJS did not later in 1822 hear anything about Tschoudy. They did so through Wolff's published journals in the Jewish Expositor. What did he write about Tschoudy? Did he write that Tschoudy was a deceiver?

WAS TSCHOUDY A CROOK AND DECEIVER?

Yaron Perry argues, in 2003, that choosing Tschoudy "was a bad bargain" for LJS. Perry even uses the term crook to describe Tschoudy. He does so with a reference to the following words by Joseph Wolff—words

---

49. Ibid., c.10, no. 351.
50. Ibid., c.10, no. 428.
51. Ibid., c.10, no. 446.
52. Jewish Expositor, 1822, 234–35.

that were not published until 1860,[53] and with reference to the British Consul-General Henry Salt, whom Wolff met on his arrival in Alexandria, September 6, 1821, on his first journey to the Levant.

> Mr. Salt complained that the London Society for Promoting Christianity among the Jews had just sent a most unfit missionary to Jerusalem, Melchior Tschudy by name, with his little wife; a man who was evidently a mere speculator. He had already offered the Pasha to drill the Arabs in military tactics in the Desert, provided he was made Governor of Arabia, and Commander-in-Chief of the troops! He played the quack also, and sold medicines to the ladies, in order that they might be blessed with children; moreover, he pretended to know witchcraft. Wolff wrote all this home, and got the fellow dismissed.[54]

If the content of the declaration about *Tschoudy* is of the same quality as the concluding sentence about *Wolff*, it is not worth much. When Wolff is credited with getting "the fellow dismissed," it is misleading. Wolff did not come to Alexandria until September 6, 1821, but already on July 24, 1821, the general committee in London had resolved "the dismissal of the Rev. M. Tschudy on his arrival at Malta."

After having cited Wolff's quote from 1860, Perry concludes the following without any critical analysis:

> Tschudy's deceptions came to the attention of his London superiors in September 1821, and they remained baffled by the

---

53. The book *Travels and Adventures* by Wolff opens with a preface, in which it is said that Wolff "lays now before the public, not an abridgment of his Travels and Adventures, but an edition, though in smaller type, enriched with many new remarks and notices. Every piece of information, the style and sentiments, the philosophical and theological views, the remarks on the heroes of his story, are his own throughout. They have been written down as he dictated them to kind friends who received them from his lips." The book alternates between the first and the third person, which not only results in an awkward literary style but also leaves the critical—and curious—reader with many unanswered questions as to who says what and who thinks what. When, for example, Wolff's mission is evaluated and praised, is it then Wolff's (self)praise? And the fact that Wolff has "dictated" the book sharpens the reader's awareness of possible slips of memory on his side and misunderstandings on the side of the recipients.
54. Wolff, *Travels and Adventures*, 173–74.

situation until April 1822, when they sent a letter to his place of residence in Aleppo stating that the employment con-tract between him and the Society was signed for a year only, and that, since this period had already elapsed, the Society needed merely to adopt an earlier decision and terminate his employment.

The person who had been informed about Tschudy's fraudu-lence and reported it to London was Joseph Wolff (1795–1862), an emissary of the society who was in Alexandria at that time.[55]

Perry's treatment of Wolff's quotation is worthy of criticism on several points:

1. Because of the tardy postal services, Wolff's superiors in London could not in September 1821 have dealt with negative information about Tschudy sent by Wolff from Alexandria from September 6, 1821, and onward.

2. LJS in London did *not* remain baffled by the situation until April 1822. As previously discussed, at the end of July 1821, they had already made their decision.

3. LJS did not at the end of *April 1822* send a letter to Tschoudy's place of residence in *Aleppo*. At that time Tschoudy was in Malta—or had perhaps left the island. Perry confuses "Mr. Barker" (LJS committee member Joseph Gibbs Barker), men-tioned in the LJS minutes, with Consul Barker in Aleppo.[56]

4. But most important, on the basis of Wolff's statement from 1860, Perry concludes that Tschoudy's so-called deceptions

55. Perry, *British Mission to the Jews*, 17.
56. Perry asserts, "In the margin of the document it was later noted that its con-tents were transmitted to Tschudy on 9 April 1822 through the British consul in Aleppo"; cf. Perry, *British Mission to the Jews*, 45n. 19. But that is a misreading of the notice in LJS Minutes no. 428, March 26, 1822; postal communication from London to Aleppo was not that fast. The meaning is, What was decided at the committee meeting on March 26, 1822, was sent "to Mr. [Joseph Gibbs] Barker [in London] 6th April 1822, who wrote Mr. Tschudy 9th April 1822 [from London]."

were known by the committee in the autumn of 1821. This allegation, however, is based solely on Wolff's statement from 1860. But until it is supported by other sources it cannot be considered historically reliable.

The above criticisms do not prove that Tschoudy was *not* "a crook." But my point is that LJS did *not* treat Tschoudy as "a crook," which is a step toward a partial rehabilitation of Tschoudy—at least until new material that might contradict this view emerges from the archives.

The challenge now is to find contemporary accounts about Tschoudy and his work, either from individuals who met him or heard about him. Joseph Wolff belongs to the latter category.[57]

JOSEPH WOLFF IN 1822 ABOUT TSCHOUDY IN 1821

On his first journey to the Levant, Joseph Wolff came to Acre on January 1, 1822, less than one year after Tschoudy was in that area. He was welcomed kindly by "Peter Abbot, Esq. British Consul of this place."

The first thing Wolff wrote in his journal is that Abbot "gave me the accounts of two Jewish converts;[58] the name of the one is E–, a *tapet* maker, and cantor of the synagogue, and the name of the other is A–, who have been secretly baptized; they continue outwardly to be Jews, and to go to the synagogue."[59]

The next day Wolff met a person with the initial "I," but who later on in the same passage became "E." Without giving a detailed account of all the factors involved, I am most inclined to read the discrepant information in the sources as if there are three different individuals: "E," "A"[Abraham], and "I" [Israel].

---

57. Three sources are available: First, Wolff's journals, published in the *Jewish Expositor*; next, the book *Missionary Journal and Memoir of the Rev. Joseph Wolf [sic]*, *Missionary to the Jews*, rev. and ed. John Bayford, Esq. F.S.A. (London: James Duncan, 1824); and finally, a revised edition of this with the same title from 1827, where his name is given as *Wolff*.

58. Peter Abbot was also British consul at Beirut. Wolff's meeting with these baptized Jews in 1822 takes place in Acre and is told as if they live there. Shortly after, Wolff refers to a couple of these as if they were from Beirut; see below. Maybe a slip of the pen from Wolff?

59. *Jewish Expositor*, 1822, 298; cf. Wolf, *Missionary Journal and Memoir of the Rev. Joseph Wolf [sic]*, 1824; in Wolff, 1827, 208 "E" has become "a tent maker."

Wolff met this "I"/"E" on January 2, 1822, and wrote,

> I-, baptized by the Rev. Melchior Tschudy, called on me today, he
> was introduced to me by Peter Abbot, Esq. I had a long conversation
> with him, and there is no doubt of that man's sincerity; although
> poor, he never desired a farthing of Mr. Abbot, and he has read
> the New Testament so thoroughly through, that he knows much
> of it by heart; he was already made acquainted with Christianity
> by an Armenian priest, and the Rev. M. Tschudy gave him a New
> Testament, and he persuaded his wife of the truth, and both have
> been baptized by the Rev. M. Tschudy, in secret, for they do not dare
> to profess publicly Christianity, on account of the Jews, who would,
> indeed, very much persecute them. His wife died soon after, as the
> husband told me, as a zealous Christian.[60]

On January 5, 1822, Wolff met the persons "A" and "E": "they
are convinced of the truth of Christianity" but "the situation" made a
public confession impossible. When Wolff asked by "what instrumentality" they had come to faith, "A" answered

> My brother E here present, was long time ago persuaded; he read
> with me the prophets, and, on the arrival of Melchior, we got the
> New Testament in Hebrew; we believed, and Melchior (which is
> Tschudy,) baptized us. After this I married a Jewish lady, who is very
> bigoted, and I fear to talk with her, and I fear likewise to profess
> Christ before our brethren the Jews.[61]

Wolff gave expression to the hope that "A" and "E" would come
with him to Jerusalem and also said, "They would be exceedingly useful
in the Jewish seminary at Stansted Park." The same day Wolff met
"Mr. Katafago, the Austrian, Russian, Swedish, and Danish Consul in
Acre. He is a very zealous Roman Catholic, but he reads the Bible very
diligently. He has bought an Arabic Psalters from Mr. Tschoudy."[62]

---

60. *Jewish Expositor,* 1822, 298; cf. Wolf, *Missionary Journal and Memoir of the Rev.
    Joseph Wolf [sic],* 1824, 206–7; and Wolff, 1827, 209.
61. *Jewish Expositor,* 1822, 300..
62. Ibid., 300–301.

In 1860 Wolff told the same story about the two Jews but in a very much different tone:

> When Wolff was going to Beyrout, he fell in, at the moment of his leaving Acre, with two Jews, believers in the Lord Jesus Christ, who had been converted to Christianity by the preaching of that unworthy subject, Melchior Tschudy by name; or rather by his simply giving them the New Testament in Hebrew. They spoke of Christ and the Gospel, with the highest enthusiasm; but whether they have remained faithful unto the end is doubtful. Still, even the Jews themselves believed them to have been sincere; and what else but sincerity could have made them make a confession of their faith in Christ Jesus?[63]

When this account, *dictated* in 1860, is compared with what Wolff *wrote* in 1822, the stories do not harmonize. In 1822 Wolff heard of, and had contact with, the above-mentioned Jews already at the beginning of his visit in Acre; in 1860 it happened toward the end of it.

In 1822 it is said without reservation that Tschoudy gave New Testaments to the mentioned individuals; in 1860 the importance of this for their conversion and baptism is played down with the words "by simply giving them the New Testament in Hebrew"; in Wolff's writings there are several examples of his "simply" giving Scriptures to people.

In 1822 Wolff wrote from Jerusalem (see below) that one of the mentioned Jews had "denied Christ." In 1860 it is doubtful if "they have remained faithful unto the end."

In 1822 they were secret believers who feared "to profess Christ before our brethren the Jews." In 1860 "even the Jews themselves believed them to have been sincere."

In 1822 Tschoudy is several times referred to as "the Rev. Melchior Tschudy"; in 1860 he is called "that unworthy subject." Even with little knowledge of Wolff, it is difficult to imagine that he would use the honorable title "the Rev." in 1822, if he already then had the information about Tschudy that he conveys in 1860.

In a letter dated Jerusalem, March 12, 1822, Wolff writes about the Jews in Beirut:

---

63. Wolff, *Travels and Adventures*, 227.

The two Jews at Barut [Beirut], who have been secretly baptized by Mr. Tschudy, continue to pass outwardly to be Jews, and one of them is fallen back into Judaism, and has denied Christ in the presence of the convert Abraham. I said to Israel, ["I"?] that he should come to Jerusalem and assist me in my work, an undertaking which he fears to bring into execution. I shall therefore remain faithful, to my rule I laid down, never to baptize one who would not publicly profess the name of Christ.[64]

Implicit in the report from Wolff is a criticism of Tschoudy's baptismal practice, not of his conduct. Wolff presupposes public profession prior to baptism. Wolff's own practice might be worth a study, but it is outside the scope of this present work.

That Tschoudy distributed the Hebrew New Testament in Jerusalem in 1821 is confirmed by Wolff.

On March 21, 1822, Wolff sends a letter from Jerusalem that further refers to Tschoudy. Wolff mentions a discussion with "Abraham, the son of David Iskawish Stifro, born at Sklow. The latter can tell

that Melchior Tschudy has given him a New Testament, which he read, and stated afterwards the objection to Tschudy, which he [= Tschudy] was not able to answer, and this was of Matthew ii.23, "That it might be fulfilled which was spoken by the prophets, he shall be called a Nazarene." Tschudy sought again and again in the Prophets, for more than an hour, and could not find that text; and I defy and challenge you to show me that prophecy. Tschudy's answer was, The devil detains the Jews from believing in Christ; but this was no answer to the point in question.

Naturally, Wolff is able to give Abraham Ben David the right explanation, and Wolff declared subsequently, "All the other objections brought forth by Abraham Iskawish, were exceedingly weak, and I was, by God's grace, able to encounter them by Jer. xxxi. 31–34."[65]

---

64. *Jewish Expositor*, 1822, 381–82; cf. Wolf, *Missionary Journal and Memoir of the Rev. Joseph Wolf [sic]*, 1824, 246; and Wolff, 1827, 250.
65. *Jewish Expositor*, 1822, 461–62; cf. Wolf, *Missionary Journal and Memoir of the Rev. Joseph Wolf [sic]*, 1824, 262; and Wolff, 1827, 265–66.

There is no reason to doubt that Wolff was superior to Tschoudy in theological matters. Wolff knew it himself and did nothing to hide it. It is more interesting to notice that when Wolff departed from Jerusalem in 1822, he left behind, in his own words, one "converted" Jew—albeit not baptized. Who? Well, the aforementioned Abraham Ben David,[66] the very man who had received a Hebrew New Testament from "our" Tschoudy about a year earlier. Nineteenth-century Bible-men who met with many disappointments when they distributed Scriptures could be expected to comment on this with the words, "Look, the word of God will not return empty!"

But it is possible to come even closer to testimonies about Tschoudy's work in Jerusalem, namely, from one who met him there.

LEVI PARSONS IN 1821 ABOUT TSCHOUDY IN JERUSALEM IN 1821

The American missionary Levi Parsons worked as a Bible-man in Jerusalem from February 17 to May 8, 1821.[67] It is certain that Tschoudy, too, visited Jerusalem in 1821. Under the date April 6, 1821, Parsons writes from Jerusalem, "A Swiss clergyman arrived with Bibles and Testaments. He informed me, that he has disposed of many Testaments, and with prospects of usefulness. He designs, after the Passover, to go to Aleppo."

The nameless Swiss missionary is without doubt Tschoudy. In fact, on April 7 they visit some Jewish synagogues together. Parsons writes this, among other things, about the meeting with some Jews:

> We showed them a Testament in Hebrew. They examined it; but dared not purchase it, without the consent of the Rabbins [sic]. We left a few tracts, which they examined; but not without hesitation. They treated us with respect; and invited us to come again.[68]

---

66. Jewish Expositor, 1822, 418; cf. Wolf, Missionary Journal and Memoir of the Rev. Joseph Wolf [sic], 1824, 294–96; and Wolff, 1827, 299–301.
67. Sherman Lieber writes, "While 'brothers' Parsons and Fisk were in Smyrna, Melchior Tschoudi, a Swiss pastor affiliated with the LJS, toured Jerusalem and distributed Bibles to its Jewish residents," Mystics and Missionaries: The Jews in Palestine 1799–1840 (Salt Lake City: University of Utah Press, 1992), 160. This is not correct, for Tschoudy came to Jerusalem while Parsons was still there.
68. Missionary Herald (London: J. Burditt & W. Button, 1822), 39.

Whether or not Tschoudy and/or Parsons later accepted this invitation is an open question. But Parsons confirms that Tschoudy at least *tried* to do something among Jews in Jerusalem.

WOLFF IN 1822 ABOUT PARSONS'S WORK AMONG JEWS IN 1821

Joseph Wolff was in Jerusalem in the spring of 1822 and had, like the American missionary Levi Parsons in 1821, a good relationship with Procopius, the representative in Jerusalem for the Greek Orthodox patriarch, who resided in Constantinople.[69] Procopius was the first agent in Jerusalem for the British and Foreign Bible Society.[70]

Under March 14, 1822, Wolff refers to a conversation he had with Procopius and writes, "[Procopius] spoke of high regard of Levi Parsons, and told me that that gentleman went every day among Jews, until he was obliged to leave Jerusalem."[71]

Wolff's utterance is important in establishing the reliability of his utterances in general. Are his unconditionally *positive* words about Parsons as unreliable as his unconditionally *negative* words about Tschoudy? This might very well be the case.

Parsons's published journals in *Missionary Herald* hold an important clue. The journals indicate that apart from the above-mentioned visit to a synagogue, he mentions only that he attended a Jewish burial in April 1821.[72] Further, in Parsons's list of distributed Scriptures in Jerusalem there is no mention of *Hebrew* Scriptures. The most natural explanation seems to be that Parsons's mission among Jews in Jerusalem was very limited and that Wolff, on this matter, does not

---

69. See Kai Kjær-Hansen, "First 'Organized' Bible Work in 19th Century Jerusalem (1816–1831)," *Mishkan*, no. 41 (2004): 25.

70. See Kjær-Hansen, "First 'Organized' Bible Work in 19th Century Jerusalem, Part IV: Procopius, Parsons, and Tschoudy (1821)," *Mishkan*, no. 48 (2006): 73–78.

71. *Jewish Expositor*, 1822, 384; cf. Wolf, *Missionary Journal and Memoir of the Rev. Joseph Wolf [sic]*, 1824, 252; and Wolff, 1827, 256.

72. Lieber, *Mystics and Missionaries*, 161, rightly draws attention to this matter. But he has not realized that the Swiss missionary is identical with Tschoudy, cf. n. 67. Parsons's published journals contain no information about his work among the Jews of Jerusalem, apart from the two matters that have been mentioned. It is not very likely that the editor should have left out positive information of Parsons's work among Jews, a matter which the supporters of the mission would be pleased to read about.

give a reliable picture of Parsons's work, even though Wolff's comments were written in 1822. The same seems to be the case with Wolff's negative comment about Tschoudy, written in 1860.

TSCHOUDY ABOUT HIMSELF IN 1826

In his letter of December 16, 1826 (mentioned previously), Tschoudy mentions that he had been employed by LJS as a "preacher" in Jerusalem "in Canaan." He continues,

> from where the local Turkish riots in 1822 had driven me out; my society called me to Malta and through an agent they dismissed me. After this I sought employment, though unsuccessfully, in Italy and Switzerland, but nowhere did I find a position. I had no shortage of moral testimonies, let alone shortage of morals. These wanderings took me rather ill with pneumonia to Basel.[73]

Tschoudy, however, does not tell the whole story. As already mentioned, the reason he was called back to Malta was, according to LJS, not political unrest in the area. He now writes as one who is ill, destitute, disheartened, and in need of help. The rest of the letter is an earnest plea for help to get another position. He claims that he is a man of morals. Does LJS have an opinion about this?

LJS IN 1827 ABOUT TSCHOUDY IN LJS'S SERVICE

In LJS minutes Tschoudy's name pops up in 1827—several years after his dismissal. Peter Treschow, who was LJS Foreign Secretary while the case was under consideration in 1820–1822 and who took part in the initial interview with Tschoudy on April 24, 1820,[74] now approached LJS in two letters concerning Tschoudy. Probably having been contacted by Tschoudy, Treschow requested a statement about him. The letters were dealt with at a meeting in London, February 13, 1827.

> Resolved that Mr. Melchior Tschudy be informed that this Committee have never had the slightest objection against his moral

---

73. Cf. n. 5 above.
74. Cf. Bodleian, CMJ, d.12, no. 82.

or religious character, but they are desirous of reminding him, that he was engaged by them for a special Mission of enquiring in Palestine on probation for 12 Months only: at the expiration of which term they did not require his further services, because they found him unfit for the duties which that situation required, and on that ground alone declined employing him further.[75]

In this resolution there is no hint that LJS felt they were deceived by Tschoudy's conduct. The statement is so clear that, if the Committee *during* the consideration of the case in 1821–1822 had been in possession of information about Tschoudy of the kind that Wolff circulates in 1860 and yet wrote as they did in the resolution above in 1827, there would be no alternative but to say that the "crook" here is the LJS committee.

So was *Wolff* a "crook"? This question cannot be settled until a reliable explanation is found of his statement in 1860 about Tschoudy, a challenge for further research. But with the observations seen so far, new sources are required if people want to go on maintaining that *Tschoudy* was a "crook."

WAS TSCHOUDY A SUCCESS OR A FAILURE?

The stark contrasts of "success" and "failure" should not be the only standards used to measure "ordinary" people and "ordinary" missionaries. If there is a category in between "success" and "failure," here is where Tschoudy belongs.

Was Tschoudy more successful in distributing Scriptures in Jerusalem than the sources we've examined give him credit for? This is an open question. But if we want to do justice to Tschoudy, we need to compare his mission in Jerusalem with what other missionaries there accomplished.

The missionary Christoph Burckhardt, for example, was the first Protestant Bible-man to visit Jerusalem. Burckhardt spent approximately ten days there in the spring of 1818, and he sold one Hebrew Testament.[76] The second Bible-man visiting Jerusalem, James Connor,

---

75. Ibid., c. 12, no. 559.
76. See Kjær-Hansen, "First 'Organized' Bible Work in 19th Century Jerusalem, Part II: Christoph Burckhardt in Jerusalem, 1818," *Mishkan*, no. 42 (2005), 62.

after about six weeks there in 1820 says, "Among the Jews I have not been able to do any thing."[77]

It is my argument that Tschoudy was misplaced as a *researcher*. The Malta committee, headed by Jowett, had the overall responsibility for error of assignment and for the way the situation developed. Tschoudy, however, did better as a Bible-man than as a researcher, which does not mean that he can be declared an absolute success. It is something of a mystery, after all, that he wrote so few letters. But how many sick days did he and his wife have during their journey, and how did that affect him? The sources are silent about this.

But being a "failure" in one point does not necessarily mean that one is a failure in all points. The high expectations of the Malta and London committees—voiced by Jowett and adopted in London by LJS—namely, that Tschoudy should be "pilot and guide" for future missionaries in Palestine, were not fulfilled. But what missionary to the Jews in Jerusalem did that in the 1820s? None!

On the title page of Wolff's *Travels and Adventures* from 1860, where the notorious words about Tschoudy are printed, Wolff has written his motto: "'Who would not travel over sea and land, to be instrumental in the salvation of one soul!' Francis Xavier." According to Wolff, in 1822, Tschoudy was at least instrumental "in the salvation of one soul," a Jewish woman who had been baptized by Tschoudy and who still, according to Wolff 1822, died "as a zealous Christian."

Not a bad testimonial about Tschoudy—a missionary ordinary, whether his success as a missionary was great or not.

Tschoudy died in 1859.[78] How his life turned out after 1826, and how his stay in the Levant in the 1820s affected him until he died, has not been answered. The challenge is still to dig out new sources.

---

77. See Kjær-Hansen, "First 'Organized' Bible Work in 19th Century Jerusalem (1816-1831), *Mishkan*, no. 44 (2005), 69.
78. Cf. Perry, *British Mission to the Jews*, 16.

6

ETHICS AND MORALITY IN MISSION WORK

JOHN R. REID

I am very pleased to be invited to contribute to this Festschrift. This very tangible expression of our appreciation of the outstanding ministry of Moishe Rosen is appropriate. Our whole Christian witness has been enriched by the evangelistic outreach of the Jews for Jesus.

In this contribution, I discuss ethics and morality in relation to mission work. For the sake of clarity, I am defining morality as the embodiment of general principles of human behavior. Moral behavior is conduct based on ethical values. The Christian who accepts the authority of the Bible in matters of faith and conduct will find that both the values or ethics and the morality that flows from them are no less than obedience to God.

Jesus is our model for ethical behavior. He was faced with a myriad of ethical and moral issues in his mission. True, his views on some ethical issues are unknown to us. For instance, what did he think of slavery as an institution? He was certainly aware of it, as he made oblique reference to it (John 8:35). We do know that he made judgments about family obligations. At the cross, his concern for his mother's welfare is a clear example of his fulfilling that obligation. When his family pressured him to leave his ministry, however, he let it be known that there were obligations that transcended those of family (Luke 8:21; 14:26). Jesus was forced to make judgments about the priorities of his ministry. His initial obligation was to the Jews, and he seemed harsh when he said to a Gentile woman, "I was sent only to the lost sheep of the house of Israel." He seemed even harsher when he added, "it is not fair to take the children's food and throw it to the dogs" (Matt. 15:24–26 NRSV).

The three temptations, which are recorded in Matthew's and Luke's Gospels, are a study of the fundamental moral choices that Jesus had to resolve before he ministered to others. The temptation to turn stones into bread confronted him with the questions, *Could he use his messianic powers for his own comfort?* and *Could he recruit followers to join him by the promise of bread?* The temptation to jump from the pinnacle of the temple probed the way in which his messianic powers were to be conducted: *Would it be possible to use dazzling signs and wonders to recruit disciples?* The third temptation was even more searching: *Could there ever be choices that made some compromise with evil? What if the choice was to be between two evils?* Jesus had to face these moral decisions, and so have his disciples ever since.

The story of Jesus is, in fact, the story of a man who squarely faced moral issues and theological questions. The issues related to, among other things, marriage, the nature of worship, and the obligations that a citizen has to a foreign and pagan invader. In dealing with these issues, what stands out is the seamless integrity of Jesus. No matter how difficult the issue, his response revealed his undeviating commitment to truth and justice.

Three significant features characterize his moral teaching. First, he did not give a host of rules and regulations. Other moral teachers have done that very thing, attempting to cover every exigency of life. Bishop Stephen Neill draws a contrast between Muhammad and Jesus in their approach to moral conduct.[1] Muhammad laid down precepts that sought to cover the whole gamut of human behavior. Because this teaching is so specific, it became difficult to observe in a different time and culture. The feast of Ramadan, for example, required that neither food nor drink should be consumed between sunrise and sunset. This is not easy to fulfill in any circumstance, but much easier to obey if you live near the equator. It is impossible to fully observe if you live in the Arctic Circle in the month of June. There may be difficulties in applying the teaching of Jesus, but they are not of this kind. His teaching was not bound by circumstances in Palestine in the first century.

Second, Jesus gave general principles that a follower can reflect on and apply to a specific situation. The principles are truth, justice, mercy, and freedom. This resulted in an attractive flexibility in Jesus' conduct. On occasion he accepted external Jewish traditions and obligations but rejected their internal motivations. He acknowledged the Temple tax, for instance (Matt. 17:24–27), but concerning the value of offerings made in the Temple, he rejected the legalism of the religious leaders (Matt. 15:1–9) because it violated the principle of mercy. He condemned as a violation of the principles of truth and justice their practice of repudiating the obligation to care for parents because of a so-called higher duty to the Temple (Mark 7:11).

Third, Jesus affirmed the presence of the Father and the guidance of the Holy Spirit. The humble and believing person can rely on the Father's knowing what we need and will give good gifts to his children (Matt. 7:25–33; Luke 12:22–32), and one of the special tasks of the Holy Spirit is to guide in the areas of truth (John 16:13).

While Christian ethics must begin with Jesus, it is in the rest of the New Testament that we see these ethics applied in a Christian community. In addition, the church had to move out of a mono-cultural setting and deal with a whole raft of new moral issues, including

---

1. Stephen Neill, *A Genuinely Human Existence: Towards a Christian Psychology* (London: Constable & Company Ltd., 1959), 136.

issues related to freedom, race, gender, and wealth. It had to deal with new questions about sexual behavior, marriage, and the resolution of legal differences in the civil courts.

Romans 14 is a classic ethical text. The disputed issues revolved around what food was acceptable and what were the days for religious observance. It is fascinating to see how the principles of the moral behavior of Jesus were applied. The obligation of mercy meant that there should not be any passing of judgment on believers who disagree. The reality of the Father's presence meant that every decision should be made in dependence on God. The value of freedom was preserved by allowing human consciences to respond differently, while moral responsibility meant that all "should be fully convinced in their own mind" (TNIV). What is of special value here are not the specific issues but the manner by which they were resolved—that is, most important is to apply the moral principles of Jesus to a concrete situation.

The personal integrity of Jesus in every area of life is basic to our understanding of Jesus and his ministry. His tremendous claims of who he was and where he came from would not have stood the test of time if he had been a failure in personal conduct. He was able to face his critics and say, "Which one of you convicts me of sin?" (John 8:46 NASB).

Personal integrity is also required of those who follow Jesus and seek to extend his kingdom. The Pastoral Letters insist that the Christian leader must be blameless, not "arrogant or quick-tempered or addicted to wine or violent or greedy for gain; but he must be hospitable, a lover of goodness, prudent, upright, devout, and self controlled" (Titus 1:7, 8 NRSV).

Let us now examine three issues in more detail.

ISSUE 1: IS MATERIAL PROSPERITY A GOSPEL PROMISE?

In recent years and in many places, a particular presentation of the message of Jesus has been made. It gives the assurance that every follower of Jesus is entitled to be rich in material possessions. While this could be illustrated from many sources, here is an Australian example. In Sydney, New South Wales, there is a remarkable Pentecostal church called Hillsong. By any standard, its attendance of more than twenty thousand is noteworthy, but in Australia this is extraordinary. One of Hillsong's outstanding achievements is its new and contemporary music, which has enriched the services of many churches throughout the world. The modern music has been one of the reasons why the young have found the services to be so appealing. But there is another reason why Hillsong finds appeal. It declares that it is God's will that all believers be rich in material things. This declaration has caught the attention of Australian secular political figures, including the then premier of NSW, the Honorable Bob Carr, who commended Hillsong on its generating of wealth. Both the prime minister and the treasurer of the Australian federal government have appeared at services and spoken words of praise. Hillsong's senior pastor, Brian Houston, has published a book that promotes the prosperity gospel.[2] "Is it God's will for you to prosper?" Houston asks on page 55. His answer is an undoubting yes.

Houston cites biblical verses that he claims promise material wealth to all believers. But he must twist the text to arrive at his destination. Typical is his comment on 2 Corinthians 8:9, one of the central proof texts for prosperity theology:

> I've heard people misinterpret this scripture to support their belief that it is biblical to be poor. They only read half of it—"that though he was rich, yet for your sake he became poor." They completely miss the crucial point because if you read on, the reason why he became poor was that "you through his poverty might become rich." This is what it says. He became poor so you could become rich. The purpose of Jesus coming to earth includes giving up a place of abundance and riches and becoming poor so that we could escape that poverty.[3]

Houston's startling argument claims that Paul is teaching that Christ died on the cross for the purpose of making us materially wealthy. But surely Houston's exegetical confidence is misplaced through a failure to distinguish between literal and metaphorical language. The question is, *Are the riches that come to us through the cross the material riches of money or the spiritual riches of salvation?* The par-

---

2. Brian Houston, *You Need More Money: Discovering God's Amazing Financial Plan for Your Life* (Castle Hill, Australia: Maximised Leadership Inc., 1999).

3. Houston, *You Need More Money*, 12–13.

able of the rich fool in Luke 12 specifically pinpoints what it means to be rich toward God; prosperity in God's eyes does *not* mean abundance of possessions. Likewise in Revelation 3:18, it is certain that the injunction to get gold refers to the grace of God.

By failing to recognize metaphor, this interpretation reduces a sublimely spiritual text to a mundanely material one. The apostle Paul is telling the Corinthians that they have been spiritually enriched through Christ's impoverishment on the cross, and therefore they should be willing to follow his example and empty themselves of their riches for their poor brothers (v. 14). Far from saying "claim it," Paul was saying "give it."

Prosperity theology also suffers from a failure to come to grips with salvation history. Many of the promises in the Old Testament refer to Hebrew history when Israel was being specifically prepared for its role as the nation from whom the Messiah would come. The author of the Epistle to the Hebrews dealt with this new situation. Moses and Joshua were to prepare a nation to enter a promised land. Since the advent of Christ, this no longer applies. It is a spiritual inheritance of rest and grace that is to be entered. Understanding this will keep us from transferring the promise of Moses ("it is he who gives you the power to get wealth," Deut. 8:18 ESV) and the promise to Joshua ("you shall make your way prosperous," Josh. 1:8 NRSV) as if nothing has changed with the coming and work of Jesus. Paul's classic passage in Romans 5 indicates that instead of prosperity, suffering is a likely outcome of the life of faith in God's will, because it is suffering that produces the character that God wants to produce in us.

The prosperity gospel is based on inadequate exegesis. But there is also a moral issue here. The moral issue is that prosperity theology fails to come to terms with the withering power of greed and covetousness. Covetousness is the striving for material possessions as a means of security. Covetousness is a real threat to the believer, for it is an idolatrous mindset (Col. 3:5) that can bring a person under demonic power. The Evangelist Luke saw this sinister threat most clearly. He recorded Jesus' warning, "Take care! Be on your guard against all kinds of greed; for one's life does not consist in the abundance of possessions" (Luke 12:15 NRSV). The way of self-seeking and materialism is not the way of the kingdom of Christ.

ISSUE 2: DO JEWISH PEOPLE NEED TO BE EVANGELIZED?

I was the foundation chairperson of the Council for Christians and Jews in New South Wales. It met regularly and consisted of the representatives of different Jewish bodies as well as representatives of mainline Christian denominations. It seemed right to build bridges of understanding between Christians and Jews since the history of our relations had been so tragic. The council sponsored a number of scholarly symposiums that were useful in fostering mutual understanding. Several Jewish members of the council, however, pressed hard that we as a council should condemn the efforts of the Jews for Jesus who were active and creative in presenting Jesus as Messiah. The rabbi of one of the largest synagogues declared that evangelism of the Jews is a misplaced exercise, as the Jews have their own covenant with God, while the Christians have a different covenant, and these two covenants are essentially unrelated to each other. The Jews' covenant goes back to Abraham and Moses, while the Christian covenant is a new covenant. Therefore, Christian evangelism directed to Jews is unnecessary and arrogant. To prove their point that the Mosaic covenant still stood in all its glory and power, proponents of this view turned to Psalm 111:7–8: "All his precepts are trustworthy; they are established forever and ever, to be performed with faithfulness and uprighness" (ESV).

Jewish evangelism is, then, a fundamental theological and ethical issue: Are Jews to be bypassed in proclaiming the salvation message of Jesus? This issue was addressed by the author of the Epistle to the Hebrews. In chapter 8 he writes that the covenant of Christ is the very covenant that had been promised by Jeremiah. It has the same basic promise that was given to Abraham and to Moses when God said, "I will be their God and they shall be my people" (2 Cor. 6:16 NRSV). But the covenant of Christ would have wholly new features. It would be an inward covenant. It would be engraved in the minds and hearts of God's people. Indeed, it was a far superior covenant to the one made with Moses and, in fact, that covenant was obsolete.

The rabbis argued, however, that the covenant of Jeremiah could not have been the covenant of Christ, because it was to be made with both the house of Judah and the house of Israel. Although the nation of Israel had disappeared in the Assyrian captivity, the expression stands in its own right as applying to every Hebrew person, with the result that for the modern rabbis the covenant of Jeremiah is still in the future and will usher in a new age of Torah or law keeping.

The Christian with all the best intentions cannot accept two different streams of relating to God. They are ultimately contradictory to each other, one being based on law and the other on grace. The evidence of Jesus and the Gospels is clear: it was to the Jews that Jesus came. They were the lost sheep he came to seek and to save. Moreover, Jesus said that salvation was "of the Jews" (John 4:22 KJV). They were, in fact, to be initial recipients of his ministry. It is not possible to infer that Jesus thought that the Jews were to be exempt from the universal appeal of his good news. At the same time, Jesus was critical of Torah observance as an appropriate way of relating to God. In fact, this was the way of labor and heavy burden (Matt. 11:28).

In his parable of the Jewish leader and the tax collector in the Temple, Jesus contrasted the man whose confidence comes from strict Torah keeping with the man who had no personal righteousness but cried out for mercy (Luke 18:9–14). One is the way of law observance, the other acknowledges moral failure but seeks mercy. Jesus was crystal clear in his presentation of the contrast and the outcome. Using the legal term *justified*, Jesus said that in the eyes of God's law the repentant man had been declared right and the charge against him removed. But how is this status attained? Did Jesus give any clue? The clue is found in the poor tax collector's cry "be merciful," which may be technically translated as "be propitious to me." The cry means that the tax collector wanted God to act toward him on the basis of the sacrifice or propitiation. Here is language taken not from the law courts but from the Jerusalem Temple, where sacrifice was offered to remove guilt and sin. The foundational concept was that God displayed an uncompromising antagonism against evil. His judicial wrath was directed against sin. The system of sacrifice was temporary, awaiting the coming of Jesus and his voluntary death. Paul wrote that God put Jesus forward as a propitiatory sacrifice to take away sin (Rom. 3:25). This short parable lays out the two ways that humankind seeks to be related to God—one is based on law, the other on grace.

Is there a moral issue here? Excluding Jews from the covenant of Christ is ultimately an act of discrimination, which would be another act of exclusion in their long and tragic history of persecution. The gospel is for all. God is creating for himself a new people, and the Jews should have the opportunity to join the new people because to them belong the adoption, the glory, the covenants, the giving of the Law, the worship and the promise is to them of belonging to the patriarchs, and from them, according to the flesh, comes the Messiah (Rom 9:4–6).

ISSUE 3: TERRORISM AND ANTI-VILIFICATION LEGISLATION

On September 11, 2001, the attack that destroyed the Twin Towers in New York City was an act of Islamic terrorism on a scale previously unknown. It constituted an act of war between democratic countries and a number of terrorists drawn from many countries. Subsequent acts of destruction have taken place in Asia and Europe. The effects of these attacks have been widespread. Security has increased and various countries have passed legislation to deal with the threats. This legislation has the potential to influence evangelism and religious dialogue.

Australia, where I live, is a multicultural country, and multiculturalism has been the declared social policy of the nation. A net addition to the population of one international immigrant occurs every four minutes. Left far behind us is the notorious White Australia policy, which operated on a policy of exclusion of those who were Asian. Now the number of Australians who were born in Asia is about the same as those born in the United Kingdom. At the Australian federal and state level there is now a history of anti-vilification legislation, which has sought to enforce tolerance by prohibiting discrimination on grounds of race, gender, sexual preference, and sexual identity. Thus, with legal sanctions we enforce the policy of multiculturalism.

The first effect on Australia of the Twin Towers attack, however, was a public questioning of the benefits of multiculturalism and a fresh look at the discarded policy of assimilation. Peter Coleman, a former leader of the NSW Opposition party, wrote in the May 2006 edition of *Quadrant*:

It is hard to open a newspaper without reading someone questioning, if not ridiculing, multiculturalism. We have moved from scepticism to disenchantment. Whatever we thought of the mandarins of multiculturalism over the years we used to be confident that, without them or sometimes despite them, the democratic Australian way would continue to work its magic and dissolve the tensions—ethnic, racial, and religious—that the multiculturalists observed or imagined. That confidence has gone.[4]

The second effect, though, was to increase the legislation to enforce tolerance. Three of Australia's state parliaments passed toleration legislation, with that of the State of Victoria as proving most significant. Interesting to note, before the legislation was brought to the legislature, consultation was held with religious bodies who endorsed the proposed law. The Racial and Religious Tolerance Act 2001 (Victoria) was passed and Section 8 provides as follows: "a person must not on the grounds of their religious belief or activity of another person or class of persons, engage in conduct that incites hatred against, serious contempt for, or revulsion or severe ridicule of, that other person or class of persons."

> Professor Patrick Parkinson of the University of Sydney has pointed out: "At the heart of the debate about these laws is religious freedom; not the freedom to be intolerant, and certainly not the freedom to vilify—neither of these are legitimate expressions of religious freedom. Rather, at issue is the freedom to express views about truth and falsehood, right and wrong, good and evil, which may offend others who have a different view on these matters. Religious vilification laws in practice, if not in theory, pose a grave danger to this freedom because of the collateral damage that can be caused by a legislative strategy to enforce tolerance."[5]

In March 2002, Pentecostal pastor Daniel Scot presented a seminar on Islam under the auspices of Catch the Fire Ministries. It was advertised that the topics would include the Qur'an and jihad. Pastor Daniel Nalliah posted a newsletter on the website of Catch the Fire

---

4. Peter Coleman, "The Good Australian and the Lure of Islam," *Quadrant (Australia)* 50 (May 2006), 102.
5. Patrick Parkinson, "Enforcing Tolerance: Vilification Laws and Religious Freedom in Australia," June 25, 2005, http://www.sydneyanglicans.net/archive/indepth/enforcing_tolerance_patrick_parkinson. I am indebted to Parkinson's excellent analysis of the legislation and have drawn on the article.

Ministries that dealt with the same subjects. Scot and Nalliah immigrated to Australia from Pakistan and are themselves converts from Islam. Among the attendees at the seminar were three Muslims. Afterward, they lodged a complaint that the seminar incited hatred against Muslims in Australia. In December 2004, the court handed down its judgment that pastor Scot was guilty of "religious vilification." He had, said the court, presented in a way that was "essentially hostile, demeaning and derogatory of all Muslim people, their god Allah, the prophet Mohammed and in general Muslim religious beliefs and practices."[6] The newsletter was judged to be in violation of the anti-vilification law. Scot and Nalliah were ordered to publish in the daily press a public apology, and not to publish or to distribute similar material any longer.

The two men have lodged an appeal against the tribunal's decision and still wait the outcome of their appeal. They have indicated that they would rather go to jail than submit to a law that they view as unjust. A number of sober-minded Christians who are well informed on Islam have said that the two men may have used extreme language, but overall their comments genuinely sought to show the nature of Islamic belief. This case has attracted attention throughout the country and overseas as well.

Professor Parkinson wrote,

> One of the significant features of the Catch the Fire Ministries is that it demonstrates the potential reach of the Victorian law to include teaching given at Christian seminars and conferences. There can be no doubt that such seminars are public rather than private within the meaning of the Victorian legislation. They are typically advertised, at least within church congregations, and any one is welcome to attend. However, no one need attend such a seminar of this kind and it is expected that the audience would be Bible believing Christians who choose to attend a seminar about another faith from

---

6. This quote was originally found at http://www.saltshakers.org but is no longer available there. Various discussions of this can still be found online. For an official report from the U.S. Department of State, see Bureau of Democracy, Human Rights, and Labor, "Australia: International Religious Freedom Report 2005" at http://www.state.gov/g/drl/rls/irf/2005/51504.htm (accessed July 7, 2009).

a Christian perspective. This does not prevent such a complaint being made by people of other faiths who choose to attend such a seminar without sharing the world view of its organizers. The possibility of a lawsuit may intimidate religious leaders of whatever faith from teaching and expressing what they believe their faith requires or from expressing a point of view which might offend.[7]

One of the dangers of anti-vilification legislation is that it may be seen as a new means of pursuing a long-existing conflict before a neutral arbitrator. The problem is that the legal system becomes another theater for the playing out of a conflict that it cannot possibly resolve, because that conflict is political or religious.

What is the moral problem here? Religious anti-vilification legislation, wherever in the world it is put forward, represents (implicitly or explicitly) the view that all religions are equal and are different paths to a relationship with God. Such legislation suggest that, although religions are different on the surface, they are fundamentally the same. There is no allowance for the possibility that one religion could be true and another false. In the effort to promote and legislate tolerance, such legislation undercuts the very existence of truth and falsehood, and thus morality.

Terrorist attacks have moved us all into a new environment for proclaiming the gospel. We must maintain that proclaiming the truth and exposing what is false is essential for the moral health of the community.

---

7. Ibid.

7

JEWISH-GENTILE COUPLES

*Some Ethical Questions Toward a New
Approach in Jewish Evangelism*

TUVYA ZARETSKY

Moishe Rosen has had an amazing ability to mobilize others to the cause of Jewish evangelism. The first time I met him, in fact, he issued a challenge to my life. I'm honored to share where that challenge has taken me.

In the fall of 1972, Moishe was working out of a modest office in Corte Madera, California. Jews for Jesus was just a movement in the thick of a holy outbreak of the gospel within the American Jewish community. I had come to faith in Jesus in Southern California less than two years earlier.

Fearing where this unexpected spiritual turn would take me, I left the United States in January 1971. I longed for a culturally safe place where I could integrate a new appreciation for the Messiah with my Jewish identity. So I moved to Israel. There, a mutual friend connected me with Moishe and we began a correspondence relationship.

He described how God was working in the lives of other young Jews like me who were coming to faith in Jesus. He invited me to join the adventure.

I returned to the United States in late 1972 and visited the San Francisco Bay area to finally meet Moishe. That very first afternoon, Moishe invited me to go with him to the Sausalito ferry terminal to hand out evangelistic literature. He was wearing cowboy boots, jeans, a turtleneck sweater, a black leather sailor's cap, and a denim jacket with the words "Jews for Jesus" embroidered on the back.

As we walked along the promenade by the ferry terminal, he carried a stack of pamphlets that he called "broadsides." It was a gospel tract that he had written. I read one; then he handed me a stack without saying a word. I watched as he offered them to passers-by. After a while, I, too, offered them to people.

As we walked back to the car, Moishe asked me a question: "So . . . what did you learn?" I offered some observations and opinions that included something like, "Well, it might be *one* way to reach Jewish people with the message of Jesus, but there must be better ways." Moishe was refreshingly humble, "You're right. This is just one way that we've found to engage Jewish people with the gospel." Then he proposed a challenge. "Why don't you stick around and help us until you find a better way."

Thirty-four years later, I am excited to suggest another approach for mission work among Jewish people. It might not be a *better* way, but it is as appropriate today as was handing out broadsides in 1972. I offer it as a tribute to a mentor and friend in the field of Jewish evangelism.

What I propose is a ministry to Jewish-Gentile couples. Major changes in demographics have take place in the American Jewish community, and social research has uncovered cultural challenges experienced by Jewish-Gentile couples. To help meet these challenges I have developed four questions to help formulate ethical guidelines for mission workers engaged in ministry to Jewish-Gentile couples.

A CHANGING AMERICAN JEWISH COMMUNITY
The Intermarriage Trend

At the beginning of the twenty-first century, the American Jewish community is quite different from the one encountered by the Jews for

Jesus movement in 1972. The Jews of my generation are part of the post-World War II baby boom. Our parents' generation had witnessed and survived the Holocaust, and we—their children—were raised around the time when the State of Israel was being established.

In terms of demography, the Jewish community in America has changed dramatically over the last thirty-five years. Assimilation characterizes American Jewry, manifested in a high rate of intermarriage, declining Jewish birth rate, and disaffiliation from Judaism.

In 1970, the Jewish intermarriage rate was below 10 percent. Recent anti-Semitic horrors in Europe had stimulated a Jewish survival instinct that sustained a traditional taboo against intermarriage. At that time, it was common for Gentile spouses to convert to Judaism. But just twenty years later, the 1990 decadal population survey reported the rate of intermarriage as having quadrupled.[1]

In 1990 the results of the National Jewish Population Survey (NJPS) hit American Jewry like a seismic jolt. It reported the Jewish intermarriage rate between 1985 and 1990 was at 52 percent.[2] That rate has been sustained at that level for almost twenty years as reported by the 2000–1 NJPS as well as by the 2000 American Jewish Identity Survey.[3] As of 2003, nearly one third of all American Jews were married to Gentiles.[4] A 2003 survey report, in fact, indicates that the majority of American Jewish parents would not be troubled if their son or daughter married a Gentile. The traditional cultural taboo clearly has collapsed.

The assimilation characterized by Jewish-Gentile marriage is a phenomenon with missiological implications. It is an opportunity for appropriate introduction of the gospel can minister hope for marital peace and spiritual harmony to Jewish-Gentile couples. This must be done without manipulating either partner while clearly presenting the only hope of eternal life in the Messiah Jesus.[5] According to the chal-

---

1. Bernard Lazerwitz, "Jewish-Christian Marriages and Conversions: 1971 and 1990," *Sociology of Religion* 56, no. 4 (Winter 1995): 443.
2. All survey data is available online at www.jewishdatabank.org.
3. Egon Mayer, Barry Kosmin, and Ariela Keysar, *American Jewish Identity Survey 2001*, "AJIS Report: An Exploration in the Demography and Outlook of a People" (New York: Graduate Center of the City of New York, 1002), 7.
4. Joe Berkofsky, "American Jewry by Numbers," JTA: *Jewish Journal*, September 12, 2003), 21.
5. John 14:6; Acts 4:12.

lenges reported by the partners in Jewish-Gentile relationships, this type of mission is clearly needed.

Defining Terms

The term *Jewish-Gentile* applies to a specific reference. *Jewish* is used in the sense of ethnicity, a blood lineage that goes back to the Hebrew patriarchs Abraham, Isaac, and Jacob. All other nations are, from a Jewish perspective, not Jewish. They are *the nations, foreigners, or simply Gentiles*. The religion of *Judaism*, however, is not a defining factor of Jewish ethnicity. Religion is, of course, regarded as a cultural component—culture's being a learned set of behaviors, practices, and beliefs—and a very important one in shaping and expressing personal identity. While Judaism is a cultural component for Jewish belief, when I speak of Jews, I mean ethnic Jewish people, without defining their attachment or involvement with the religion of Judaism. When I speak of *Christians*, I mean anyone who is a follower of Jesus the Messiah and Savior. Thus, *Christian* is a religious and cultural identification, and it can describe the faith of Gentiles *and* Jews. I use the term *Jewish-Gentile* to refer to a heterosexual couple who are dating, cohabiting, or married, and with one partner's being Jewish.

Threats and Challenges

What are the challenges that Jewish-Gentile couples face? First, social research on interfaith marriages of any kind shows them to be at greater risk of dissolution (divorce) than same-faith marriages.[6] For intermarriage in which partners are even from a similar but not identical Christian tradition, research reports significant spiritual and social tensions.[7] It is not difficult, then, to imagine how much greater the ethnic and religious differences are for an interfaith marriages between Jewish-Gentile couples. Little wonder the divorce rate within this population is twice as high as among the Jewish inmarried population.[8]

---

6. V. R. Call and T. B. Heaton, "Religious Influence on Marital Stability," *Journal for the Scientific Study of Religion* 36, no. 3 (1997): 382–92.
7. L. M. Williams and M. G. Lawler, "The Challenges and Rewards of Interchurch Marriages: A Qualitative Study," *The Journal of Psychology and Christianity* 19, no. 3 (Fall 2000): 205–18.
8. A. Clamar, "Interfaith Marriage: Defining the Issue, Treating the Problems," *Psychotherapy in Private Practice* 9, no. 2 (1991): 79–83; and S. C. Eaton, "Marriage Between

Interfaith marriage tensions also increase the inability to find spiritual harmony in a marriage relationship. Qualitative research has attempted to measure marital satisfaction and marital spirituality. At least one study found that both satisfaction and spirituality diminished dramatically when marriage partners could not share the same spiritual belief.[9]

My own qualitative research into the challenges described by interfaith Jewish-Gentile couples reported five key challenges to marital harmony.[10]

1. Confusion over identity differences
2. Tensions over religious differences
3. Disagreements over life-cycle celebrations
4. Challenges to family harmony
5. Discord over training children

These challenges were observed as surfacing during four different stages of relationships: during dating, around the occasion of the wedding ceremony, during the marriage period without children, and then when children came into the family. In addition to these four periods in interpersonal relationships, couples described tensions that developed around specific crisis experiences.

As noted in the preceding list, interfaith couples identified five challenges as leading to marital tension; these challenges fall within categories of cultural experience that relate to self-identity, religious identity, life-cycle events, family identity, and the enculturation of children.[11] Looking at the relational stages along with the cultural categories of experience reveals a complex spiritual phenomenon among these couples.

In mission workers' responding to this phenomenon, it is important to begin by seeking to understand the challenges, as Jewish-Gentile couples describe them. We are then better able to formulate

---

Jews and Non-Jews: Counseling Implications," *Journal of Multicultural Counseling and Development* 22, no. 4 (1994): 210–14.
9. Paul R. Giblin, "Marital Spirituality: A Qualitative Study," *Journal of Religion and Health*, Winter 1997, 321–32.
10. Enoch Wan and Tuvya Zaretsky, *Jewish-Gentile Couples: Trends, Challenges, and Hopes* (Pasadena, CA: William Carey Library Publishers, 2005).
11. Ibid., 43.

appropriate missiological responses to address the spiritual needs of this unique population.

In speaking of *appropriate* missiological responses, we turn to the matter of ethics in ministry.

ETHICS IN MINISTRY

Ethics

When I first met Moishe he was preparing a manuscript for a small, tongue-in-cheek book of pithy sayings later published as *The Sayings of Chairman Moishe*.[12] Those humorous musings reflected a passion for ethics in ministry and life, a passion he passed on to the rest of us mission workers.

One serious philosophical book that Moishe recommended to all of us was Mortimer Adler's *Six Great Ideas*.[13] Adler's insights about the nature of goodness and ethical choices are helpful in formulating a philosophy of ministry. Adler distinguishes between truth as descriptive statements that assert what is, and those prescriptive statements—value judgments—that teach what is true and ought to be done.[14] He wrote, "Our motivation for seeking ethics in our work is that we ought to seek . . . that which is really good for us."[15]

So, too, ought we to seek what is really good for the people to whom we as workers minister. The term *ethics* means "manner of life," "conduct," "custom," or "practice," as prescribed by a knowledgeable authority.[16] The aim of the mission worker, then, is to seek what is really good for the Jewish-Gentile couple.

Traditional Jewish Communal Responses

If Jewish-Gentile marriages are prone to marital dissatisfaction, what is the best policy for ministry response? Since release of the 1990 NJP survey, traditional Jewish communal policy has been in debate, back and forth between *outreach* and *conversion*. In 2003, an American

---

12. Moishe Rosen, *The Sayings of Chairman Moishe* (Carol Stream, IL: Creation House, 1975).
13. Mortimer J. Adler, *Six Great Ideas* (New York: Macmillan, 1981).
14. Ibid., 69–71.
15. Ibid., 79.
16. Walter C. Kaiser Jr., *Toward Old Testament Ethics* (Grand Rapids: Zondervan, 1983), 2.

Jewish Committee public opinion poll found that American Jews no longer saw intermarriage as a tragedy. The taboo against intermarriage had collapsed. So the public policy debate intensified, concluding that efforts to stem intermarriage had been fruitless.

In 2007, Jewish sociologist Steven M. Cohen issued a paper that described the Jewish community as two distinct entities: *inmarried* and *intermarried*.[17] He concluded that the Jewish future in America rests with Jewish-Jewish inmarried couples, since they will more likely participate in Judaism and raise their children as Jews.

Cohen's reasoning is that intermarriage is "contributing to a weakened Jewish identity." When the child of a Jewish-Gentile couple marries a Jewish offspring from an inmarried couple, their children are raised as Jews 71 percent of the time. By contrast, when a child of intermarried Jews—a Jewish-Gentile couple—marries another offspring from a Jewish-Gentile couple their children are raised as Jews in only 10 percent of the cases. Therefore, says Cohen, communal resources should be focused only on those who will make up almost three quarters of the American Jewish future.[18] Others who support Cohen's view include Sylvia Barack Fishman of Brandeis University, Steven Bayme of the American Jewish Committee, and Jewish Theological Seminary Provost Jack Wertheimer.

It seems that Cohen's proposed response to intermarried couples is motivated by communal preservation and a religious basis for defining Jewry. A Brandeis University study in 2005 sought to understand how intermarried couples made Jewish choices.[19] The research was aimed to show how intermarried couples defined Jewish life through attachment to Judaism and traditional behaviors. We have already seen that Jewish-Gentiles couples, along with the larger American Jewish population, are trending away from affiliation with Judaism.

American Jewish communal response to intermarriage has been divided. The Steven M. Cohen group advocates outreach that focuses on the conversion of Gentile spouses. An "opposition" view is advocated by

---

17. Steven M. Cohen, "A Tale of Two Jewries: The 'Inconvenient Truth' for American Jews" (Jewish Life Network: Steinhardt Foundation, 2006) is available at www .jewishlife.org/pdf/steven_cohen_paper.pdf.
18. Sue Fishkoff, "Latest Salvo in Intermarriage Debate Suggests a Split in Jewish Community," *JTA: Jewish Journal*, February 10, 2007.
19. Sylvia Barack Fishman, *Double or Nothing? Jewish Families and Mixed Marriage* (Waltham, MA: Brandeis University Press, 2004).

leaders like Edmund Case of InterfaithFamily.com, Rabbi Kerry Orlitzky of the Jewish Outreach Institute, Bethamie Horowitz of the Mandel Foundation, and Len Saxe at Brandeis's Cohen Center. In their view, outreach to Jewish-Gentile families should include them in Jewish communal life. They urge intermarried couples to pursue Jewish behaviors and attitudes as well as participation in traditional services. Synagogues are advised to embrace Jewish-Gentile couples in membership and community.

Rabbi Orlitzky argued that forcing conversion on the intermarried is inappropriate. He asked, "What happens to the 800,000 (intermarried) families already in the Jewish community?"[20] These couples have already opted out of traditional institutions and are found to be less inclined toward an "unambiguous" relationship to Judaism. What ministry is appropriate to their needs?

As mission workers consider ethics for ministry to Jewish-Gentile couples, we must be committed to a relationship that is safe for both partners. Christian partners must not fear that their conscience regarding faith in Christ is in jeopardy. Gentile partners ought not feel they are judged for uncertainty about their personal faith or beliefs. Jewish partners must not sense that they are targets for conversion to a foreign belief. Jews should not be made to feel guilty for their choice to marry Gentiles. Those of us in ministry ought to hold out hope to Jewish-Gentile couples that they may find a mutually beneficial spiritual solution to their longing for religious harmony in their marriages and homes.

To that end, mission workers ought to ask ourselves some basic questions to help refine our strategy and orientation for evangelistic outreach as a spiritual service to Jewish-Gentile couples and their families. It is to those questions that we now turn. More lengthy discussion is warranted, but these questions are offered as an introduction in the hope of encouraging more missiological thinking, and with the intent of arriving at some guidelines for ethics in ministry to these couples.

SUGGESTED ETHICS IN JEWISH-GENTILE COUPLES MINISTRY
Should We Be for or Against Intermarriage?

Intermarriage is a fact of American Jewish life. Social research finds that Jewish-Gentile marriages are twice as likely to end in

---

20. Ibid.

divorce as are endogamous Jewish marriages.[21] Would it, therefore, be right to oppose Jewish intermarriage? An opinion from *the* competent authority on the subject of marriage would be beneficial. I therefore turn to the biblical basis for marriage and then the reasons for any prohibition on Jewish intermarriages.

Biblical Guidance

God's design for marriage is provided in the Bible. Marriage between a man and a woman was given to provide the appropriate social structure for the family.[22] Marriage within the long history of Israel has set the stage for questions about Jewish intermarriage.

The Jewish people were set apart by God as a holy people and a special "treasure" for God's purposes.[23] Through the Jewish people would come the family that would yield "the seed of the woman," a savior promised in the Garden of Eden.[24] That child, from among the Jews, would fulfill God's promise to Abraham that "in you all the families of the earth shall be blessed."[25] It seems reasonable to assume that the line of messianic promise had to be preserved through means of an endogamous community.

Participation in the messianic blessing was conditioned on the faith of those Jewish people who trusted in the promises of God.[26] So Abraham and his immediate heirs were committed to endogamy. The patriarchs sought spouses for their children from among the Semites of the East, at least among their own Aramean people.[27] By the generation of Abraham's great-grandchildren, however, at least two had already married out of the clan. Jacob's son Judah (*Yehudah ben Ya'akov*) took a Canaanite wife, and Joseph married Asenath, an Egyptian.[28]

After the exodus from Egypt, the Lord cautioned that marriage to foreign idol worshippers could turn the hearts of Israelites away from their love

---

21. Pini Herman, *Los Angeles Jewish Population Survey '97* (Los Angeles: Jewish Federation of Greater Los Angeles, 1998), 10–11.
22. Genesis 2:18, 24.
23. Exodus 19:5–6a; Deuteronomy 7:6–9.
24. Genesis 3:15.
25. Genesis 12:3 NKJV.
26. Genesis 15:5–6; 17:9–10a. For a fuller discussion see H. Wayne House, "Israel the People," in *Israel: The Land and the People* (Grand Rapids: Kregel, 1998), 45–49.
27. Genesis 24:3–4.
28. Genesis 38:1; Genesis 41:45.

of Yahweh, a God who is jealous for his own people.[29] God was concerned for the spiritual welfare of His people, and about the potential negative influence on Israelites' faith as a result of marrying foreign spouses.[30]

Joshua confirmed the ban on intermarriage with Canaanites at the time of the conquest of their land. It was not a matter of racism. Nor was it to insure the survival of the Jewish people. That covenant promise was already insured by the name and reputation of Yahweh. The prohibition against marrying the former proprietors of Canaan was to insure the spiritual sanctity of the Jewish people.[31]

King Solomon's disregard for the warning against taking foreign wives displayed repeated bad judgment. The otherwise wise king set a horrible example to the subjects of his kingdom, which eventually led to the demise of the unified kingdom of David. The Scripture reports the predictable results. "As Solomon grew old, his wives turned his heart after other gods, and his heart was not fully devoted to the LORD his God, as the heart of David his father had been."[32]

In the fifth century B.C., Nehemiah championed spiritual reforms during the return of the Jewish people from captivity in Babylon. Upon discovering that many of the religious leaders had married foreign wives in the Diaspora, he verbally chastised them, cursed them, and even physically attacked them for their moral failure.[33] They were disqualified from providing spiritual leadership for the people, and they were a risk to Israel's trust in Yahweh God.

Successful intermarriage relationships are, of course, reported in the Bible. Moses was married to Zipporah, a Midianite woman. Her people, though related by blood to Abraham, eventually became enemies of Israel and were judged by God during the ministry of Gideon. In the period of the Judges, Samson married a Philistine woman. Samson returned to the Lord, however, and was used of God. The Bible says that his intermarriage union was "of the Lord" and within God's sovereign plan.[34]

---

29. Exodus 34:11–16; Deuteronomy 7:3.
30. Genesis 24:3–4; Exodus 34:11–16; Deuteronomy 7:3.
31. Joshua 23:12.
32. I Kings 11:4 NIV.
33. Nehemiah 13:23–26.
34. Judges 14:1–4.

A whole book of the Bible is dedicated to Ruth, a Moabitess who joined the Jewish people through marriage. Though Moab was an enemy of the Jews, Ruth stands out from her nation for her turning to faith in Yahweh God. Her faith was honored among the line of Jewish people that leads to Messiah Jesus.[35]

It is easy to overlook a Jewish-Gentile marriage in the tragic story of Uriah the Hittite. Here is a biblical case where a Gentile male is married to a Jewish woman.[36] Esther is another book of the Bible that is dedicated to a Jewish woman who was intermarried to a Persian king.

The New Testament reports many Jewish-Gentile marriages in the era of the Roman Empire. Timothy, for example, was the son of Eunice, a Jewish follower of Jesus, and his father was a Gentile pagan man.[37]

Intermarriages are found throughout the Bible. The question of ethics in intermarriage between Jews and Gentiles concerned the potential negative effect that foreigners might have on the faith of Jews who would otherwise trust in Yahweh God.

Contemporary Guidelines for Ministry

The American Jewish community is guided in forming policy about intermarriage by a survival instinct for Jewry and for the preservation of Judaism. It is consistent that public policy, then, focuses on bringing Gentiles into the Jewish community through conversion or reattachment to Judaism. Such an approach, however, seems out of step with the fact that American Jews are intermarrying because they have not found sufficient satisfaction within Judaism. Dissatisfaction with Judaism, though, is not a useful motivation that we should adopt in Jewish evangelism.

Unlike traditional Jewish communal policy, mission workers should be focused on how to minister to these couples according to their real needs and not from an external agenda. Based upon their spiritual need and the sociological threats to marital satisfaction, the motivation for Jewish evangelism must be founded in the hope of introducing the couple to truth and spiritual resources in Christ, the Messiah.

---

35. Matthew 1:5.
36. 2 Samuel 11.
37. Acts 16:1; 2 Timothy 1:5.

We have already pointed out that continuity of the Jewish people is established in the faithfulness of God. That is ensured by the reputation of Yahweh. So we need not be motivated by a concern that Jewish-Gentile marriage would undermine the survival of the Jewish people. The kingdom of Messiah will continue to grow according to the sovereign plan of God, and the Jewish people are part of that holy program.

If those who minister to the Jewish people are going to be *against* intermarriage or interfaith marriage at any time, it should be *before* a couple marries. When Jewish-Gentile couples seek advice before marriage, we have a moral obligation to tell them that marriage without God is difficult. Marriage, when only one partner knows the Lord, will put pressure on the believing spouse and places the believer's testimony in jeopardy. There is simply no practical wisdom in "missionary dating."

Once a couple is married, however, and comes to us for ministerial help, we have an obligation to accept them and approach their spiritual needs. Christian ministry to Jewish-Gentile couples can introduce them to the oneness that God intended in marriage. Mission workers can point out to these couples the "one flesh" relationship as described in the Bible. We can give them hope for spiritual harmony when a couple is joined together through their faith in the Messiah.

Jewish-Gentile couples generally see themselves as marginalized. They see themselves as outsiders to the Jewish community. The Christian church unintentionally leaves the Jewish partners feeling culturally alienated. Messianic congregations might be culturally more appealing to Jewish-Gentile couples if the issue of Jesus is not a barrier. Nevertheless, the approach for evangelical ministry should be guided by the commitment to accept intermarried couples without expressing disappointment or opposition for their choice to be intermarried.

Workers in Jewish evangelism are obligated to be available to these couples without judging them. We must be able to help them see the special status of their situation as the growing majority in the Jewish community, and not the minority. We are able to provide insight regarding the sources of their cross-cultural pressures. We may affirm them as potential members of God's eternal family, since that community is multi-ethnic and multicultural.

So should we be for or against intermarriage? The primary ethical guideline for us is that Jewish-Gentile couples present a unique opportunity for ministry. We should be concerned for the potential cross-cultural strains that result when couples intermarry. When couples come to mission workers before marriage, we ought not minimize the difficulty encountered when a Christian chooses to marry with *any* non-Christian. Once the wedding has taken place, however, we should not encourage a violation of marriage vows. How, then, should we respond when a Jewish-Gentile couple asks for advice about a wedding when one is already a believer in Jesus and the other is not?

HOW SHOULD WE ADDRESS THE ISSUE
OF BEING UNEQUALLY YOKED?

Terminology: Jews and Gentiles

Before considering the subject of binding believers and unbelievers, we need to review some definitions. Recall, the term *Jewish-Gentile couples* indicates the differences between partners based on ethnicity. Religion is a separate subject. Ethnicity comes from the bloodline, the people of the parents. Jewish people are an ethnicity, a people. From the Jewish perspective, all other ethnic groups are *Gentiles*, the "other nations." We use that perspective in this chapter.

If ethnicity were our hardware, then culture would be our software or operating system. All culture is learned, and religion is a component of culture. Religion explains origins of life and the universe. It provides people with a notion of their worth. It establishes the bases for truth and moral choices. Religious faith is based on what we have learned and eventually come to embrace. Like all aspects of culture, religious belief can change when new information is learned.

We distinguish between *nominal* believers and *confessing* believers. When I speak of *Christian* partners in this chapter, I mean those who believe that Jesus rose from the dead and confess him as Lord, their Savior.[38] When I speak of Gentiles, I refer to those who regard themselves as even nominally Christian.

Bound Together with Unbelievers

In the previous section, we noted that God warns that a non-believer could hinder or have a detrimental effect on the faith of a

---

38. Romans 10:9.

believer in the living God. How should mission workers advise those who come to us and are considering being *unequally yoked* or who have already entered such a relationship?

First, a word of explanation is appropriate for those who might not be aware of the concept under discussion.

> Do not be unequally yoked together with unbelievers. For what fellowship has righteousness with lawlessness? And that communion has light with darkness? And what accord has Christ with Belial? Or what part has a believer with an unbeliever?[39]

In context, the apostle Paul was admonishing believers in the congregation at Corinth to turn from false teachers. Paul used the example of God's jealousy for Israel as his illustration that the believer should be sanctified to the Lord.[40]

Unequally yoked is a New Testament description for those who love God, yet have joined themselves to others who do not share that faith.[41] The point is often applied as a warning against interfaith marriage.

Christian ministers often teach about the potential for oneness in Messiah though spiritual harmony. That subject has to be approached differently with a Jewish-Gentile couple in which one is already a believer in Jesus. Christian partners may be dating, already cohabiting, or married to a non-believing Jewish person. Christians that I interviewed reported surprisingly often that they are aware of this New Testament caution even while already in a dating relationship with a Jewish non-Christian. Mission workers have an ethical obligation to remind them that their faith and testimony to the unbeliever are in peril as they open themselves to the potential for marriage with an unbeliever.

I have ministered to quite a number of Christians who, while dating a Jewish person, were looking for a way to reconcile their relationships with the warning against being unequally yoked. In the face of strong romantic attraction, Christians do understand that they are

---

39. 2 Corinthians 6:14–15 NKJV.
40. Ezekiel 37:26–27; Isaiah 52:11; 2 Samuel 7:14
41. Alice Fryling, *An Unequal Yoke: In Dating and Marriage* (Downers Grove, IL: InterVarsity Press, 1979) provides a good discussion; "Unequally yoked" is used in KJV, NIV and NRSV versions. The NASB uses "bound together with unbelievers."

at a watershed point in their Christian walk if they marry someone who cannot share their faith.

While interviewing Jewish-Gentile couples for research, I met Barbara and Sam (all names used for examples in this chapter are pseudonyms). Barbara is a Christian who was in love with Sam, her Jewish boyfriend. Their relationship tested her faith. She was not at peace about marrying Sam, because he was not yet a believer in Jesus. She knew in her heart that she could not marry him. She could not bring herself to explain her hesitancy about going any further than dating with their relationship. He was interested in discussing marriage and she could not.

Barbara did not want to pressure Sam, so she suggested that they separate amicably, at least for a while to think. During that period Sam came to faith in Jesus. He would not tell Barbara of his new faith, however, since now he was not sure about the depth of her commitment to Jesus. Only after she finally confessed that she would not marry him if he were not a Christian did Sam tell her of his belief in Jesus Christ. They eventually married and enjoyed many years of successful and joyous marriage together as Jew and Gentile in Christ, equally yoked together.

Mission workers bear a ministerial obligation to discuss with dating Jewish-Gentile couples the potential disharmony from being unequally yoked. In one case, a mature Christian, Carol, asked me to meet with her and her non-Christian Jewish boyfriend, Philip. During our appointment, it was quickly obvious that both of them were deeply attracted one to another. I also heard from them that they had not been very candid about their different motives or agendas.

I asked Carol, in front of Philip, if she would be willing to marry him if he did not become a believer in Jesus. She responded, "No." I asked her if she was likely to have sex with him before they were married. Again, she answered, "No."

I turned next to Philip to ask if he understood that Carol wanted us to meet so he could hear about Jesus from another Jewish person. In truth, Philip was not interested in a discussion of the gospel. He would have done almost anything to satisfy Carol, even to the point of marriage, so he could eventually have sex with her. He had not been particularly candid with her about that and, to be fair, may not have understood the depth of his own desire for her. Evidently, that became the most candid conversation the two of them ever had together. Forty-eight hours later, Carol called me to let me know the relationship had ended by mutual agreement.

We should be open to meet with and minister to couples who are considering being "unequally yoked." It may be their only opportunity to receive truth and biblical wisdom. Christians may benefit from the reminder of their obligation to live for the Lord and the potential peril to their own faith from being joined with a nonbeliever. The mission worker may be the only voice telling the nonbeliever about hope for spiritual harmony in a marriage relationship.

Mission workers are, I believe, ethically bound not knowingly to perform a wedding ceremony in which one partner is already a believer and the other one is not. In such a case, I think the admonition against binding believers and unbelievers is clear. Consideration of all the potential exceptions to this rule is beyond the scope of this chapter. But ethical standards should be in place for the purpose of guiding ministry to Jewish-Gentile couples. The clear challenges from an unequally yoked partnership are significant enough to warrant candid discussion based on biblical wisdom and trends from social research. It seems only right that we have an obligation to minister with consideration for both of the partners involved. That brings us to the next ethical question.

WHOSE SIDE SHOULD WE TAKE—THE JEW'S OR THE CHRISTIAN'S?

Often, we hear from Christians who need help talking to their Jewish partner about Jesus. In this case, we are talking about committed Christian believers who are dating or are already married to non-Christian Jews. What are some ethical guidelines as we minister to both the unbelieving Jewish partner and the Christian?

Shouldn't we, who minister in the name of Messiah Jesus, be in partnership with Gentile believers to help witness to their non-Christian Jewish partners? Of course; but our actual ministry is to both partners. God cares about both the saved and the unsaved partner in the Jewish-Gentile relationship. Our ministry ought to be equally extended to both of them.

A Jewish-Gentile couple seeking spiritual help needs assistance to communicate cross-culturally. Thus, one aspect of our ministry must be as cross-cultural translators. One of the five key challenges experienced by Jewish-Gentile couples that I identified previously is confusion over identity differences. Effective Christian ministry to both partners involves helping them communicate about their cultural differences. The minister, in this situation, should understand both cultures and be able to translate between the partners to create a new understanding.

It is often new insight to Jewish persons, for example, when it is explained to them that the term *Christian* literally means a "follower of Messiah." Anyone, from any ethnicity, can be a follower of the Messiah. That is different from the common Jewish misunderstanding that the word *Christian* is synonymous with *Gentile*. The Christian/Gentile distinction is important, since the Jewish understanding is that Jews and Gentiles are mutually exclusive people groups. That small but significant distinction can create a new understanding and possibility for a Jewish person.

On the other side, many Gentiles think of Jewishness as a religion. As I have pointed out, however, Jewishness is an ethnic identity that is apart from any belief. While Judaism is called a Jewish faith, and it is a religion that is practiced by some Jewish people, there are many Jews who do not believe or practice it. They are nonetheless still considered Jews. When Gentiles convert to Judaism that does not erase their ethnic heritage even when Jewish people embrace them as one of their own. It is helpful when mission workers can facilitate cross-cultural communication for Jewish-Gentile partners and thereby create new understanding between them.

Shouldn't our emphasis be to assist a Christian witness to the Jewish partner? Of course, but that must be in the context of a holistic care for both partners. In one case, Shirley and Rodney called, asking for help. Jews for Jesus doesn't provide marriage counseling, but we do offer spiritual resources for Jewish-Gentile couples. Shirley, a Gentile Christian, wanted me to help her tell Rodney, her Jewish husband, about Jesus. Rodney was open to that, but he particularly wanted me to explain her Christian faith from the Jewish perspective.

Much of the initial effort with Rodney was going to be pre-evangelistic. He was doing his best to understand her faith, but his own culture made it difficult for him to comprehend her Christian terms. When she said "Christ" he was hearing Jesus' last name! Neither she nor Rodney realized that *Christ* means "Messiah." Now, *Messiah* is a term that Rodney understood. Yet, when he grasped that concept, Shirley was disappointed in him, because he did not know the messianic prophecies of his Old Testament Scriptures.

He was trying to learn as fast as he could. Shirley was impatient with him, and her comments about his intelligence were getting embarrassing. She was looking to me as if to make Rodney understand. I had to tell Shirley, in front of Rodney, "I won't be your hammer to beat Rodney with the gospel." That comment made him feel safer in our meeting. At first, it disappointed Shirley, but she understood the need to be fair with Rodney and a bit more patient in the process.

We do have an obligation to protect the Jewish partner from an unseemly or aggressive witness. When well-meaning Gentile Christian partners press the matter, they are often motivated by deep love and anguish for their unsaved partners, whom they realize face eternity without Christ. It is only right to comfort the Christian. We can discreetly affirm the truth of the gospel and its implications while urging forbearance based in our trust that the Holy Spirit will, in his time, work in the life of their Jewish spouses.

As mentioned earlier, mission workers should not practice marriage counseling unless they are adequately and professionally trained to do marriage and family counseling. Beyond being cross-cultural translators, however, we can minister spiritual help to both partners. Often, Jewish-Gentile couples are overwhelmed by the religious disharmony at the core of their marriage.

Donna and Barry were part of a small group of Jewish-Gentile couples who met for most of a year in our home. I loaned a Christian video made for intermarried couples to Barry. In the video he heard that a Jewish-Gentile couple could not find harmony without Jesus in their marriage. He commented, "So, if I don't come to believe in Jesus, we're screwed!" I did my best to reassure him that if they both draw near to the God of Abraham, Isaac, and Jacob, the Lord would draw each of them to himself. The Bible clearly teaches the only way to have a relationship with the Father is through the Son of God.[42] The couple's situation turned out sadly; even as Barry was slowly

---

42. John 14:6, 17:3; Acts 4:12.

opening to the gospel, Donna came to the end of her patience over his progress toward faith and divorced him.

Without taking sides, mission workers are obligated to extend ministry to both partners. Each partner has unique needs. In that sense, ministry to Jewish-Gentile couples is a holistic ministry. We can be cultural translators to create understanding between them. We can minister hope to both of them and trust in God to provide the resources necessary to heal their marriage. We must not, however, become the Christian partner's witnessing hammer, nor should we ever soft sell the uniqueness of the gospel, its reconciling power with God, and the spiritual harmony it can bring to the family.

IS A CHURCH OR A MESSIANIC CONGREGATION THE ANSWER FOR JEWISH-GENTILE COUPLES?

From the earliest days, Moishe spoke of our Jews for Jesus ministry as an *arm of the local church*. We serve the church, and we minister to Jewish people. When either or both partners in a Jewish-Gentile couple comes to faith in Jesus we expect the believer to eventually become maturing participants in a local body of Christians. That can be in a church or a Messianic congregation, whichever is most comfortable for the new believer.

Often, our ministry relationships with Jewish-Gentile couples begins with one partner looking for a church, a Messianic church or Messianic congregation. Often, Gentile Christian partners are looking for a place to bring their non-Christian Jewish spouses. They hope that the nonbelieving spouses will hear the gospel and learn about Jesus in religious services.

At that point, our first step is to ask some diagnostic questions. "You are a Jewish-Gentile couple. So tell me how each of you identifies yourself and what religious practices each of you observes." That line of questioning usually reveals some of the cross-cultural tensions over religious differences. I have found from my research that such tension was one of the five key challenges to interfaith marriage.[43] Rarely does a couple identify "the failure to find spiritual harmony" as the reason for seeking out a common place for worship. A mission

---

43. Wan and Zaretsky, *Jewish-Gentile Couples*, 93.

worker has to deduce as much from the way the couple describe their religious practices and identities.

Next, I find it helpful to tell the couple how they fit into the demographic data about Jewish-Gentile marriages since 1985. They are generally surprised by the high percentage of intermarried Jews, though most have anecdotal observations of other couples like them. They are usually comforted by the notion that they are part of a larger community that is just like them.

Many Jewish-Gentile couples believe they are marginalized from the Jewish community, and the Jewish partners are often alienated from Christian church culture. It is most important at this stage, however, to address the underlying needs for spiritual harmony as a couple, and family harmony in the home. The conversation can turn more naturally from locating a congregation to finding spiritual hope for their relationship.

Some in the Messianic congregational movement in America believe that the Messianic synagogue is the best and perhaps only place for Jewish-Gentile couples. While I do believe that Messianic congregations can provide a unique and culturally comfortable community for Jewish-Gentile couples, I believe mission workers are obligated to provide more than just a community if couples are going to find spiritual harmony.

David J. Rudolph has been an advocate for Messianic Judaism as a good option in meeting the needs of intermarried couples. I might be inclined to agree that Messianic congregations can be an excellent option for some Jewish-Gentile couples. I would disagree, however, when he says, "Loss of Jewish identity is almost certain in the local church."[44] A broad, sweeping statement like that is both unnecessary and untrue.

I reject the notion that the *only* place for ministry to a Jewish-Gentile couple would be in a Messianic, or indigenous, culturally Jewish congregation. By its definition, a Jewish-Gentile couple is not 100 percent Jewish. There must be sensitivity to the cultural needs of both partners.

Finding community is important to Jewish-Gentile couples for it provides a safe place to make cross-cultural discoveries. Our chief resource,

---

44. David J. Rudolph, *Growing Your Olive Tree Marriage: A Guide for Couples from Two Traditions* (Baltimore: Lederer Books, 2003), 49, 59.

however, is in teaching couples how they may find the oneness in marriage that God intended. The only hope for spiritual harmony for a Jewish-Gentile couple is when both partners learn of and believe in the Messiah Jesus. A full explanation is beyond my current purpose, but I would suggest to a Jewish-Gentile couple that they consider attending a small group or *havurah* as an intermediate step between going it alone and full congregational participation.[45] It is a comfortable place to explore beliefs and to find community for Jewish-Gentile couples. Where they go after that, whether to a church or Messianic congregation, is up to them.

The four questions we have just explored help us to think about what is appropriate missiological strategy in ministry to Jewish-Gentile couples. These questions are intended to help refine ministry orientation for evangelistic outreach as a spiritual service to Jewish-Gentile couples and their families. Let us summarize, then, the missiological implications of the data presented.

MISSIOLOGICAL IMPLICATIONS

1. Jewish-Gentile couples and their families are a strategic population for focused Jewish mission allocation of resources and application of efforts.

2. Ministry to Jewish-Gentile couples requires multidimensional understanding and a cross-cultural approach. Formulation of ministry strategy should begin with consideration of the challenges and needs of the couple. Traditional Jewish public policy toward intermarried Jews seems to be driven by instincts for preservation of the Jewish people and Judaism. Our ethical obligation is to trust God for the preservation of the Jewish people and to provide spiritual resources that meet the mutual needs of Jewish-Gentile partners.

3. Mission workers should be prepared to accept Jewish-Gentile couples without judging them, whether they are

---

45. *Havurah* is a small affinity group for discussion and learning.

dating, cohabiting, or intermarried. The conversation has to begin somewhere. It starts with the first meeting. We do not need to be prophetic about the projected success of Jewish-Gentile marriages or opponents of intermarriage. We must be able to address each couple's underlying spiritual needs while counting on the Holy Spirit to speak to their consciences regarding their choices.

4. Mission workers have an ethical responsibility to remind Christians who are dating unsaved Jewish people that "missionary dating" is generally a futile effort. It places in question the believer's testimony of fidelity to the Lord. This sort of dating is an optimistic risk that could potentially harm the believer's walk with the Lord. It is appropriate to remind a Christian of the biblical warning against being bound together with unbelievers while he or she is dating. Once a couple is married, however, we are obligated to respect their marriage vows and offer ministry within that context.

5. We have a responsibility to both partners in a Jewish-Gentile couple. We ought not take sides with the Jewish partner or the Gentile/Christian partner. Rather, our ministry should aim to provide cross-cultural translation and improved understanding between the partners. They must feel that we are there for both of them. They should not be defending themselves against any alleged secret agenda. We ought to be open about our appreciation for Jewish culture and our conviction regarding the unique axiomatic hope in Messiah Jesus. At the same time, both partners should be made to feel they are held in equal esteem. We can provide spiritual resources without pressing them to conform to the truth.

6. Local churches and Messianic congregations can be adequate spiritual communities for Jewish-Gentile couples. Partners who desire community might find that in either

social setting. They also may explore synagogue participation or a small group *havurah* for a time. It is important to help them focus on finding spiritual harmony. That longing will be satisfied only when both partners know the Savior Jesus.

CONCLUSION

There is great potential for ministry to Jewish-Gentile couples, and I've presented some ethical guidelines for doing so. Ministering to Jewish-Gentile couples is certainly not the *preferred* setting in which to do Jewish evangelism, but it is a *fresh* approach in light of current trends within American Jewry.

Amazing demographic changes are occurring in the American Jewish community. Social research shows that, as a result, Jewish-Gentile couples describe several cultural challenges they face. The four questions presented may well aid in formulating ethical guidelines for mission work with Jewish-Gentile couples.

I appreciate the example of Moishe Rosen's passion for Jewish evangelism. He has been used by God to guide many of us in fulfilling our destiny in service to the Lord. I pray that this offering of my work might be useful for helping Jews and Gentiles find their spiritual home in Y'shua (Jesus).

8

THE MOSAIC LAW AND CHRISTIAN ETHICS

Obligation or Fulfillment?

JIM CONGDON

Torah observance has long been accepted as permissible for Jews who have come to faith in Yeshua, and even for Gentile believers as well.[1]

---

1. That Gentiles often greatly outnumber Jews in their synagogues poses an added theological difficulty for messianic rabbis who preach law obligation. David Kling-hoffer, in a recent issue of the Jewish women's magazine *Hadassah*, names a Messianic rabbi in Seattle who admitted to him that only about 2 percent of his Beit Tikvah congregation of 200 are Jewish-born. *Hadassah* 88, no. 9 (May 2007).

But recently some Messianic leaders have asserted that Torah-centered living is *normative* for Messianic Jewish congregations.[2]

In an atmosphere of requirement, it is helpful to remind ourselves that God's people are no longer under obligation to the Law of Moses. Two lines of evidence are linked by the enigmatic word "fulfill." Jesus said that He came to "fulfill" the Law; Paul wrote that believers "fulfill" the Law. Both statements indicate that the believer is free from the Law.[3]

JESUS "FULFILLED" THE LAW BY INAUGURATING A NEW AGE

Jesus teaches in Matthew 5 that he is the new and living Torah—the realization of the Old Testament, the culmination of the Law of Moses. Paul affirms the same truth in Romans 10:4.

Matthew 5:17–48

Matthew 5:17–20 is the critical text for the question of the abiding force of the Mosaic Law in the life of the believer. This passage is often summoned as the expert witness to prove the Law-obligation view, but the witness itself destroys the case, for it says "too much" for that view, whether offered in its Reformed theological form or its Jewish Torah-observant form.

Matthew 5:17–18 says "too much" for the traditional Reformed view, which would neatly resolve this *crux interpretum* by dividing the Law into "abiding" (moral law) and "abrogated" (civil, ceremonial) parts—for Jesus is declaring that the *entire* Mosaic Law remains in force. This idea that Jesus was referring only to the moral laws—especially the Decalogue—within the Torah is unable to handle the all-embracing sweep of Jesus' next words in verse 18, which, he

---

2. This is the argument of Mark Kinzer, *Post-Missionary Messianic Judaism* (Grand Rapids: Brazos Press, 2005). The use of *Judaism* is deliberate by Kinzer, for whom Jews in rabbinic Judaism rest under God's redemptive favor and may be saved through Jesus, even if they do not believe in him (p. 25).

3. This does not mean we are lawless, of course. To broadly summarize, using distinctions as old as Thomas Aquinas, (1) *everyone* is under the law of Nature; (2) *no one* is under the Law of Moses, (3) *believers* are under the law of Christ. See J. Budziszewski, *Written on the Heart: A Case for Natural Law* (Downers Grove, IL: InterVarsity Press, 1997). When referring to the Law of Moses in this article, "law," is capitalized to distinguish the Law of Moses from the laws of God, nature, and Christ.

declares, gather "every iota and dot" of the Law into that which will not pass away "until all is accomplished."[4]

Similarly, Matthew 5:18 says too much for the Messianic Jewish view that compliments itself on correctly noting that the Law is an indivisible unit—for confronted with the actual 613 laws themselves, Torah-observant believers are compelled to "take the absolute value" of each, removing multiple iotas here, dots there—of sacrifices, purifications, and penalties for disobedience, for much of the Law requires Temple, priesthood, and presence in the Land.[5] Westerholm is right to ask: "How can Christians be said to 'fulfill' the law when a significant number of its commands are disregarded?"[6] Once again, this is a reductionist interpretation of verse 18 that fails to honor the inclusive sweep of Jesus' words.

Instead, Jesus must be saying that the Mosaic Law *in toto* remains in force. But how can this be, since we are told that he abolished the food laws (Mark 7:19) and that the sacrificial system is abolished (Heb. 8:13; 10:1–18)? The explanation must be "eschatological": Jesus is claiming that he is the climactic figure of history, and that the Law and Prophets remain in force *in himself*. He has come to inaugurate a new age in salvation history—not an age in which the old age is abolished, but the age to which it pointed and in which it is fully realized.[7] An analogy to this realization might be the way in which a graduate student looks back on her undergraduate years of schooling. Are those university days

---

4. Paul is unaware of the threefold division of the Law upon which much of the modern argument for the continuing validity of the Law is based. This division would have been repugnant to the Jews, for whom all 613 commands were moral, and it is spurned by them to this day. While general comparisons were drawn in biblical times between "weightier and lighter matters of the law" (Matt. 23:23), sharp lines were not drawn until postbiblical times. When the New Testament refers to "the law," it generally means the entire Mosaic corpus of law.

5. "For the most part, the emphasis is on holy days, Sabbaths, and festivals, with perhaps some attention given to other parts of the Law. In essence, these are not so much Torah-observant as festival-observant groups." Rich Robinson, *Havurah* 8, no. 4 (Winter 2005): 2.

6. Stephen Westerholm, *Israel's Law and the Church's Faith: Paul and His Recent Interpreters* (Grand Rapids: Eerdmans, 1988), 202, citing E. P. Sanders in support. He adds on page 221 that "it was Paul who realized that when the sanctions of the law have been removed, its demands have no force."

7. The first thorough delineation of this "salvation-history" interpretation is usually attributed to Robert Banks, *Jesus and the Law in the Synoptic Tradition*, Society for New Testament Studies Monograph Series 28 (Cambridge: Cambridge University Press, 1975).

now abolished? Never! They will always be cherished, yet only as the preparation of the advanced study to which they intentionally pointed.

Two textual witnesses support this exegesis: the verb "fulfill" (v. 17) and the six "words" that follow (vv. 21–48). Our Lord's choice of verb (*pleroō*, "fulfill") is critical: "The antithesis is not between 'abolish' and 'keep' but between 'abolish' and 'fulfill.'"[8] While many interpretations have been suggested, the best is that which sees it as part of the promise-fulfillment theology of Matthew, which pictures the entire Old Testament as promising and anticipating Jesus.[9] Indeed, that theology mirrors Jesus' statement a few chapters later: "The Prophets and the Law prophesied until John" (11:13 NIV).[10] It is *in* Christ that all that the Law anticipated is about to be "accomplished" (v. 18)—in his teaching, his ministry, and especially in his death and resurrection.

"Jesus does not conceive of his life and ministry in terms of opposition to the Old Testament, but in terms of *bringing to* fruition that toward which it points. Thus, the Law and the Prophets, far from being abolished, find their valid continuity in terms of their outworking in Jesus. The detailed prescriptions of the Old Testament may well be superseded, because whatever is prophetic must be in some sense provisional. But whatever is prophetic likewise discovers its legitimate continuity in the happy arrival of that toward which it has pointed."[11]

This interpretation of Matthew 5:17–18 is also confirmed by the six "words" that follow (vv. 21–48), in which Jesus sets himself up as the new Torah giver. Those who view the Law as still binding argue that Jesus is simply giving the "deeper, original meaning" of the ancient laws here, but while this explanation will do for his third word (on adultery), it will not suffice for the others. Others respond that

---

8. D. A. Carson, "Matthew," in *The Expositor's Bible Commentary* (Grand Rapids: Zondervan, 1984), 8:243.

9. Douglas J. Moo, "The Law of Christ as the Fulfillment of the Law of Moses: A Modified Lutheran View," in *Five Views on Law and Gospel*, ed. Stanley N. Gundry (Grand Rapids: Zondervan, 1996), 347–53.

10. It may be helpful to observe that for Matthew, Jesus is here thinking of the Hebrew Scriptures, and especially the Torah, not as a "code" or even primarily as an "ethic" but as a "promise"—a promise that reaches forward to its fulfillment in himself, the new and living Torah. See Darrell L. Bock, *Luke 1:1–9:50* (Grand Rapids: Baker, 1994), 39, who draws these distinctions in the third Gospel.

11. D. A. Carson, *The Sermon on the Mount: An Evangelical Exposition of Matthew 5–7* (Grand Rapids: Baker, 1978), 37.

Jesus is "expanding the meaning" of the old laws, but while that will do for his first and second words (on murder and adultery), it will not suffice for the others. Instead, the point that Matthew wants us to see, by repetition, is that Jesus is the new Lawgiver, who alone has the authority to say "you have heard that it was said . . . but I say unto you."[12]

The transfiguration story (17:1–8; cf. Mark 9:2–8; Luke 9:28–36) is probably meant to illustrate this replacement theme. In Exodus 24:16, Moses had gone up into a high mountain on the seventh day; in Matthew 17:1, "after six days" Jesus goes up into a high mountain. Moses had been accompanied by Aaron and a pair of brother priests, Nadab and Abihu; Jesus was accompanied by Peter and the brothers James and John. As Moses had entered the cloud and divine light with the result that his face shone, so Jesus shone with heaven's light, and before him appeared Moses and Elijah, the only Old Testament saints to receive a revelation on "the mountain." As tents had been part of the ritual of Moses receiving revelation (Exod. 33), so Peter suggests that tents be erected for the three recipients of revelation. But at this juncture there is a sharp discontinuity meant to catch our attention. At Sinai, God had revealed himself with "I am Yahweh," and then given the Ten Words to Moses; but here and now, God introduces his Son, "This is my beloved Son," and then says, "Listen to *him*." The Gospel writer could not present it more clearly: Jesus has become the revealed Word. The old Torah has given way to One who himself is the new and living Torah.

Where, then, is the code of conduct for "life in the kingdom" here and now? According to verses 19–20, our ethic is found in "these commands" of Jesus, which assume and advance the Old Testament law, and last forever (cf. Exod. 33).[13] The Law and Prophets no longer govern God's people directly—only Christ does that—but when filtered through the lens of Jesus' works and words, provide principles

---

12. Moo, *Five Views*, 347–50.
13. By "these commands" Jesus must not be referring not to Old Testament law *per se*, to which the Pharisees and scribes who will not enter the kingdom (v. 20) adhere, but to his own words in their fulfillment of the Law (vv. 18–19), words that will never pass away (Matt. 24:35; 28:20). See A. T. Lincoln, "Sabbath, Rest, and Eschatology in the New Testament," in *From Sabbath to Lord's Day: A Biblical, Historical, and Theological Investigation*, ed. D. A. Carson (Grand Rapids: Zondervan, 1982), 219n. 82; and followed by Carson, *From Sabbath to Lord's Day*, 78.

"for teaching, rebuking, correcting, and training in righteousness" (2 Tim. 3:16 NIV). This exegesis explains the relatively few number of times that Jesus cites the Law to support his demands, as well as supports statements such as "the Son of Man is Lord even of the Sabbath" (Mark 2:28 NIV), and the fact that Jesus leaves his disciples with the command to take *his* teaching to the world (Matt 28:20).

Romans 10:4

In his most famous statement on the Law, Paul affirms that Jesus is the goal and end of the Law. He writes, "Christ is the end of the [L]aw so that there may be righteousness for everyone who believes" (Rom. 10:4 NIV). The apostle seems to be declaring a "full stop" to the Law of Moses, but both of the words in the phrase *telos nomou* are debated, and the study leads us to the same conclusion as in Matthew 5.

Some proponents of Law obligation deny that Romans 10:4 refers to the Law at all. Instead, they say, Paul declares that Christ is the end of *legalism*, the Law's misuse as a way of salvation. But this escape route is closed, for Paul nowhere else uses *nomos* to mean legalism, while its normal use is the Mosaic Law.[14]

Most proponents of Law obligation instead note that *telos* can take the meaning "goal" rather than "end," and argue that this is what Paul means here.[15] The Law could then remain in full force for believers today. These two translations are sometimes presented as options in stark contrast: either Christ has terminated the Law, or the Law remains in full force.

We do not need to choose between these two opposite poles, however, and should not do so here. In this context Paul seems to be saying that Christ is both "goal" and "end": Christ is the "goal" of the Law, in the sense that the Law has always looked forward to him (10:2–3). But he is also its "end" in connection with righteousness, because through him comes faith as the new means to righteousness (9:30–32;

---

14. Douglas J. Moo, "'Law,' 'Works of the Law,' and Legalism in Paul," *Westminster Theological Journal* 45 (1983): 73–100.

15. C. E. B. Cranfield, *A Critical and Exegetical Commentary on the Epistle to the Romans*, 2 vols. (Edinburgh: T. & T. Clark, 1975, 1979), 2:516–19; Daniel P. Fuller, *Gospel/Law: Contrast or Continuum?* (Grand Rapids: Eerdmans, 1980), 82–85; and Frank Thielman, *Paul and the Law: A Contextual Approach* (Downers Grove, IL: InterVarsity Press, 1994), 207.

10:4b).[16] By *telos*, then, Paul means that Jesus is the Law's "point of culmination."[17]

Therefore Paul is saying the same thing about Christ that Christ said about himself—he is the culmination of the Law. Its permanence is guaranteed, yet not in its own continued existence but rather in its fulfillment in his teachings and in the new age of life in the Spirit.

BELIEVERS "FULFILL" THE LAW, EVEN WHILE THEY ARE FREE FROM IT

Paul is adamant that believers are no longer subject to the Law of Moses, yet he also expects that believers must comply with the moral demands of the Law. This conundrum is resolved by the apostle himself, who declares that believers comply with the Law's demands not by "doing" the Law but by "fulfilling" it, when they walk by the Spirit in love.

Believers Are Free from the Law

A heavy burden of proof rests upon those who would teach Law obligation today, for Paul declares unequivocally that believers are no longer subject to the Law: they have "died to the law" (Rom. 7:6; Gal. 2:19); they have been "set free" from the Law (Rom. 7:6); they are no longer "under" the Law (Rom. 6:14–15); they have been "redeemed" from the Law (Gal. 4:5).

As a Pharisee, Paul had understood the Torah to be the highest revelation of the will of God to man. But in his vision of the risen Jesus on the road to Damascus, Paul recognized in him a fuller, eschatological revelation of God. In other words, Christ, the bearer of the image of the invisible God, has superseded the Torah as the revelation of God and of his will for mankind (2 Cor. 4:4–6). The age of the Law has been replaced by the age of Christ (Gal. 3:19–4:5). And so while the Jews to whom he preaches are under obligation to observe the Law's demands, Paul says that he is not (1 Cor. 9:20).

---

16. Walter Bauer, W. F. Arndt, and F. W. Gingrich, *A Greek-English Lexicon of the New Testament and Other Early Christian Literature* (Chicago: University of Chicago Press, 1957), 818–18.
17. Douglas J. Moo, "The Law of Moses or the Law of Christ," in *Continuity and Discontinuity: Perspectives on the Relationship Between the Old and New Testaments* (Westchester, IL: Crossway, 1988), 207.

Finding scant support in Paul, those who teach Law obligation often sift the early church narratives of Acts for help. Finding Torah observance by Peter, James, and even Paul himself (!), they commandeer it as ground for the doctrine that believers—at least the Jewish ones—are still subject to the Law.[18] But early church practices will not bear this heavy theological weight. Thoughtful readers of Luke/Acts will remind themselves of several factors: (1) the early church of the Gospels and Acts occupied a kind of salvation-historical transitional phase as the old covenant was still in effect even as the new was in the process of inauguration; (2) the Jewish Christian therefore belonged to two communities—to the new covenant people as a believer, but to the Old Testament civil and social legislation as a Jew; (3) according to Luke, the early church merely rolled on in the well-worn grooves of Jewish piety, only gradually working out the full implications of the new covenant; (4) Stephen and other early Christians were accused by antagonistic Judaism of challenging the centrality of the Law and the Temple for God's people, and they did not deny it; (5) the gospel was preached beyond the boundaries of Judaism, and those who believed were admitted to the church without becoming proselytes; (6) Peter opposes nomism in Acts 15:10–11 with a programmatic statement that dismisses the imposition of Torah observance as "a yoke that neither we nor our fathers have been able to bear" (NIV); (7) the Sabbath, holiday, and purity practices of the apostles are therefore best seen as arising not from Law-obligation theology, but from one or more of the following factors: habit, religious conservatism, social pressure, avoidance of persecution, and missionary policy ("to the Jew I become as a Jew" [1 Cor. 9:20]).[19] From these factors, it is necessary to conclude that the continuing first-century practice of the Law by believing Jews falls into the category of liberty, not law. The Willowbank Declaration agrees: "We affirm that Jewish people who come to faith in Messiah have liberty before God to observe or

---

18. Kinzer, *Post-Missionary Messianic Judaism*, is the most recent example of resting one's case for abiding Torah observance on the narratives of Acts, rather than the teaching of Jesus and Paul.
19. Max M. B. Turner, "The Sabbath, Sunday, and the Law in Luke/Acts," in *From Sabbath to Lord's Day*, 121–26; and Arnold G. Fruchtenbaum, *Israelology: The Missing Link in Systematic Theology*, 2nd ed. (Tustin, CA: Ariel Ministries, 1994), 648.

not to observe traditional Jewish customs and ceremonies that are consistent with the Christian Scriptures."[20]

Paul's certainty that believers are free from the Law would be perfectly straightforward were it not also clear that he expects believers to comply with its moral demands (Rom. 8:4; 13:8–10; Gal. 5:14). How is this seeming contradiction resolved?

Believers Who Walk by the Spirit in Love Automatically "Fulfill" the Law

Paul says that believers must "fulfill" the Law (Rom. 8:4; 13:8–10; Gal. 5:14). But nowhere does he require that believers "do" the Law. This distinction is more than semantic. To "do" the Law, the believer would need to perform its individual and specific commands (Gal. 5:3). To "fulfill" the Law—described by Paul as walking by the Spirit in love—does not require performance of the specific legal requirements. Yet, says Paul, it completely satisfies what is required. But how is it possible to "fulfill" the Law without actually "doing" the Law?

Consider an illustration. A foreign exchange student from Greece enrolls in Introductory Greek at a school in the States. The instructor soon realizes that the student more than adequately "fulfills" the requirements of the course, and releases her from "doing" the assignments.[21] According to Paul, the Christian who walks by the Holy Spirit in love bears a similar relationship to the Law. He "fulfills" its demands without ever actually "doing" its specific requirements.

Romans 7:5–6 is definitive.[22] Believers have been set free from the Law (the "moral" law is included, v. 7), so that they now serve God in the new way of the Spirit rather than in the old way of the written

---

20. In a nice turn of phrase, the position statement of Jews for Jesus "affirms Jewish believers who, for the sake of honoring our heritage and developing a Jewish testimony, *choose to give up some of what grace allows* to conform to dietary standards and various other Jewish practices" (italics mine).

21. Westerholm, *Israel's Law and the Church's Faith*, 203, uses the illustration of a concert pianist who enrolls in an undergraduate music course. The argument here is indebted to Westerholm, "The Law and Christian Behavior," in *Israel's Law and the Church's Faith*, chap. 10.

22. This is the text that Mosaic Law scholar Frank Thielman confesses finally "converted" him to the view that "Paul considered the Mosaic covenant obsolete"; see *Paul and the Law: A Contextual Approach* (Downers Grove, IL: InterVarsity Press, 1994), 242.

code.[23] Paradoxically, the results of the new way—fulfillment of the Law, service in love (Rom. 8:4; Gal. 5:13)—are better than the results of the old way—sinful passions, disobedience, and death (Rom. 7:5; 2 Cor. 3:6; Gal. 3:19).

Both Jesus and the believer, then, are said to "fulfill" the Law. In neither instance is "doing" the Law in view; yet in both instances, the demands of the Law are fully satisfied. In the case of Jesus, the whole Law finds fulfillment—complete satisfaction and permanent validity—in his person and words. In the case of Jesus' followers, the whole Law finds fulfillment—complete satisfaction of all require-ments—in their submission to the person and words of Christ.

Christ, then, is the heart of New Testament ethics. He is every-thing that Judaism has claimed for Torah, and much more. He, rather than the Law, is the Wisdom of God, the Bread of Life, the Word, the Instrument of God's creation, the Light of the world, the Way, the Truth, the Life, the Glory, the Shepherd, and the Teacher. God speaks: "This is my beloved son; listen to him."

---

23. Space does not permit discussion of the essentials of the new covenant ethic: the central command of love, the law of Christ, walking by the Spirit.

9

THE CURRENT STATE OF
MESSIANIC JEWISH THOUGHT

RICHARD HARVEY

Since the early 1970s significant numbers of Jewish people have come to believe in Jesus. For me, as a Jewish believer in Jesus, and for the whole church, the phenomenon of Messianic Judaism has raised several questions concerning Jewish evangelization as well as Jewish and Christian identity and theology.[1] Those questions in-

---

1. The modern Messianic Jewish movement began after the Second World War, the Holocaust, and the establishment of the State of Israel. Jewish believers in Jesus from a new generation were concerned to rediscover their ethnic roots and express their faith from a Jewish perspective. In the wake of the Jesus movement of the 1970s, "Jews for Jesus" moved from a slogan used on the streets of San Francisco

clude, What are the most effective ways to share the good news of the Messiah with both Israel and the nations? What has been the effect of Messianic Jewish thought on Christian thinking? What has been the effect of Christianity on the development of Messianic Jewish thought?

MESSIANIC JUDAISM

A first reasonable question, however, might be, *What is Messianic Jewish thought?* That might best be answered by beginning with yet another question: *What exactly is meant by Messianic Judaism?*

Messianic Judaism is the religion of Jewish people who believe in Jesus as the promised Messiah.[2] It is both a Jewish form of Christianity and a Christian form of Judaism, challenging the boundaries and beliefs of both. *Messianic Jewish movement*[3] refers to the movement of Jewish people who have come to believe in Jesus (Yeshua).[4] Messianic Jews construct a new social and religious identity that they express communally in

---

to an organization of Jewish missionaries to their people. At the same time, the Messianic Jewish Alliance of America encouraged the establishment of Messianic congregations and synagogues. In Israel a new generation of native-born Israelis (sabras) were finding the Messiah, and starting Hebrew-speaking congregations. By the end of the twentieth century an international network of Messianic groups had been established, with denominational, theological, and cultural distinctives, but united in belief in Yeshua.

2. Other expressions of Jewish Messianism are not part of the present study. Eugene Fisher, "Divided Peoples of the Covenant" review of *After the Evil: Christianity and Judaism in the Shadow of the Holocaust*, by Richard Harries, *The Tablet*, August 23, 2003 (at http://www.thetablet.co.uk/review/144): "All branches of rabbinic Judaism, of course, are 'messianic,' so one wonders at the usage of the term in this title. Likewise, why the insistence on claiming to be a form of 'Judaism'? Does being ethnically Jewish give these Jewish Christians (or Christian Jews), the right, once they have accepted Christ as their saviour, to redefine for other Jews what forms of 'Judaism' are valid? Somehow the name, for me, breaches both common sense and common courtesy." Also Michael Wyschogrod, *The Body of Faith*, 2nd ed. (Northvale, NJ: Jason Aronson, 1996), 254–55: "Messianic Judaism is Judaism that takes seriously the belief that Jewish history, in spite of everything that has happened, is prelude to an extraordinary act of God by which history will come to its climax." Cf. Aviezer Ravitzky, *Messianism, Zionism and Jewish Religious Radicalism* (Chicago: University of Chicago Press, 1996) for discussion of Messianic expectation in religious Zionism.

3. Frequently shortened to "Messianic movement."

4. Yeshua, alternatively *Y'shua*, is the preferred way of referring to Jesus, and will be used interchangeably with *Jesus* throughout. See Moishe Rosen, *Y'shua: The Jewish Way to Say Jesus* (Chicago: Moody Press, 1995).

Messianic congregations and synagogues, and in their individual beliefs and practices.

Some 150,000 Jewish believers in Jesus practice worldwide, according to conservative estimates.[5] More than 100,000 are in the United States, approximately 5,000 in Israel, the remainder being found throughout the approximately 13.2 million worldwide Jewish population.[6] More than 200 Messianic groups practice in the United States and more than 80 in Israel and many other countries. While not uniform in their beliefs and expression, the majority of Messianic groups adhere to orthodox Christian doctrines on the uniqueness and deity of Christ, the Trinity, and the authority of Scripture. They express these doctrines, however, in a Jewish cultural and religious context while affirming the continuing election of Israel (the Jewish people), with whom they identify.

To varying degrees Messianic Jews observe the Sabbath, keep the kosher food laws, circumcise their sons, and celebrate the Jewish festivals. While many Messianic Jews are influenced by the charismatic movement, an increasing number are opting for more formal styles of worship using the resources of the Jewish prayer book, and integrating standard liturgical features such as the wearing of prayer shawls (*tallit*) and the use of Torah scrolls.

---

5. Tuvya Zaretsky, ed., *Jewish Evangelism: A Call to the Church*, Lausanne Occasional Paper No. 60 (Thailand: Lausanne Committee for World Evangelisation, 2005), 5–11; and Kai Kjær-Hansen and Bodil F. Skjøtt, *Facts and Myths About the Messianic Congregations in Israel*, Jerusalem: United Christian Council in Israel/Caspari Centre for Biblical and Jewish Studies, *Mishkan* 30–31 (1999): 71.

6. Sergio DellaPergola, *World Jewish Population 2000*, vol. 100 (New York: Division of Jewish Demography and Statistics, American Jewish Year Book). "We define as the core Jewish population all those who, when asked, identify themselves as Jews; or, if the respondent is a different person in the same household, are identified by him/her as Jews. This is an intentionally comprehensive and pragmatic approach. Such definition of a person as a Jew, reflecting subjective feelings, broadly overlaps but does not necessarily coincide with Halakhah (rabbinic law) or other normatively binding definitions. It does not depend on any measure of that person's Jewish commitment or behaviour—in terms of religiosity, beliefs, knowledge, communal affiliation, or otherwise. The core Jewish population includes all those who converted to Judaism by any procedure, or joined the Jewish group informally, and declare themselves to be Jewish. It excludes those of Jewish descent who formally adopted another religion, as well as other individuals who did not convert out but currently refuse to acknowledge their Jewish identification." While Della Pergola's definition excludes some Messianic Jews, who are considered to have "formally adopted another religion," this estimate of the world Jewish population is more reliable than others.

Messianic groups look to the practice of Jesus and the early church of the Book of Acts as their model and example. They celebrate Passover, pointing to Yeshua's coming as the Passover Lamb, and practice baptism, linking it to the Jewish *mikveh* (ritual bath). They worship with their own liturgies, based on the synagogue service, reading from the Torah and the New Testament.

The hermeneutic of Scripture recognized by Messianic groups repudiates the tradition of Christian anti-Judaism that "the Jews killed Christ."[7] It repudiates as well the metanarrative of supersessionism, which claims that the church replaces Israel as the "new Israel."[8] Messianic Jews thus argue for continued Torah observance that witnesses to the presence of Jewish members within the church, and for the presence of a believing remnant in the midst of Israel.

As might be expected, the Messianic Jewish movement has experienced opposition from the Jewish community, and misunderstanding in some Christian quarters. It is nonetheless widely recognized as an important expression of contextualized theology, being, in fact, a case study in ethnotheology.[9] While Jews as a whole are far from being a homogenous unit, the solidarity recognized among Jewish believers in Jesus does promote the need for an ethnic church that remains part of the universal body of Christ, while at the same time remains connected to the majority of the Jewish people who do not yet believe in Jesus.

WHAT IS MESSIANIC JEWISH THOUGHT (MJT)?

Messianic Jewish thought cannot be articulated apart from Messianic Jewish theology. That theology has developed in the light of its Protestant evangelical background and its engagement with Jewish concerns. So while the doctrinal statements of Messianic Jewish organizations are uniformly orthodox, they are more closely linked to Jewish concepts and readings of Scripture[10] and are often expressed in Jewish, rather than Hellenistic, thought forms.

---

7. Rosemary Ruether, *Faith and Fratricide* (New York: Search Press, 1974).
8. R. Kendall Soulen, *The God of Israel and Christian Theology* (Minneapolis: Fortress, 1996).
9. Harvie Conn, "Ethnotheologies," in *Evangelical Dictionary of World Missions*, ed. A. Scott Moreau (Grand Rapids: Baker, 2000), 328–30.
10. Most Messianic Jews are premilliennial in their eschatology, seeing God's purposes for Israel being played out with various degrees of linkage to the present political

Messianic Jewish theology is both the process and product of theological reflection that articulates and explains the beliefs and practices found within the Messianic movement.[11] It addresses both its own adherents and the Jewish, Christian, and wider communities to which it relates, presenting itself as both an authentic form of Jewish discourse and as an expression of faith in Jesus as Messiah.

The key concerns of Messianic Judaism are the nature and functions of the Messiah, the role of the Torah, and the place of Israel in the purposes of God. Its manifesting and applying of theological activity is evident in the fashioning of Messianic Jewish identity, self-definition, and expression in lifecycle and liturgy. Messianic Jewish theology is thus theoretical and theological reflection that arises from the faith and practice of Messianic Judaism. It is a theology of Jewish identity linked to belief in Jesus as Messiah.

As such, it coheres around the messiahship of Jesus and the Jewishness of following him. It resonates with, and relates to, a variety of points of contact with forms of Judaism and Christianity, and with various Jewish and Christian identities. It thus seeks to articulate itself intelligibly and intelligently within Jewish and Christian contexts.

What, then, does MJT say in response to its Christian and Jewish audiences? How do both traditions affect it, and how does it respond? Answering may best be accomplished by considering three key topics—God, Jesus, and Torah. First, though, are some brief observations on

---

events in the Middle East. Many advocate Aliyah (immigration to Israel) for Messianic Jews, although the majority of Messianic Jews live in the Diaspora. A growing number are concerned for Reconciliation ministry with their Arab Christian neighbors. See Richard Harvey, "Eschatology in Messianic Jewish Thought," in *Mapping Messianic Jewish Theology: A Constructive Approach* (Carlisle: Paternoster, 2009).

11. Mark Kinzer defines Messianic Jewish theology as disciplined reflection about God's character, will, and works, and about God's relationship to Israel, the nations, and all creation, in the light of God's irrevocable election of Israel to be a kingdom of priests and a holy nation, and God's creative, revelatory, and redemptive work in Messiah Yeshua. Messianic Jewish theology is rooted in divine revelation (Torah), pursued in the context of Jewish communal life and tradition and in respectful conversation with the entire Christian theological tradition, and informed by prayer, by experience of the world, and by all available sources of human knowledge and understanding. In "The Shape of Messianic Jewish Theology [Session 1]: What Is Messianic Jewish Theology?" (Paper presented at Messianic Jewish Theological Institute, Fuller Theological Seminary, 2005).

the theological method that MJT follows in contrast with, and challenge to, much Christian thought.

Messianic Jewish thought is holistic, not dualistic. Much of Western Christian theology has been influenced by Aristotelian dualism, Enlightenment rationalism, and contemporary materialism. Jewish or Hebraic thought does not dichotomize the soul from the body, the spiritual from the physical and the material, or the individual from the community. It keeps all in relationship, as aspects of a whole, rather than parts that can be divided up. Greek thought, often described as Hellenism, separated the body from the soul, the idea from the manifestation. Although Judaism was greatly influenced by Hellenism, and the greatest medieval Jewish philosopher, Moses Maimonides (1135–1204), combined a biblical worldview with Aristotelian thought, the general trend of Jewish teaching is to put forward a holistic view of life. Messianic Jewish thought does not separate the sacred from the secular, and the holy from the normal.

Like Jewish thought generally, Messianic thought is not systematic in the sense that it is bound to abstract philosophical concepts that result in tight philosophical systems. This can be very frustrating for those who like their theology, like their thinking, neatly tied up. This exploratory thinking does not mean, however, that Jewish people do not engage in philosophy or theology. Far from it! But Jewish thought is always practically oriented and not always clear what the theoretical base is for much practical discussion.

Nowhere is this more true than in the main corpus of Jewish teaching, the Talmud. This massive corpus of discussions on everything—from the detection of mold in the walls of a house to how to say prayers correctly—is unsystematic, repetitive, and difficult to follow. Studying the Talmud (an orthodox Jew studies one page a day and takes seven years to complete the cycle) is like your setting sail on an ocean. You are carried along by its discussions, but you never arrive at your destination. It is the journey itself that teaches, and the composite of hundreds of years of tradition as well as the discussion of hundreds of rabbis on a multiplicity of topics adds up to a comprehensive, if not systematic, presentation on God, humanity, and the world.

Messianic Jewish thought is biblical. It sees the Scriptures as

God's revelation in written form, and as having final authority in all matters of faith and conduct. But Messianic Jews do not limit their hermeneutical procedures to a historic-critical approach, which dissects Scripture on the operating table of the human sciences without allowing the theological vitality of the text to challenge the reader with its own authority as God's living Word for us today. Messianic Jews bring a theological reading to Scripture, which is both canonical (the whole Bible, not just the New Testament), Christological (seeing Yeshua [Jesus] as the Messiah and fulfilment of promise), and community-based (received and interpreted in both the Jewish, and the Christian and Messianic Jewish communities). Their hermeneutic often employs *midrashic*[12] methods of exegesis and interpretation, using the interpretive grid of the first Jewish believers in Jesus. Those first believers read the Torah (the Law of Moses) in the light of the prophetic traditions, and the fulfilment of the promise of the Hebrew Bible (the Tanach) in the light of the coming of the Messiah. Messianic Jews also read the whole Bible as the story of Israel, the people of God, with the inclusion of the nations in the promises God makes to Israel through belief in the Messiah. This "enlargement theology" does not exclude the Jewish people today from the promises of God to Israel, but sees the promises as fulfilled by faith in Yeshua as Messiah.

Messianic Jewish interpretation of the Scriptures sees Israel not just as a concept, but a living, present reality of the covenant people of God. In order to understand the ministry and message of Jesus, we have to understand him in the context of his first-century Palestinian Jewish background, and in the context of the salvation history of Israel from the time of the exodus from Egypt. Reading the life and teaching of Jesus in the context of his Jewishness is a challenge, and many critical scholars have reconstructed a Jesus who is against the Judaism of his day, or a Jesus who is not God and Messiah but just a special rabbi, prophet, or miracle worker. Messianic Jews see Yeshua as fully Jewish, fully human, and fully divine.

---

12. Midrash (interpretation) is the pre- and post-critical exegesis and interpretation of Scripture, which looks primarily at the "plain meaning" of the text (*p'shat*), but also at the allusive (*remez*), interpretive (*derash*), and mystical/allegorical (*sod*) meanings of a text. The rabbinic tradition says there are "a hundred ways" of interpreting each biblical verse!

Messianic Jewish thought reacts against supersessionism and anti-Judaism. The teaching that God has replaced the Israel of the Old Testament by the church of the New Testament as the people of God oversimplifies the complex relationship between Israel and the nations in the body of Christ, and was often used for polemical purposes in the early church's struggle to define itself in the Roman empire in contradistinction to the Jewish people.[13]

Finally, Messianic Jewish thought is both principle-driven and pragmatic. There is nothing as practical as a good theory, and Messianic Jews—with their three thousand years of survival as Jews, and two thousand years of survival as the faithful remnant within the house of Israel, a minority within a minority—need a theology that is based on sound biblical, missiological, and theological principles, that is culturally relevant and sensitive, and is practically oriented. Messianic Jews need practical and direct applications or our theology is too abstract. We require sound principles or our methods are too situational. Quite a challenge!

GOD

Turning now to the doctrines of God, Jesus, and Torah in Judaism, Christianity, and Messianic Judaism, we begin with God, because in both Judaism and Christianity the doctrine of God is central. The *Shema* (Deut. 6:4) declares the existence, identity, unity, and authority of God, as do the first five articles of Maimonides' 13 Articles of Faith.[14] The Jewish understanding of God is seldom presented as systematic theology, but is addressed philosophically.[15] Christian theology pursues similar investigative pathways, with the doctrine of the Trinity lying at its heart.

Creedal Statements

Where Messianic Jews have discussed God, the emphasis has been on the Trinity and the incarnation, while other aspects of the subject

---

13. See Daniel Boyarin, *Border Lines: The Partition of Judaeo-Christianity* (Philadelphia: University of Pennsylvania Press, 2004); and Martin Goodman, Adam H. Becker, and Peter Schafer, eds., *The Ways That Never Parted: Jews and Christians in Late Antiquity and the Early Middle Ages* (Minneapolis: Fortress, 2007).
14. Louis Jacobs, *Principles of the Jewish Faith: An Analytical Study* (New York: Basic Books, 1964), 14.
15. Louis Jacobs, *God in Contemporary Jewish Religious Thought*, ed. Arthur A. Cohen and Paul Mendes-Flohr (New York: Macmillan/Free Press, 1988), 290.

have followed the lines of Protestant dogma.[16] The creeds and articles of faith produced by Messianic Jewish organizations are, from a Christian perspective, uniformly orthodox. The first modern Messianic Jewish creed, composed by Joseph Rabinowitz for the Israelites of the New Covenant, affirms traditional aspects of God's nature.

> There is but one true and living God, not corporeal, without divisions, cannot be apprehended by the bodily senses, of great goodness, power and wisdom beyond comprehension, who creates, forms, makes and upholds everything by His Word and by His Holy Spirit. All things are from Him, all things in Him, and all things to Him.[17]

Rabinowitz adopted the Hebrew translation of the Anglican Book of Common Prayer, omitting the phrase "three persons of one substance in the godhead."[18] While Gentiles, who are accustomed to polytheism, need instruction that the three persons in the Holy Scriptures are one, Jews find it very difficult to use the number three, although they know from Scripture that the one God is three persons or personalities.

> The believing Gentiles call the three persons in the Godhead: "Father, Son and Holy Ghost"; we name them: "One God, and His Word, and His Holy Spirit," which is the same. Why should the

---

16. While half of Louis Jacobs's A Jewish Theology (Springfield, NJ: Behrman House, 1973) is given to discussing God (pp. 21–151) and Alister McGrath's Christian Theology: An Introduction (Malden, MA: Blackwell, 1993) devotes some eighty pages (pp. 265–344), Messianic Jews give little space in their published works to this fundamental topic. David Stern devotes just two pages to the nature of God. Daniel Juster does not even have a section on God in his Jewish Roots: A Foundation of Biblical Theology for Messianic Judaism (Rockville, MD: Davar Publishing, 1986) although he devotes ten pages to the question "Is the Messiah Divine?" The subjects of God, the Trinity, or the nature of Messiah do not appear in Voices of Messianic Judaism, ed. Dan Cohn-Sherbok (Baltimore: Messianic Jewish Publishers, 2001), a collection of essays by Messianic Jewish thinkers "confronting critical issues facing a maturing movement." Similarly Dan Cohn-Sherbok, The Jewish Faith (London, SPCK: 1993), 29–71; and Kaufman Kohler, Jewish Theology: Systematically and Historically Considered (New York: Macmillan, 1918), 29–205.
17. Kai Kjær-Hansen, Joseph Rabinowitz and the Messianic Movement (Edinburgh: Handsel Press, 1995), 103. Cf. Dan Cohn-Sherbok, Messianic Judaism (New York: Cassell, 2000), 21.
18. Kjær-Hansen, Joseph Rabinowitz, 98.

Christian Church burden Israel with doctrines, which were taught them from false conceptions of the Godhead?[19]

Messianic Jewish organizations make similar statements. The Messianic Jewish Alliance of America (MJAA) basis of belief affirms,

> GOD—We believe that the Shema, "Hear, O Israel: the LORD our God, the LORD is one" (Deut. 6:4), teaches that God is Echad, as so declared: a united one, a composite unity, eternally existent in plural oneness.[20]

The Union of Messianic Jewish Congregations (UMJC) similarly asserts, "We believe that there is one G-d, eternally existent in three persons."[21]

Detailed Presentations

Five extended considerations on the doctrine of God reflect various approaches, methods, and concerns.[22] Baruch Maoz's presentation begins with God's existence, essence, and attributes.[23] The fatherhood of God, the divine and human natures of the Son, and the person of the Holy Spirit follow. Maoz refutes "important but wrong views,"[24] including heretical Christologies.[25] Acknowledging his sources, Maoz invites readers to adopt a Reformation approach to Scripture, as found in Calvin, the Puritans, and contemporary Reformed dogma. The Westminster Confession is also included.[26] Apart from translation

---

19. Ibid., 107–8.
20. MJAA, "MJAA Doctrinal Basis, Article 2," http://mjaa.org/StatementofFaith. html (accessed August 8, 2005).
21. UMJC, "UMJC Doctrinal Statement, Article 2," http://www.umjc.org/main/ documents/DoctrinalBasis.pdf (accessed August 8, 2005). The spelling "G-d" is retained in Messianic Jewish materials where it occurs. It expresses concern that even in translation the name of God might not be defaced.
22. Many others were approached, but have not produced material on the topic.
23. Baruch Maoz, *Lessons on the Doctrine of God: A Tutorial on the Biblical Doctrine of God* (Rishon Le Tzion, Israel: Grace and Truth Congregation, 1997).
24. For example, atheism, agnosticism, polytheism, dualism, and pantheism.
25. Docetism, ebionism, modalistic monarchianism, Arianism, Nestorianism, Eutychianism, and Appollinarianism.
26. "There is only one living and true God. He is infinite in his substance and perfection, a most pure spirit, invisible, without body, parts or passions, unchangeable,

of concepts into Hebrew, however, Maoz offers little engagement with Jewish sources.

Arnold Fruchtenbaum expounds God as Father of the Son, of creation, of heavenly beings, Israel, and all believers.[27] He considers the love and revelation of God through the Son and the Scriptures.[28] The Trinity is explained in opposition to its heresies.[29] Fruchtenbaum, however, does not interact with Jewish philosophical tradition or Christian theological debate. Rather, his method is biblical exposition with little use of secondary sources.

David Stern finds the traditional Christian and Jewish understandings of God are sufficient, up to a point, at which they then divide.

> In theology proper, the study of the nature of God, one can begin with the elements common to Jewish and Christian understanding or "Judeo-Christian tradition—for example, the oneness, eternality, omnipotence, and holiness of God. But soon one must deal with the two chief issues which divide, the divinity of the Messiah and the inner nature of God.[30]

For Stern the historical developments of Judaism and Christianity bring non-Messianic Judaism to the point of "utterly denying the possibility of the incarnation and insisting on the absolute unity of God in a way that negates most Christian assertions about the trinity."[31] Yet Stern insists that there are "hints within Judaism" that the opposition "is not

---

immense, eternal, incomprehensible, almighty, most wise, most holy, most free, most absolute. He causes everything to work according to the determination of his unchangeable and most righteous will for his own glory. He and his will are most loving, gracious, merciful, long-suffering, abundant in goodness and truth. He forgives evil, rebellion and sin; the rewarder of those that diligently look for him, as well as most just and terrible in his judgments. He hates all sin and will by no means pronounce the guilty innocent." Maoz, *Lessons on the Doctrine of God*, 73.

27. Arnold G. Fruchtenbaum, *God the Father* (Tustin, CA: Ariel Ministries, 1985).
28. Ibid.; idem, *The Bible and Divine Revelation* (Tustin, CA: Ariel Ministries, 1983); idem, *The Inspiration of the Scriptures* (Tustin, CA: Ariel Ministries, 1983).
29. Arnold G. Fruchtenbaum, *The Trinity* (Tustin, CA: Ariel Ministries, 1985). The heresies are Arianism, Sabellianism, Socinianism, Unitarianism, and tritheism
30. David Stern, *Messianic Jewish Manifesto* (Jerusalem: Jewish New Testament Publications, 1988), 93.
31. Ibid.

so monolithic." While Stern does not give a systematic presentation of the doctrine of God, his theological reflections are found in comments on several biblical passages in his *Jewish New Testament Commentary*.[32]

Louis Goldberg's contribution, "Specific Observations on the Doctrine of God," engages with the classical sources of Jewish and Christian debate.[33] He first formulates and explains propositions about God from the biblical material. He then addresses problems related to those propositions, as well as emphasizes the "practical value" of them for the believer. The material is well-suited for discipleship and catechesis.

Mark Kinzer's unpublished lectures on "God and the Messiah" incorporate classical and contemporary Jewish and Christian material, demonstrating a reflective approach to the task of MJT in addition to the articulation of the nature of God.[34] Kinzer's published work does not address the doctrine of God directly, but his recent *Postmissionary Messianic Judaism* has a section on the nature of revelation.[35] In the light of this material, Messianic Jewish understandings of God are presented, with due consideration of the method, content, and resources used, and with awareness of the creativity and originality of the discussion.

The above five studies are of interest to readers wishing to further investigate the doctrine of God from diverse Messianic Jewish viewpoints. What, though, do these Messianic Jewish understandings of God have to say to the church? They challenge the direct relevancy of the Aristotelian and Platonic formulations of the creeds. Jewish thought is functional, not ontological. God is known through his redemptive acts in history, not through Aquinas's five proofs for his existence. Yes, God exists, as the Holy One of Israel, the Ruler of

---

32. David Stern, *Jewish New Testament Commentary* (Jerusalem: Jewish New Testament Publications, 1992), *passim*.

33. Louis Goldberg, *A Messianic Jewish Theology* (manuscript, Jews for Jesus Research Library, 2003). At the time of his death in 2003 he had assembled some 47,000 words of material for a Messianic Jewish theology, due to be edited and published posthumously by Rich Robinson of Jews for Jesus.

34. Mark Kinzer, "God and the Messiah: Course Outline, MJ518" (Messianic Jewish Theological Institute, Fuller School of Theology, 2004).

35. Mark Kinzer, "Theology and History: Divine Action in Human History," *Postmissionary Messianic Judaism: Redefining Christian Engagement with the Jewish People* (Grand Rapids: Baker Academic/Brazos, 2005), 38–46.

all nations, and the Savior of humanity. A Messianic Jewish under-standing of God sets his being in the light of his creation, redemption, and consummation of all things.

JESUS

Jacob Jocz, a Hebrew Christian of the last century, wrote,

> At the centre of the controversy between Church and Synagogue stands the Christological question. This is not a question whether Jesus is the Messiah, but whether the Christian understanding of the Messiah is admissible in view of the Jewish concept of God. Here lies the dividing line between Judaism and Church. On this point neither can afford to compromise.[36]

Most Christians, however, when they understand the doctrine of the Trinity, do not explain it in Jewish terms. Lev Gillet wrote, "What is needed is a 'translation of meanings.' A re-thinking of Christology in Jewish terms, i.e. not only in Hebrew words, but in Hebrew catego-ries of thought."[37]

Today there is great discussion about the divinity of Jesus in the Messianic movement. In 2003, Gershon Nerel wrote,

> Like in ancient times, also the modern movement of Jewish Yeshua-believers is shaping its corporate identity through theological de-bates and doctrinal definitions. Particularly during the last two years we are observing unceasing discussions concerning the topic of Yeshua's divinity.[38]

The Need for a Messianic Jewish Christology

Messianic Jews stand astride Jocz's "dividing line," refusing the par-tition of Judaism and Christianity into mutually exclusive theological

---

36. Jacob Jocz, "The Invisibility of God and the Incarnation," in *The Messiahship of Jesus*, ed. Arthur Kac, rev. ed. (Grand Rapids, Baker: 1986), 189. Reprinted from *Canadian Journal of Theology* 4, no. 3 (1958).
37. Lev Gillet, *Communion in the Messiah: Studies in the Relationship Between Judaism and Christianity* (London: Lutterworth Press, 1942), 73.
38. Gershon Nerel, "Eusebius, *Ecclesiastical History* and the Modern Yeshua Move-ment: Some Comparisons," *Mishkan* 39 (2003): 80.

systems.[39] Nowhere is this more apparent than in their belief in Jesus, which appears blasphemous to Judaism and heretical to Christianity, either clashing with the fundamental tenets of Jewish monotheism or compromising the uniqueness of Christ. The nature of Yeshua as Messiah and Son of God has always been a matter of controversy between Jews and Christians. It is bound to be a focal point for MJT.

The divine nature of Yeshua was again brought to prominence in the Messianic movement by a November 2002 articles in *Israel Today*.[40] In that issue, twelve Messianic Jews were asked their views on the divinity of the Messiah, and some of the answers given "were made to seem to state that Yeshua is not God."[41] Tzvi Sadan notes the uncertainty that is found in the Messianic movement on the issue.[42] Joseph Shulam of *Netivyah* in Jerusalem is also concerned at the level of heat generated by the controversy on the divinity of Christ.[43] As is Elazar Brandt:

> Those who question the deity of Yeshua but serve him faithfully ought not to be labelled as heretics or unsaved for their ideas alone; likewise, Trinitarians ought not be labelled idolaters by non-Trinitarians if their intent is to worship and serve one G-d. If we cannot grant each other some room for fresh thought, we will never advance beyond Nicæa in our concept of G-d.[44]

39. Cf. Daniel Boyarin, *Boundary Lines: The Partition of Judaeo-Christianity* (Philadelphia: University of Pennsylvania Press, 2004).
40. A. Schneider, ed., "Messianic Jews Debate the Deity of Jesus," *Israel Today* 22 (November 2001): 21.
41. David H. Stern, "Israel's Messianic Jews and the Deity of Yeshua: An Update," *Israel Today* 23 (July 2002): 23, http://mayimhayim.org/Academic%20-Stuff/David%20-Stern/Article.htm (accessed May 24, 2007).
42. Tzvi Sadan, e-mail message to author, June 5, 2003. "As far as the Trinity is concerned, the truth is that there are as many opinions as there are people. I have talked to many and sometimes it was scary to find out what some of them believe in."
43. Joseph Shulam, e-mail message to author, March 3, 2003: "The question . . . is one of the hottest in all of Christianity and especially among the brothers and sisters in Israel. There have been inquisitory actions taken here by some brothers as if they were Savonarola or Torquemada during the darkest periods of Christian history, but with God's help we shall overcome this wave of tyrannical leadership with the love of the Lord and the Grace of the Cross."
44. Elazar Brandt, e-mail message to author, March 10, 2003.

David Stern recognizes the need for Messianic Jews to develop their Christology:

> I challenge Messianic Jews, especially those of us who feel in our gut the need for staying Jewish, to get enough training in theology to deal seriously with the complex data underlying the Church's affirmation of Yeshua's deity—which can even be supported by material in the Talmud and other classical Jewish writings.[45]

Christology in Doctrinal Statements

The creeds and doctrinal statements produced by the Messianic movement reflect an orthodox Christian understanding of Jesus and the Godhead. All are uniformly Trinitarian, but expressed with varying degrees of Jewish content.[46] The MJAA *Basis of Belief*, for example, affirms the triune nature of God and the deity of the Messiah.[47]

> GOD—We believe that the *Shema*, "Hear, O Israel: the LORD our God, the LORD is one" (Deut. 6:4), teaches that God is *Echad*, as so declared: a united one, a composite unity, eternally existent in plural oneness (Gen. 1:1 [*Elohim*: God]); Gen. 1:26 "Let us make man in our image"; Gen. 2:24 Adam & Eve were created to be as one flesh (*basar echad*)], that He is a personal God who created us (Gen. 1 & 2), and that He exists forever in three persons: Father, Son, and Holy Spirit, as mentioned in Romans 8:14–17 (Father, Spirit, and Messiah-Son) and Matt. 28:18–20 (immersing in the name of the Father, Son, and Holy Spirit).

---

45. Stern, "Israel's Messianic Jews," 2.
46. Gershon Nerel, "Creeds among Jewish Believers in Yeshua," *Mishkan* 34 (2001): 61–79. Nerel examined the creeds of the Hebrew Christian Alliance of America (HCAA) (1915); the International Hebrew Christian Alliance (IHCA) (1925); the IHCA Hebrew Christian Church Commission (1932); Abram Poljak's "Jewish Christian Union" (1939); and the Warsaw Hebrew Christian Community, published by Jacob Jocz (1939).
47. Michael Schiffman, "Messianic Jews and the Tri-Unity of God," in *The Enduring Paradox: Exploratory Essays in Messianic Judaism*, ed. John Fischer (Baltimore: Lederer, 2000), 93–104. "Belief in the triune nature of God is not merely held by a group within the Messianic community, but is believed by every Messianic organisation of the community: the Union of Messianic Jewish Congregations, the Fellowship of Messianic Congregations and the Messianic Alliance of America."

A. GOD THE FATHER (*Abba*)—John 6:27b; 1 Cor. 1:3; Gal. 1:1; Rev. 3:5, 21; Jer. 3:4, 19; 31:9; Mal. 1:6; Matt. 6:9, 32; Luke 10:21–22; John 1:14; 4:23; 5:17–26; 6:28–46; Rom. 8:14–15.

B. GOD THE SON (*HaBen*)
1. God does have a Son (Ps. 2; Prov. 30:4–6 [cf. Heb. 1]; Luke 12:35–37; John 1:29–34, 49; 3:14–18).
2. The Son, called *Yeshua* (Jesus), meaning salvation, came to this world born of a virgin (Isa. 7:14 [cf. Luke 1:30–35]).
3. The Son is God (deity), and is worshipped as God, having existed eternally (Ps. 110:1 [cf. Heb. 1:13]; Isa. 9:6–7; Matt. 28:18–20; Phil. 2:5–11; Col. 1:15–19; Rev. 3:21 [Heb. 1—worshipped by angels]; Rev. 4:8, 5:5–14).
4. This One is the promised *Mashiach* (Messiah) of Israel (Isa. 9:6–7; 11:1; Dan. 9 [esp. verses 20–26]; Isa. 53; John 1:17, 40–41, 45, 49; Mark 8:29).
5. He is the root and offspring of David, the bright and morning star (Num. 24:17; Rev. 22:16).
6. He is our Passover, the Lamb of God (1 Cor. 5:7; Rev. 5; John 1:29).[48]

The Development of Christology

Christological methods and resources in the Messianic movement are derived from previous approaches. Amos Funkenstein has identified five phases in the history of Jewish-Christian encounter and the presentation of the Messiahship and divinity of Yeshua.[49] The first phase was the early debate on the interpretation of the Hebrew Scriptures, the *Tanach*. The use of *Testimonia*, collections of texts from the Hebrew Scriptures confirming the messiahship of Jesus, may be seen in some of sermonic material in the New Testament writings, and the *Dialogue of Justin Martyr with the Jew Trypho* is an example of this type of apologetic. A second phase developed with the use of Jewish sermonic material, the *Aggadah*, in

---

48. MJAA, "MJAA Doctrinal Statement," http://www.mjaa.org/statementoffaith .html (accessed March 3, 2003).
49. See Amos Funkenstein, "Basic Types of Christian Anti-Jewish Polemic in the Middle Ages," *Viator* 2 (1971): 373–82.

the context of mediaeval debate, as exemplified by Raimundus Martini's manual for Christian Preachers, the *Pugio Fidei*.[50] The debate between Paulus Christiani and Nachmanides in 1264 in Spain illustrates this approach. The third phase of development was the use of the Jewish mystical tradition, the *Kabbalah*, to prove the messiahship and divinity of Jesus.

The fourth phase combined modern critical methods of study of Scripture with changing views of the historical Jesus. In some cases this led to a liberal and rationalist perspective on Jesus, setting him within the Jewish context of his day, but not recognizing his messiahship or divinity.[51] The Jewish reclamation of Jesus and the loss of confidence in the uniqueness of Christ both emerged in the light of this development of nineteenth- and twentieth-century critical studies. At the same time arose the development of the modern missionary movement, and Hebrew-Christian apologetics were developed and propagated by writers such as Frey, Delitzsch, Hengstenberg, and Reichardt.[52]

A fifth postmissionary phase can be detected in recent presentations of Messianic Jews employing post liberal and postcritical readings of the biblical and rabbinic materials.[53]

Emerging Christologies

Previous studies have emphasized the uniformity of the orthodox (Christian) Christologies within Messianic Judaism.[54] The presence

---

50. Cf. Richard Harvey, "Raymundus Martini and the Pugio Fidei: A Survey of the Life and Works of a Medieval Controversialist," MA diss., University College, London, 1991.

51. Cf. Donald A. Hagner, *The Jewish Reclamation of Jesus* (Grand Rapids: Zondervan, 1984).

52. Cf. J. C. Frey, *The Divinity of the Messiah* (Jerusalem: Keren Ahavah Meshichit, 2002).

53. The term *postmissionary* is employed by Mark Kinzer, but typifies a less adversarial and apologetic approach to Jewish tradition. Cf. Mark Kinzer, *Postmissionary Messianic Judaism: Redefining Christian Engagement with the Jewish People* (Grand Rapids: Baker Academic/Brazos, 2005). This approach is eclectic, and as yet undefined, but may allow for a rediscovery of Jesus as both Jewish Messiah and incarnate deity. It is concerned with the construction of Jewish identity and "Messianic Jewish social space" as much as with the nature and being of the Messiah. The materials of the Jewish tradition, Torah, Talmud, and Kabbalah are all resources from which a contemporary Jewish expression can be formulated, but these are filtered through the lens of modern and postmodern Jewish thought, which deconstructs, challenges, and re-addresses age-old problems of Jewish existence.

54. For example, David A. Rausch, *Messianic Judaism: Its History, Theology, and Polity* (Lewiston, NY: Edwin Mellen, 1982), 125–26.

of heterodox views has caused some embarrassment within the move-ment.[55] It is clear that within Messianic Judaism considerable variety can be found on the nature of the Messiah. Five emerging Christologies can be identified, which represent the spectrum of thought within the movement. The first reflects Protestant Reformed and evangelical tra-dition. The second recontextualizes the Nicæan formulation without losing its substance. The third articulates the deity of Christ in terms of the Kabbalah and the Jewish mystical tradition. The fourth attempts a new Christological method in its handling of the traditional mate-rials. The fifth arises from Unitarian thought that denies the deity of Jesus and echoes adoptionist Christology.[56]

All these approaches accept that Yeshua (Jesus) is the Messiah, and are happy to base this on his fulfillment of prophecy in the Hebrew Scriptures. They acknowledge his Jewishness, atoning work, and resur-rection. The question is rather what kind of Messiah he is, and how to express this in response to both Jewish tradition and Christian teaching. The focus of the current debate is the relationship of Yeshua's messi-ahship to the nature of God.[57] The redefinition of the Christology of the Nicene and Chalcedonian creeds challenges Messianic Jews to link Jewish and Hellenistic ways of thinking about the uniqueness of Christ.

Transcending Hebrew and Greek Categories

Daniel Juster recognizes that

> to raise the question of Yeshua's divinity is to open one of the greatest debates between Jews and Christians. This question leads to the whole

---

55. John Fischer, "Yeshua—The Deity Debate," Mishkan 39 (2003): 27. The theme of the issue is "the Divinity of the Messiah," with seven significant articles on the topic.

56. Developments in Christology outside the Messianic movement are not part of the present study except where their contributions have been adopted by MJT, e.g., N. T. Wright, Larry Hurtado, Richard Bauckham, Oscar Skarsaune, and Risto San-tala. Also not included are those who have written on Christology in the context of Messianic Judaism and Jewish-Christian relations, but are not actively part of the Messianic movement such as Rosemary Ruether and John Pawlikowski. Jewish scholars such as Geza Vermes and Pinchas Lapide are also not included.

57. Other aspects of the person and work of the Messiah, such as Yeshua's self-con-sciousness, Jewish identity, revelatory presence, saving work (sin and atonement) and example for life are beyond the scope of the present study.

debate about the Trinity, since the Messiah is said to be divine as one part of the Triune God.[58]

Juster rejects the "widely held conclusion of modern scholarship" that sharply differentiates between Hebraic and Hellenistic modes of thought as functional and ontological. For him the real question is rather

> how a metaphysic that is implied by biblical teaching compares and contrasts with a Greek metaphysic. Because all human beings are created in the image of God, communication and evaluation with regard to metaphysical views is cross-culturally possible.[59]

This recognition gives the debate on Christology a more fruitful foundation. The Nicæan statement is neither "totally Greek and unacceptable" nor an absolutely "accurate metaphysical statement of biblically implied truth." The affirmations of Nicæa which are implied by the Bible, are that Yeshua is "Son of God"; "only begotten from the Father"; "begotten not made (created)" and "light from light."[60]

Juster reformulates the truths safeguarded by Nicæa in order to better communicate to the modern Jewish mind. He urges Messianic Jews to look to the original Jewish roots that influenced the Nicene Creed and from these roots speak afresh to our day. Juster defends a perspective of the plural nature of God in the Tenach, and follows this with discussion of the Angel of the Lord, the superhuman nature of the Messiah (Isa. 9:6–7) and discussion of New Testament passages

---

58. Juster, *Jewish Roots*, 181.
59. Ibid.
60. Ibid. According to Juster, other dimensions of the Nicæan formula, although biblically defensible, are unhelpful in a Jewish context because they lend themselves to connotative misunderstanding. "'God from God' and 'true God from true God' are phrases that too easily lend themselves to misconception. These statements emphasize divinity to such a degree that the humanity of the Son and His submission to the Father are eclipsed (e.g., a danger of Docetism). New Testament Christology, at least with regard to the relationship of the incarnate Messiah to the Father, in all biblical language and in all apocalyptic pictures of the Father and the Lamb in heaven, reflect[s] subordinationist overtones. 'One substance' language is difficult philosophically even if there are reasons for its use. He is in His divine nature everlastingly one in being with the Father. Perhaps other language such as 'one in essence' or 'one in His divine being' could be more helpful."

that show the divinity of Yeshua. He then gives his own understanding of Yeshua's two natures.

> He is one person or aspect of that plural manifestation of God (from the Tenach) who became a human being. He, therefore, is a man who depends on the Spirit, prays to the Father, gets weary and dies. His divine nature never dies, but he is human as well as divine. As such, prayer in the New Testament is not primarily addressed to Yeshua but to "Our Father" in the Name of Yeshua. For Yeshua is the human revelation of the Father[61] [very important].

While there is a suggestion of *patripassianism* here, Juster warns against the Christomonism that loses sight of God the Father, calling for full recognition of Yeshua's divinity while recognizing that God is more than just Yeshua. He then calls for a deeper expression of the Trinity in Jewish terms:

> Jewish ways of expression are needed, ways more consistent to the New Testament, if Jews are to penetrate Christian rhetoric to see the Truth of Yeshua's divine nature.[62]

There are several reasons why it is important to accept the "uni-plurality of God" and the divine nature of Yeshua. Only a perfect man could bring a full revelation of God, as humanity is made in the image of God. The revelation of God's love in the form of a human being is the greatest way possible to show God's love. Such revelation has unique redemptive significance, as the Messiah's suffering is the revelation of the suffering love of God himself. Because the Messiah is divine, his suffering has infinite redemptive value. So for Juster "the divinity of the Messiah is not idolatry, but reflects the fullest revelation of God."

> The scriptures thus communicate to us the impression of one great divine reality of three inseparable manifestations of God. The

---

61. Ibid., 187.
62. Ibid., 188.

relationship of love and accord blends the three into eternal one-ness beyond human comprehension. . . . The reciprocal *giving rela-tionship* of love is eternally existent within the plural unity of God.[63]

Juster responds to the argument that, in the distinction between Hellenistic and Hebraic thinking, Jerusalem and Nicæa can be so easily juxtaposed. In reality, the interaction and interdependence of Jewish and Hellenistic thought is complex and varied.

The bifurcation of Hebraic thinking and Greek thinking as respec-tively functional and metaphysical-ontological is a widely held con-clusion of modern scholarship (cf. O. Cullman, *Christ and Time*, also Bishop J. S. Spong, *The Hebrew Lord*). Yet, in my view, this abso-lute separation of functional thinking as Hebraic and metaphysical thinking as Greek can not be maintained. Functional thinking at least implies statements about the nature of being or it would lend to relativism in questions concerning the nature of reality. (This distinction has been used to bolster relativism in theology.) The real question is rather one which raises the issue of how a metaphysic that is implied by biblical teaching compares and contrasts with a Greek metaphysic. Because all human beings are created in the image of God, communication and evaluation with regard to meta-physical views is cross-culturally possible.[64]

In regard to MJT on the doctrine of God and Jesus, the UMJC position paper on the Tri-Unity of God summarizes the biblical data for the plurality of God, the basis in Jewish tradition for plurality in the divinity, then goes on to state,

It has also been pointed out that traditional Judaism has always re-jected the concept of the tri-unity of G-d, interpreting the Shema in a narrower sense as an absolute oneness. This traditional view is in no way monolithic. The biblical data is also [part of] Jewish

---

63. Ibid., 189–90.
64. Daniel Juster, "The Christological Dogma of Nicaea—Greek or Jewish?" *Mishkan* 1, no. 1 (1984): 54.

175

thought. Within Jewish thought, albeit mystical, the Zohar contains a Trinitarian concept of G-d. While the Zohar is not our authority, it does demonstrate that the Trinitarian understanding of G-d is NOT non-Jewish. Regardless of traditional views, we must not look to traditional Jewish teaching to tell us what is proper for us to believe. Our authority is the Word of G-d. Traditional rejection of the tri-unity is not based upon what we believe, but based upon their erroneous interpretation of what we believe. We in no way affirm the existence of three gods, but ONE G-d eternally existent in three persons.[65]

It concludes with the strong affirmation of the deity of Jesus and the plural unity of God:

Because the tri-unity of G-d has a central bearing upon the rest of our theology, and the scriptures do support it as a biblical doctrine, Messianic believers need to affirm the tri-unity of G-d as a central part of our faith and not relegate it to secondary importance or opinion for the sake of palatability to others.[66]

Messianic Jews need to avoid both an "arid biblicism and a shallow Trinitarianism"[67] in their search for an appropriate Christology and Trinitarian theology.[68]

---

65. UMJC, "The Tri-Unity of G-d from a Messianic Perspective," UMJC position paper, http://www.umjc.org/aboutumjc/theology/triunity.htm (accessed March 12, 2003).
66. Ibid.
67. A phrase borrowed from N. T. Wright.
68. An adoptionist Christology is also found in some parts of the Messianic movement. This is reminiscent of the Ebionites and Arius of the early church and denies the divinity of Jesus. According to Ray Pritz, an extremely small minority of congregations in Israel (I would estimate no more than 5 percent) would hold a formal doctrinal position that does not affirm the divinity of Jesus.

Uri Marcus, a member of the *Heftzibah* congregation in Israel, summarizes this position:

Myself as well as our entire congregation of Believers in *Ma'aleh Adumim*, completely reject the Trinitarian notions of plural unity, and will not acquiesce to any theology which challenges the ONE-ness of HaShem in any fashion . . . Yeshua is the Son of the living G-d, never G-d the Son, in our view.

TORAH

Many Jews and Christians consider Christianity to be a religion of grace, and Judaism to be one of law. Trude Weiss-Rosmarin summarizes a common misconception:

> The laws of the Torah are to Judaism the quintessence of permanent goodness. Christianity, on the other hand, advances its claims on the strength that the "Law" is superseded and abrogated by "Faith" in Jesus.[69]

Michael Schiffman notes the importance of the topic:

> The relationship between Messianic Jews and the law is an important issue in the Messianic movement because the law is not solely a theological issue to be debated, but part of Jewish culture, heritage and worship. At the same time, Messianic believers recognise their relationship to the law is not the same as that of traditional Jews because the center of a believer's life is not the law, but the Messiah.[70]

David Stern realizes that the question of the Law is important not just for Messianic Jews:

> The lack of a correct, clear and relatively complete Messianic Jewish or Gentile Christian theology of the Law is not only a major impedi-

---

Marcus argues against the deity of Jesus on the grounds that the Hebrew Scriptures and Jewish tradition forbid idolatry; the Christian understanding of the incarnation is idolatrous, and Trinitarian doctrine is a Hellenistic misreading of the biblical data. Trinitarians misread Scripture without taking into account their original Jewish background and frame of reference. This is given by rabbinic tradition, which provides the authoritative understanding of the nature of God, the meaning of idolatry, and the nature of the Messiah. Only with the use of this interpretive tradition can the early church's excessive reliance on an anti-Semitic Hellenistic influence be avoided. Daniel Juster responds appropriately to these arguments (see above). Cf. Richard Harvey, "Jesus the Messiah in Messianic Jewish Thought," *Mishkan* 39 (2003), 4–19.

69. Trude Weiss-Rosmarin, *Judaism and Christianity: The Differences* (New York: Jonathan David, 1943), 81.

70. Michael Schiffman, *Return from Exile: The Re-emergence of the Messianic Congregational Movement*, 2nd ed. (New York: Teshuvah Publishing, 1991), 72.

ment to Christians' understanding of their own faith, but also the greatest barrier to Jewish people's receiving the Gospel.[71]

The term *Torah* means more than just "law."[72] It includes teaching, instruction, and revelation. It refers both to the Pentateuch and Mosaic Law, the Hebrew Scriptures of the Old Testament, the Jewish religious tradition (the Mishnah, Talmud, and later Rabbinic writings), and is a general term for revelation or teaching. Thus the intended sense of *Torah* is not always clear. Jewish religious groupings, too, interpret *Torah* differently. Orthodox Jews are strict in their observance of the laws of the Pentateuch, which are further expanded, interpreted, and applied by rabbinic tradition. Conservative Jews modify this traditional observance in the light of modernity. Reform, Liberal, and Reconstructionist Jews adopt a humanist and revisionary position that looks to the Torah for moral principles and cultural norms, but these may be renegotiated, and there are few absolutes. Most Jewish people observe some aspects of the Mosaic Law as customary and traditional rather than out of the conviction that God commands them.

Within the Messianic Jewish movement, *Torah* is both a key concept and a matter of controversy. There is no agreed-upon definition within the movement, which leads to a lack of clarity in the discussion. *Torah* may mean one or several of the following in Messianic Jewish discussion: the Pentateuch (the Mosaic Law), the Hebrew Scriptures (the Old Testament), the written and oral law, Jewish tradition (including its Orthodox, Conservative, Reform, Liberal, and Reconstructionist expressions), the New Testament and the teaching of Jesus, "law" as opposed to "grace," and individual statutes and commandments.

---

71. Stern, *Messianic Jewish Manifesto*, 125.
72. Ariel Berkowitz and Devorah Berkowitz, *Torah Rediscovered: Challenging Centuries of Misinterpretation and Neglect,* 3rd ed. (Littleton, CO: First Fruits of Zion, 1998), 144. Berkowitz lays down the challenge: "We have seen how theological error and misinterpretation of the Brit Chadasha have led to an outright neglect of the Torah at best, and a stiff-necked rejection of it at worst. Let us now attempt to do what no other generation has ever done. Let us be the first generation of Jewish believers since the early days of our history to begin turning back the tear-drenched pages of our history and again to follow the covenant which the Holy One made with Moshe Rabbenu."

The term *Torah* thus functions as theological shorthand for various understandings of Jewish law, from the most flexible to the most rigorous halachic requirements. The relationships between law and grace, between Yeshua and the Torah, and between the practice of the early Jewish Christians and today, are all matters of debate.

Among Messianic groups, several rationales are given for Torah observance. It has value in witness to, and cultural identification with, the Jewish people. It sheds light on the life and teaching of Yeshua. For some it has a validity of its own, in that the Torah remains in effect as the grounds for the life of the covenant people, leading to ethical and spiritual wholeness and preserving the distinct witness of Israel to her God. Others share a deep concern that all talk of Torah observance may lead to legalism and bondage to the Law.

Below, I present a full range of opinion on Torah observance. Some in the Messianic Jewish movement would exclude certain observances as "Hebrew Christian" (Baruch Maoz and Arnold Fruchtenbaum), but failing to express all views gives a distorted picture of the breadth and diversity of opinion found within the movement. At present there is no normative view of Torah, although all seek legitimacy for their positions.

Messianic Jews believe that the Law has been fulfilled by Yeshua (Matt. 5:17) and that he is the "goal of the law" (Rom. 10:4). But just as there are different understandings of Torah in the Jewish community, so too it is among Messianic Jews. Some see the Law of Moses as obsolete. Yeshua has inaugurated the *new* covenant. The old has gone. The laws of sacrifice have been fulfilled in Christ. The civil laws were only relevant to ancient Israel. Only the universal moral law as exemplified in the Ten Commandments is still applicable. It is therefore misguided to observe aspects of the Mosaic Law that lead back to bondage in legalism. If Messianic Jews observe the Mosaic Law they are denying the grace of God and justification by faith alone. They rebuild the "middle wall of partition" (Eph. 2:14 ASV), attempting to justify themselves by works of the Law.

A second view affirms the cultural and social practices of the Mosaic Law, yet this is not for religious reasons. Over the centuries, customs that make up Jewish identity have been incorporated by tradition into Jewish life, such as the calendar, circumcision, and the food laws. These are still normative for ethnic, cultural, and national identity but have no theological merit and do not add to righteousness. Consequently, they are not prescriptive on Jewish believers in Jesus, who are free to observe them if they choose.

A third approach recognizes the continuing validity of Jewish tradition as the interpretative context for understanding the biblical Torah of the Tenach and new covenant. Yeshua, in his teaching and example, and the practice of the early church defined a new *halacha* for the new covenant community. This *halacha* is developed today following the first Messianic Jews' example in the book of Acts. They observed Jewish lifestyle and practices, adapted some, abandoned others, and applied only a few to the nations. Messianic Jews who observe Torah in this way acknowledge its value but challenge its interpretation by the main branches of Judaism. They propose a new interpretation of Torah based on the teaching and practice of Yeshua and the first disciples.

A fourth position argues that Messianic Jews should observe the Torah according to Orthodox or Conservative tradition, with only a few exceptions. Torah observance is a necessary response of gratitude and obedience in the light of God's election of Israel, which has not been abrogated, diminished, or substantially altered with the coming of Yeshua. Torah observance preserved the Jewish community through its rabbinic leaders over the centuries, and Messianic Jews should accept their normative authority and work within this. This will enable them to develop their primary identity within the Jewish community rather than the mainstream church. They should see themselves as members of the community of Israel, even if others do not accept them.

This fourth position challenges Messianic Jews to identify fully with their cultural and religious heritage rather than deny, ignore, or approach it in an adversarial manner. A few, however, would extend this approach to a complete identification with non-Messianic Judaism in its observance of Torah. Those who promote this complete identification claim that the Jewish tradition is itself the inspired, God-given vehicle for the preservation of the Jewish people and should not be criticized except from within, by those who already adhere to it.

The problem raised by this approach is the potential compromise on the significance of Yeshua and his soteriological role. While such an option may be attractive for those wishing to receive a validation of their identity from the Jewish community, it can lead to a diminishment of effective testimony. The self-understanding that may be gained from such an approach leads to isolation from other believers. Torah observance at the cost of the visible unity of the body of Messiah made up of Israel and the nations can only result in loss of fellowship and faith.

MJT has yet to reflect seriously on these options, which are still at an early stage of presentation and debate. The manifold values behind some form of Torah observance will continue to challenge and inspire the movement. Living a godly life, following the example of Yeshua, having a culturally sensitive lifestyle and witness, demonstrating the freedom given to observe or not observe aspects of *halacha*, taking up the responsibilities of Israel, reacting against assimilation, all are motivations to be integrated in "taking up the yoke of Torah." What is needed for the future development of MJT is further reflection on the theological assumptions, hermeneutical methods, and exegetical processes that Messianic Jews bring to the subject of Torah. Also needed is a systematic development and working out in detail of what a Messianic *halacha* will look like.

At the beginning of this current work, I presented the question, *What has been the effect of Messianic Jewish thought on Christian thinking?* Messianic Jews have much to contribute to the church's understanding on many matters vital to its life, faith, and witness. The Hebrew Bible and the Jewish understanding of life sees it lived as a member of a community, not as an isolated individual. The community has a corporate personality and bears a corporate responsibility for its members before God. Its holiness must be preserved collectively and its sinfulness collectively atoned for on Yom Kippur, the Day of Atonement. The family is the building block of this society under God, and the family, through the clan and the tribal unit, makes up the people of God. The church today urgently needs to recover what it means to celebrate the life of the people of God as a community, and not just a collection of individuals.

Messianic Jews see the purpose of this community as witness to the nations. The community gathers for worship and scatters for witness. It witnesses to God's character and standards through its obedience to Torah, not as an act of self-justification, but as a response of gratitude for God's grace, and as an act of humble obedience and recognition of its responsibility to be a light to the nations. Only with Yeshua, the light that lightens every person, can Israel live up to this covenant responsibility. Even when she fails, God graciously forgives through the atoning love of the Messiah.

Messianic Jews see God's faithfulness to his people Israel as a reminder of his faithfulness to all who believe in the name of Jesus. The character of Israel as the people of God, bound together by the Torah, is a reminder to all those who believe that we are called into new covenant relationships with God and our brothers and sisters in the Messiah.

Yet Messianic Jews long for their people, and all nations, to know the Messiah, and pray earnestly for that to happen. A venerable Jewish anecdote describes a man hired by his *shtetl* to sit at the outskirts of town and alert his village should he see the Messiah coming. When asked why he had accepted such a monotonous form of employment the watchman would invariably reply, "The pay is not so good, but it's a lifetime job." Judaism considers waiting for the Redeemer a lifetime job, and Jewish people are obligated not only to believe in the coming of the Messiah but also to yearn for his coming.[73]

But waiting and yearning are not enough. Messianic Jews, and the whole church, are called to put the watchman out of business by announcing that the Messiah is here, and is no longer hidden. We can recognize him now, and know his presence with us. It may still be a lifetime job (unless he returns first), but our task has changed from that of watchmen to being heralds of good news. Messianic Jews, like the whole church, exist to make the good news of the Messiah known to Israel and all nations. Thus, we all need to be challenged in our thinking about, and in our practical witness to, Jews as we respond together to our Lord's challenge to "go and make disciples of all nations" (Matt. 28:19 NIV).

---

73. Meir Soloveitchik, "Redemption and the Power of Man," *Azure* 16 (Winter 2004), http://www.azure.org.il/magazine/magazine.asp?id=172.

PART 3

ESCHATOLOGY

10

EZEKIEL 37 AND THE PROMISE-PLAN OF GOD

The Divine Restoration of Israel

WALTER C. KAISER JR.

The thirty-seventh chapter of Ezekiel is one of the most amazing chapters in the *Tanak*. Yet, opined L. E. Cooper, "[f]ew other passages have suffered more from the extremes of interpreters who see either too much or too little in both the meaning and application of the figures, symbols and types."[1] Noting a similar extreme in interpretation, Charles Feinberg pointed out that some of the church fathers, such as Jerome, and a good number of recent commentators "have taken the passage in verses 1–10 to be a *locus classicus* for the doctrine of the [individual] resurrection of the dead."[2] Others see this passage as a description of a general resurrection of the dead in the last day, while still others relate it to Israel's awakening to life from death in their return from the Babylonian captivity. This latter view is in part more faithful to that part of verse 11 that refers to the whole house of Israel: "Our bones are dried up and our hope is gone; we are cut off" (NIV [used throughout this chapter, unless otherwise specified]). The text of Ezekiel 37:1–14 also speaks, however, of a spiritual restoration of the nation Israel in the final day, much as the prophet Hosea did in Hosea 6:2.

These alternative views raise once again a central question in the promise-plan of God:[3] Was the promise-plan of God given to the patriarchs (e.g., Gen. 15) and David (e.g., 2 Sam. 7) a conditional, bilateral type of agreement (i.e., pending Israel's obedience) or was that promise-plan offered to the nation as an eternal promise without condition on any of the mortals involved, but resting solely on the word and reputation of God himself?

This chapter of Ezekiel is noteworthy because it speaks directly to this question of the future of Israel in the land God promised. In this regard, the vision of the valley of dry bones (Ezek. 37:1–14) and the symbol of the joining of the two sticks (Ezek. 37:15–28) are, in fact, two of the most straightforward texts one will find in the *Tanak*.

THE CONTEXT OF EZEKIEL 37

One day, during the "twelfth year of [Israel's] exile"[4] (Ezek. 33:21–22), devastating news reached the exiles in Babylon; the city

---

1. Lamar Eugene Cooper, *Ezekiel*, The New American Commentary (Nashville: Broadman & Holman, 1994), 319.

2. Charles Lee Feinberg, *The Prophecy of Ezekiel: The Glory of the Lord* (Chicago: Moody Press, 1969), 212.

3. In *The Promise-Plan of God: A Biblical Theology of the Old and New Testaments* (Grand Rapids, Zondervan, 2008), I argue that the Greek word *epangellia* is the unifying term for a cohesive plan of God in both Testaments.

4. Some (e.g., H. L. Ellison, *Ezekiel: The Man and His Message* [Grand Rapids:

of the Jerusalem had been destroyed. Just the night before, the Lord had given to the prophet Ezekiel a series of six prophecies. Each of the six prophecies dealt with God's future relationship with the land and people of Israel. These prophecies spoke to the following themes:

1. *Idolatry.* First was given an explanation as to why God had laid waste Israel's land; it was due to her idolatrous practices (Ezek. 33:23–33).

2. *The Good Shepherd.* Then God would remove the self-centered leaders who had robbed the people. In their stead, the Lord would himself be the Good Shepherd, who would care for them as the Messiah and who would come in the Davidic line (Ezek. 34:1–31).

3. *Fruitfulness.* The Lord would fight against Edom and all similar nations that had harbored hostility against his people. He would not only devastate those nations, he would repopulate the land of Israel again and make the land fruitful once more (Ezek. 35:1–36:15).

4. *Cleansing and renewing.* Then the people themselves would be cleansed and renewed by the Spirit of God, revived as a nation once more (Ezek. 36:16–37:14).

5. *Reuniting.* The people would be not only dramatically revived, they would be reunited as a single nation, no longer separate powers consisting of a northern group of ten tribes

---

Eerdmans, 1956], 118; and Peter C. Craigie, *Ezekiel* [Philadelphia: Westminster, 1983], 239) emend the "twelfth year" to the "eleventh year," which would make it six months after the fall of Jerusalem in 586 B.C., rather than eighteen months— the latter period judged by most to be too long for the news to reach the exiles. However, the evidence for this textual change seems too weak to some (e.g., Daniel I. Block, *The Book of Ezekiel* [Grand Rapids: Eerdmans, 1998], 2:254). There are only eight Hebrew manuscripts, some LXX manuscripts, and the Syriac that read the "eleventh." Block favors resolving the date by reconciling Ezekiel 24:1 and 2 Kings 25:3–4 with the observation that the calendar was based on the king's regnal year, that is, his first full year in office and not that portion that he began before the full year began.

and two southern tribes, known as Judah and Benjamin (Ezek. 37:15–28), but all one kingdom once again.

6. *Dwelling place.* Finally, God would thwart the concluding act of the enemies of Israel led by Gog and would securely establish for Israel a dwelling place in their own land (Ezek. 38–39).

At the heart of these six blocks of text are messages—contained in themes four and five—that took up the question of the future of the people. How could they be presented any picture of hope given their constant penchant for unholiness and rebellion against God? The answer was that they must first be punished with exile for defiling the land and themselves (36:17–20). But then they would be regathered back in their land (36:22–24), cleansed from their iniquities (36:25–33a), and given a new heart and a new Spirit (36:26–27). The central vision to this restoring work of God, however, came in the vision of the valley of the dry bones.

THE VALLEY OF DRY BONES (EZEK. 37:1–10)

As already noted, the vision of the valley of dry bones in Ezekiel 37:1–10 is at once one of the most dramatic and one of the best-known passages of the *Tanak*. If for no other reason, it is best known by the lyrics of the well-known spiritual: "the leg bone connected to the knee bone and the knee bone connected to the thigh bone, thigh bone connected to the hip bone. . . . Now hear the Word of the Lord. 'Dem bones, 'dem bones, 'dem dry bones . . . are 'go'in' to walk all around" once more by the power of God.

Many modern interpreters have steered away from an interpretation that depicts a literal reappearance of the nation Israel in the eschatological days. Strong evidence can be presented, however, for a genuine resurrection to life in the nation Israel from the old order to a whole new order for that ethnic group. So dramatic will be the restoration of the nation of Israel, it will be akin, in fact, to a resurrection from the dead. This work of God will come, however, only after the three earlier predictions of renewal in themes 14a have been completed. The new community will live in a renewed land (Ezek. 35:1–36:15), have a renewed community that has a new heart and a new spirit (Ezek. 36:16–38), and experience the leadership of a new shepherd (Ezek. 34:1–31).

As mentioned, this vision of the valley of the dry bones was part of a group of messages that were received just prior to the news of Jerusalem's destruction. The interpretive setting for these messages, then, is one of dispelling the despair of the people upon hearing that Jerusalem had fallen and that the throne and kingdom of David no longer seemed to exist!

"The hand of the LORD was upon me," the prophet would begin his prophecy (37:1). But just as abruptly as it began, in the style seen in other vision passages in the book of Ezekiel (1:1–3; 8:1; 40:1), we are told that the "Spirit of the LORD" "brought" the prophet and "set [him] in the middle of a valley; it was full of bones" (37:1).

The chapter begins, remember, by claiming that the "hand of the LORD was upon [Ezekiel]," a phrase used also by Elijah and Elisha when describing God's power being levied against Israel for her sin, or against her enemies, as sign of hope for Israel. This phrase occurs in the book of Ezekiel seven times (1:3; 3:14, 22; 8:1; 33:22; 37:1; 40:1).[5] In this context, then, it is the power of God that rests on the prophet to announce the prospect of hope for the nation.

The prophet is taken in a vision to a valley filled with dried, bleached bones, which litter the valley floor. While the text does not tell us where the valley is or even why the vision had to take place in a valley, it was probably the same valley where Ezekiel had received his first vision in Ezekiel 3:22–23 and again in 8:4. The prophet was guided "back and forth"[6] among the bones of those who had been "slain" (v. 9) in the valley before the "Spirit of the LORD" asked him the question: "Son of man, can these bones live?" (v. 3).

What could the prophet say? God alone knew the answer to that question (v. 3b). Therefore, without further ado, Ezekiel was commanded to "Prophesy to these bones and say to them, 'Dry bones, hear the word of the LORD!'" (v. 4).

Immediately Ezekiel obeyed as he began to prophesy (v. 7). It appears that even before he finished prophesying, Ezekiel heard the

---

5. See other places for the "hand of the LORD" in Exodus 9:3; Deuteronomy 2:15; 1 Samuel 5:6; 1 Kings 18:46; 2 Kings 3:15; Isaiah 8:11; and Jeremiah 15:17.
6. Literally, "around."

"noise" or "rattling" as bone after bone of these anatomical remnants came together. The prophet's obedience produced immediate, but startling, results (v. 7): "there was a noise" (*qol*) as he was prophesying, "a rattling sound," (*ra'ash*), or even better, "an earthquake" or a "shaking" (as in the AV of 38:19–20). Thus, one bone made its way to its corresponding bone under the duress of the power of God and the action of the earthquake.[7] Yet despite the marvel of this event, the bones still were not living: "there was no breath in them" (v. 8c). The bones were without vitality.

Daniel Block has noted that the bones on the valley floor do not represent merely the victims of Nebuchadnezzar's wars, who were left out in the fields. "They represent the entire house of Israel, including even those who had been exiled by the Assyrians more than 130 years earlier."[8]

There stood the assembled bones, tendons with skin and flesh on them, "but there was no breath in them" (v. 8) until the prophet prophesied (i.e., preached) the second time. Once again, the prophet was told, "Prophesy to the breath; prophesy, son of man, and say to it, 'This is what the Sovereign LORD says: Come from the four winds, O breath, and breathe into these slain, that they may live'" (v. 9). The result was "they came to life and stood up on their feet—a vast army" (v. 10). The God of the whole universe had already announced in verses 5–6 that he would cause breath to come into these bones, and that he would attach sinews to them, and cover them with skin. This in itself would be startling enough, but there was more: all would see that the power of the word of God to effect his will would be as awesome in the future as it was in the days of Ezekiel two millennia ago!

THE MEANING OF THE VISION (EZEK. 37:11–14)

The pivotal verse eleven of Ezekiel 37 declares,

> Then he said to me, "Son of man, these bones are the whole house of Israel. They say, 'Our bones are dried up and our hope is gone; we are cut off.'"

---

7. Ellison, *Ezekiel*, 130–31.
8. Daniel I. Block, *The Book of Ezekiel: Chapters 25–48* (Grand Rapids: Eerdmans, 1998), 379.

What could be clearer? Rather than the vision's representing a resurrection of individuals, as is spoken of elsewhere (Isa. 25:8; 26:19; Dan. 12:2), it was a bringing to life of the nation of Israel once again, just as Hosea 6:2 affirmed. Hosea taught that "after two days he will revive us; on the third day he will restore us, [so] that we may live in his presence."[9]

The Ezekiel passage divides itself, then, into two parts: the description of what Ezekiel saw in the vision of the valley of dry bones, verses 1–10, and the interpretation of the vision in verses 11–14. To reject the interpretation offered in verses 11–14 is to jeopardize one's ability to understand verses 1–10. The very same rule of interpretation occurs in other prophets from this same period such as Zechariah and Daniel: the prophetic analysis that follows a prophetic discourse supplies its own interpretation, thereby helping the reader to understand the meaning of the prophecy.

This two-stage prophetic act reminds us of God's work in creation: first, God formed man out of the dust of the earth, then he breathed into his nostrils the breath of life, and man became alive (Gen. 2:7). In Ezekiel, however, the breath does not come directly from God, as it did in creation, but from the "four winds" (v. 9). The "four winds" usually indicate the four corners of the earth (cf. Isa. 43:5–6; Jer 31:8). Thus, according to some, the two-step restoration of the bones could well refer to Israel's returning to her land in the last days in an unconverted state without spiritual life and vitality.

Charles Feinberg noted, in fact, "Apparently the reference to the absence of breath in the bodies indicated that when Israel will be returned to the land in the latter days, they will be unconverted. Surely the general tenor of Scripture points in this direction (see Zech. 13:8–9). Otherwise it is difficult to see how a covenant could be made nationally with such a godless one as the Roman prince of the end times" (cf. Dan. 9:27).[10]

O. Palmer Robertson, however, emphasizes the "two stages involved in this process of resurrection" as being an "obvious parallel

---

9. See also the theology of a general resurrection in Deuteronomy 32:39: "I kill, and I make alive" (ESV); 1 Samuel 2:6; Psalm 30:3.
10. Feinberg, *The Prophecy of Ezekiel*, 213–14.

between this account on the infusion of life [as recorded] in Ezekiel and the creation account in Genesis 2:7." For Robertson this "makes it plain that Ezekiel's vision of a return to life refers to a single event."[11] What Robertson draws from this is that

> However the establishment of the state of Israel [in 1948] may be viewed, it does not fulfill the expectation of Ezekiel as described in this vivid prophecy. Instead, this picture of a people brought to newness of life by the Spirit of God leads to a consideration of the role of the land in the context of the new covenant.[12]

Robertson then translates the old covenant concept of the land into what he considers categories of new covenant fulfillment. This process of fulfillment is a movement, we are assured, of going from shadow to reality, of the general resurrection of all of the dead.

That meaning, however, needs to be weighted against the interpretation given by the Lord himself in verses 11–14. It is apparent to all who heed this section that the vision does not intend to symbolize the general resurrection of all the dead. It simply points to the raising up of the nation of Israel, which lies slain and without any human sources of hope.

Robertson feels that Peter Walker has a similar analysis of Ezekiel's vision in regard to Israel's restored Temple. Walker concludes that the New Testament writers

> were presumably not expecting Ezekiel's prophecy to be fulfilled literally at some future point in a physical Temple. Instead this prophecy became a brilliant way of speaking pictorially of what God had now achieved in and through Jesus. Paradoxically, therefore, although Ezekiel's vision had focused so much upon the Temple, it found its ultimate fulfillment in that city where there was "no Temple," because "its Temple is the Lord Almighty and the Lamb." (Rev 21:22).[13]

---

11. O. Palmer Robertson, *The Israel of God: Yesterday, Today, and Tomorrow* (Phillipsburg, NJ: P&R Publishing, 2000), 24.
12. Ibid., 25.
13. P. W. L. Walker, *Jesus and the Holy City: New Testament Perspectives on Jerusalem* (Grand Rapids: Eerdmans, 1996), 313.

Using this same type of analogy, Robertson sees the New Testament fulfillment of the revived "House of Israel" as the promise made concerning Abraham spoken of in Romans 4:13—that he would be "heir" not just of "the land," but of "the world." Thus, the "image" of the "House of Israel" becomes the "Church" and the Old Testament image of the "land" is in turn equated in Romans 4:13 with "the world." Robertson adds to this the promise in Romans 8:22–23, where the whole creation groans in travail, waiting for the rejuvenation of the whole earth! Therefore, Robertson concludes, "By this renewal of the entire creation, the old covenant's promise of land finds its new covenant realization."[14]

Finally, Robertson asks what Jesus meant when he declared that the meek would inherit the earth (Matt 5:5). The amazing thing is not his answer, for he does see all believers, regardless of their ethnic roots, inheriting in the world in which they live. What is startling is that he should make this text figure into the discussion of the promise made to Ezekiel when God announced that "these bones are the whole house of Israel" (Ezek. 37:11). It was these bones that God would bring out of their graves (in Ezekiel's mixed metaphor) and bring back to their own land. By this act, those same "bones" would know that Yahweh was none other than the Yahweh himself.

The rest of the divine interpretation in Ezekiel is this:

> They say, "Our bones are dried up and our hope is gone; we are cut off." Therefore prophesy and say to them; "This is what the Sovereign LORD says: O my people, I am going to open your graves and bring you up from them. . . . I will put my Spirit in you and you will live, and I will settle you in your own land. Then you will know that I the LORD have spoken, and I have done it, declares the LORD" (Ezek. 37:12b, 14).

The condition of Israel when God would do this new act is one in which they were dead and cut off from God. They would be without hope. God himself would intervene, however, "open" their graves, and "bring" them "back" into "the land of Israel." As Charles Feinberg noted,

---

14. Robertson, *The Israel of God*, 26.

By a change of figure the bones . . . [are now] seen [as] buried in graves instead of [being] scattered and strewn upon a valley. God's bringing them into the land of Israel is further evidence that the passage is speaking figuratively of the resurrection of the dead nation, and not of a physical resurrection of dead persons.[15]

Peter Craigie, too, is just as clear that the meaning of this text is not about the resurrection of dead persons. He warned, "The prophecy, in other words, is not concerned with any theology of resurrection from the dead; . . . rather its focus is on the restoration of moribund exiles to new life in their original homeland."[16]

The act of revivification includes the promise of the land (Ezek. 37:12, 14, 'adamah). But it also includes placing God's Spirit in them so they could "live." That God will "bring" (hebi') them into the land and grant them rest (hinniach) demonstrates that the work of the Spirit is not a divine act differing from the raising of the dead to life in this nation. Thus, there are not three events announced in these verses, but two: (1) the bringing of a nation out of its grave; (2) the leading of them back to their land again. There does not seem, at least in this prophecy, to be a separate communication of the Holy Spirit distinct from the impartation of the breath of life to the dead corpses.

It is well worth noting that the figure of a resurrection had real meaning for the people of Ezekiel's day and did not need to be explained. Resurrection of the body is not as foreign to the Old Testament listeners in those ancient times as many modern interpreters of the Old Testament have opined. After all, in Genesis 5 a mortal, such as Enoch, "the seventh" from Adam, had gone directly into the immortal presence of God, as had Elijah the prophet in 2 Kings 2:11 by his ascension to heaven in a whirlwind. Moreover, Elijah had restored to life the widow's son (1 Kings 17:22), just as the prophet Elisha had restored to life the Shunnamite's son (2 Kings 4:34–35). The eighth century B.C. prophet Isaiah had also declared that God would one day "swallow up death forever" (Isa. 25:8), and he announced that "your dead will live; their bodies will

---

15. Feinberg, The Prophecy of Ezekiel, 214.
16. Peter C. Craigie, Ezekiel (Philadelphia: Westminster Press, 1983), 261.

rise . . . the earth will give birth to her dead" (Isa. 26:19). In like manner, Hosea, in that same eighth century, had mocked death and the grave (Hos. 13:14), asking them where their victory rested, while the prophet Daniel, a contemporary of Ezekiel in the sixth century B.C., had announced that "multitudes who sleep in the dust of the earth will awake: some to everlasting life, others to shame and everlasting contempt" (Dan. 12:2). Therefore, the doctrine of a resurrection of the body was not all that novel or foreign to Ezekiel's listeners or to those who had preceded them.

THE REUNIFICIATION OF ISRAEL (EZEK. 37:15–28)

In a new vision, which is a sequel to the vision of the valley of dry bones, Ezekiel performs another of his symbolic actions to get his message across. He is told by the Lord to take two sticks of wood and identify them: one he is to mark as belonging to "Ephraim"—standing for the ten northern tribes as signified by the house of Joseph—and the other as belonging to "Judah"—and presumably the tribe of Benjamin. Then he is to "join them together into one stick so they [would] become one in [his] hand" (Ezek. 37:17).

The meaning of this symbolic action is immediately given in verses 18–28. All of this must have been done in a public display, for the people asked, "Won't you tell us what you mean by this?" (v. 18). The prophet explained that God was going to join the kingdom divided since the days of 931 B.C. into one nation once again.

> I will take the Israelites out of the nations [note the plural; therefore they would come not just from Babylon] where they have gone. I will gather them from all around and bring them back into their own land. I will make them one nation in the land, on the mountains of Israel. There will be one king over all of them and they will never again be two nations or be divided into two kingdoms. They will no longer defile themselves with their idols, . . . for I will save them from all their sinful backsliding, and I will cleanse them. They shall be my people and I will be their God. (vv. 21–23).

The word "one" ('ehad) occurs ten times in this text. There would be "one nation," "one king," "one shepherd," and by implication, one

God among this revived and restored people. Not only that, but two new elements are added: (1) the people would be restored to their land "forever"[17] (v. 25, cf. 34:25); (2) a sanctuary would be constructed among them that would remain "forever" (vv. 26c, 28). This passage could not, then, be referring to the return from the Babylonian exile, for the extent mentioned here is "forever."

The key point to be repeated here is this: it is clear from our vantage point that not all of these promises were fulfilled after the return of the Jewish people from their exile in Babylon. The nation never was reunited into one kingdom, nor did they ever have only one king or shepherd over them. But the most telling feature is that the Messiah, the Davidic "Servant of the LORD," did not come to rule over them and they have not as yet ceased from all of their sinful backsliding. Israel is not yet "holy," nor is God's eternal sanctuary among them. While there have been some immediate and limited fulfillments, as there always are in a "now, but not yet" inaugurated eschatology, the long-range and complete fulfillments still await a future day.[18]

A wide range of contemporary believing scholars and laity disparage the claim that Ezekiel contains reference to future events. Nonetheless, this passage does embrace thirteen promises that illustrate God's determination to revive, restore, and reestablish the nation of Israel. They include that

1. God will regather Israel from among all the nations (v. 21a).
2. God will bring Israel into its own land again (v. 21b).
3. God will make one nation of the two divided kingdoms (v. 22a).
4. God will place one king over the nation (v. 22b, 24).
5. God will see to it that the nation is never again divided (v. 2c).

---

17. The word *forever*, Hebrew *'olam*, is used five times in this passage: vv. 25 (bis), 26 (bis), 28.
18. For further development of these and related hermeneutical ideas on interpreting prophecy, see Walter C. Kaiser Jr., *Back Toward the Future: Hints for Interpreting Biblical Prophecy* (Grand Rapids: Baker, 1989; reprint, Eugene, OR: Wipf & Stock, 2003), esp. 117–24.

6. God will make sure that Israel will never again serve idols (v. 23a).
7. God will save Israel from all their sinful backsliding (v. 3b).
8. God will enable Israel to walk in obedience to his law (v. 24b).
9. God will establish Israel in their land forever (v. 25).
10. God will establish a new covenant of peace[19] with Israel (v. 26a; cf. 34:25; Jer. 31:31–34);
11. God will multiply them in their land (v. 26a).
12. God will establish his sanctuary among the Israelites and will personally dwell there forever (vv. 26c–27).
13. God will make Israel a testimony to his saving grace (v. 28).

CONCLUSION

It is difficult to conclude that God has transferred solely to the New Testament church all the promises, in their entirety, that he made with the patriarchs, David, and the prophets. A passage such as the one investigated here is too explicit and too detailed to provide for that interpretation. It is one thing to recognize some of the symbolic elements in a prophecy, but it is another to spiritualize them into something quite other than what they were understood to mean in the original designations as well as in the scriptural interpretations given at the time of writing.

Hans K. LaRondelle likewise is too one-sided in his approach when he declares that the prophecies in Ezekiel 36:2–33 and 37:22–26

> stress that God's central concern with Israel is her restoration, not as a secular, political state, but as a united theocracy, a spiritually cleansed and truly worshiping people of God. Ezekiel's focus in his

---

19. See Bernard F. Batto, "The Covenant of Peace: A Neglected Ancient Near Eastern Motif," *Catholic Biblical Quarterly* 49 (1987): 187–211. The "Covenant of Peace" centers on three prophetic texts: Isaiah 54:10; Ezekiel 34:25; 37:26. Numbers 25:12 uses the same expression, but it should not be considered with the above three texts. For similarities in content, see Hosea 2:18–25 and Leviticus 26:3–13.

restoration promises is not primarily on Israel's return to her home-land, but on her return to Yahweh.[20]

There is no question that the promises made in the Old Testament were meant to include all who believed in all ages and among "the people of God," not just the believing in the nation of Israel. That is what has been strenuously argued for in promise-plan theology. Nor is it to be doubted that a central concern in both Testaments is how the heart is related to God. But these spiritual components in no way de-tract from the holistic view of redemption, which includes the material side of the promise of God in the covenants. In this way, Israel acted as God's sign that all the nations, indeed, in all times, and that all physical things as well as those that are of a spiritual nature belong to God.

LaRondelle urges us to use the New Testament and Christ as the "true interpreter" of Old Testament prophecies rather than "seeking our own independent solution"[21] to these texts. Based on Matthew's word from Jesus that the meek would inherit the earth, LaRondelle boldly goes on to apply "Israel's territorial inheritance to the Church by enlarging the original promise of the land of Canaan to include the whole earth made new."[22]

But such advice seems to forget that the same Lord gave the Old Testament revelation and attached his own divine interpretations to the original words of prophecy. To act otherwise is to set up a supra-sessionist model of interpreting the Bible, in which the later passages not only *supplement* the previous ones—which is correct—but that they also now are said to *supersede* what had been given in olden times, even when there were no indications of a built-in obsolescence in the Old Testament. Such a model is dangerous. It leads to a canon within a canon and a tendency toward a Marcionite approach to hermeneu-tics, especially in the realm of eschatology.

On the contrary, God is not finished with the physical side of

---

20. Hans K. LaRondelle, *The Israel of God in Prophecy* (Berrien Springs, MI: Andrews University Press, 1983), 90.
21. Could this mean that we should not follow the prophet's truth assertions as the route to discerning what it is that God wanted to communicate to his people then and now? That hardly seems correct in the face of the biblical claims made by the prophets.
22. LaRondelle, *The Israel of God in Prophecy*, 138.

creation or with any other aspects of his holistic view of persons and things. He will conclude his work in history just as he said he would in order to show that he is Lord of all history, persons, and nations. His sovereignty will not entail a dualism in which he designates Israel as a separate people, or that he has a dual purpose for history that involves an earthly as well as a heavenly calling. Promise theology[23] holds that God has one "People of God" forever, comprised of both Jewish and Gentile believers yet with many discernable and distinguishable aspects, and he has one program of the "kingdom of God" forever, even though we may isolate several aspects (such as an earthly and a spiritual aspect) in that single program of the kingdom of God.

As a tribute to the grace of God and his own faithfulness to his own promise, the Lord of all history will bring Israel back to the land he originally promised to them as far back in time as the days of the patriarchs. Nothing in Israel will merit this action, nor will this action indicate a form of partiality or chauvinism by God. It will only signal that God is able to complete in space and time what he has pledged. It will also indicate that he is sovereign over the nations of the world, over the physical aspects of the universe, just as he is sovereign in sending his Messiah and providing redemption for all the families of the earth. Holistically, the promises that appear in the one Abrahamic-Davidic covenant cannot be separated, divided, or interpreted independently so as to contrast with each other. The promise of (1) the Seed, (2) the land, and (3) the gospel—which announced that in the Seed all the nations of the earth would be blessed (Gen. 12:2–3; etc, Gal. 3:8)—was all of one piece, one promise-plan, and in concert and continuity with both testaments. And herein lies both a theology and a philosophy of history at the heart of this continuous story of God's promise-plan, working through the ages.

---

23. See Walter C. Kaiser Jr., *Toward Old Testament Theology* (Grand Rapids: Zondervan, 1978) for an early discussion of promise theology. This volume is now in its 27th printing. Also see idem, *The Christian and the "Old" Testament* (Pasadena: CA: William Carey Press, 2000) for a more popular, but more recent discussion of the features of promise theology. It is neither dispensational or covenantal in its approach, though it shares features with both in so far as biblical support can be found to substantiate the various features. A new edition was released titled *The Promise-Plan of God: A Biblical Theology of the Old and New Testaments* (Grand Rapids: Zondervan, 2008).

11

THE BASIS OF THE SECOND COMING OF THE MESSIAH

ARNOLD G. FRUCHTENBAUM

The basis of the second coming of the Messiah consists of two main pillars. First is the rejection by Israel of the messiahship of Jesus, and the second relates to the prerequisite to his second coming.[1]

Closely connected with God's kingdom program is the first coming of the Messiah. Both John the Baptist (Matt. 3:1–2) and Jesus (Matt. 4:17) came proclaiming *the kingdom of heaven is at hand.* Neither John

---

1. A detailed study of this topic may be found in Arnold G. Fruchtenbaum, *The Footsteps of the Messiah*, rev. ed. (San Antonio, TX: Ariel Ministries, 2004).

nor Jesus, according to the Gospel writers, felt the need to define the nature of this kingdom, apparently expecting the audience to under- stand what they meant by that term. And well they might. Jewish audiences had common knowledge of the Old Testament and under- stood the nature of the messianic kingdom. In first-century Israel the common Jewish understanding of the kingdom was that of a literal earthly kingdom centered in Jerusalem and ruled by the Messiah. The obvious origin of such a view was the literal understanding of the Old Testament prophets.

If either John or Jesus had meant something totally different, as all covenant theologians insist (including covenant premillennial- ists), then their silence is inexplicable. We must conclude that the common Jewish understanding of the coming kingdom was a correct one. Toussaint and Dyer come to the same conclusion:

> Suddenly in Matthew 3 John the baptizer, the Lord's forerunner, appears on the scene. His message was, "Repent, for the kingdom of heaven is at hand." What does the word *kingdom* mean here? It certainly cannot be some *spiritual* kingdom in the hearts of people. That kingdom was always present (cf. Psalm 37:31). Furthermore, the fact that John never explained what the term meant when the Jews clearly expected an earthly kingdom would imply that he was expecting the same type of kingdom.[2]

The common Jewish understanding, however, that "all Israel has a share in the age to come" was an incorrect one. So both John and Jesus proclaimed that the need to repent for righteousness was the means of entering the kingdom. Furthermore, agree Toussaint and Dyer, to see the messianic kingdom established in their day required Israel's acceptance of Jesus as the messianic King.

> "The gospel of the kingdom" proclaimed by Christ in Matthew 9:35 must be the same as that preached by him in 4:23. It was the good news of the nearness of the kingdom and freedom of access by

---

2. Stanley D. Toussaint and Charles H. Dyer, *Essays in Honor of J. Dwight Pentecost* (Chicago: Moody Press, 1986), 24.

repentance. The kingdom was proximate in two senses. First, the Messiah was here on earth, and second, the kingdom's coming was contingent on Israel's response to her Messiah.[3]

When Jesus was rejected, a key change took place in the kingdom program. Toussaint has stated the dispensational viewpoint quite well:

> Very often the dispensationalist school of interpretation will refer to "the offer of the kingdom" to Israel. By this is meant the contingency of the coming of the kingdom to Israel in the first century based on Israel's acceptance of Jesus as its Messiah. This concept is clearly found in the New Testament. For instance, Peter openly states the coming of the Messiah rests on Israel's repentance (Acts 3:19–21). The Lord Himself said that John the Baptist could have been the fulfillment of the Elijah prophecy of Malachi 4:5–6 if Israel had repented (Matthew 11:14). . . .
>
> However, dispensationalists may want to clarify their terminology. The New Testament does teach the contingency of the coming of the kingdom premised on the response to the Jews. But every Israelite wanted the kingdom to come. To say Christ offered the kingdom to Israel is true, but it leaves the impression the Jews did not want the kingdom to come. It would be far better to say Jesus offered himself as Israel's Messiah and the coming of the kingdom was contingent on their acceptance or rejection of him.[4]

The King was rejected and, along with him, the messianic kingdom. This point, so important to Israelology, needs to be explored further.

THE REJECTION OF HIS MESSIAHSHIP

To fully understand the basis of his coming, one must first understand what occurred when the messiahship of *Yeshua* (Jesus) was rejected. In the layout of Matthew's gospel, Jesus began His ministry in chapter

---

3. Ibid., 27.
4. Ibid., 22.

4, and from chapter 4 until chapter 12, he is seen going around Israel proclaiming the kingdom, preaching the gospel of the kingdom of the Jewish prophets, and performing many miracles. The purpose of the miracles recorded in chapters 4–12 is to authenticate his Person and his message. They are signs to force the nation of Israel to come to a decision regarding two things: first, his Person, that He is the Messiah; secondly, his message, the gospel of the kingdom.

Then in Matthew 12, the purpose of his miracles and his ministry undergoes a radical change. The rejection of his messiahship occurs.

The Unpardonable Sin: Matthew 12:22–37
Among the many miracles Yeshua performed was the casting out of demons. According to Matthew 12:27, Judaism also had exorcists. The exorcist established communication with the demon in order to find out his name. Then, using that demon's name, the exorcist could cast him out. On some occasions Yeshua used the Jewish method, as in Luke 8:30. When demons speak, they use the vocal cords of the person under their control. Therefore, in the case of the demon that caused dumbness, Jewish exorcism was to no avail, for communication with the demon was impossible. The Jewish observation that demons of dumbness were a special case is validated by the Messiah in Mark 9:17, 25, and 29.

But the Messiah was able to exorcise that demon in Mark 9:22: "Then was brought unto him one possessed with a demon, blind and dumb: and he healed him, insomuch that the dumb man spake and saw" (ASV). Mark's point is that Jesus performed a miracle that had never been performed before.

This caused the people to begin asking, *Can this be the son of David?* The question was, "Can Yeshua really be the Messiah?" Indeed, the miracle was intended to bring them to see that he was indeed *the son of David.* The people, however, were not willing to judge his person by themselves, but were looking to their religious leaders to declare their judgment of Jesus. They were waiting for the Pharisees to conclude either that he was the Messiah or that he was not the Messiah. And if he was not the Messiah, then the Pharisees must offer some alternative explanation for his many miracles, especially the miracles that were never done before.

The Pharisees chose the latter course: "But when the Pharisees heard it, they said, This man does not cast out demons, but by Beelzebub the prince of the demons" (v. 24 ASV). They refused to accept Jesus as the Messiah because he did not fit their idea of what the Messiah should say and do. Their explanation of how he was able to perform miracles was that he himself was possessed by Beelzebub. Their explanation became, then, the official basis of the rejection of the messiahship of Yeshua. It was "the leaven of the Pharisees" (Luke 12:1), about which the Messiah would warn his disciples—the Pharisaic claim that Jesus was not the Messiah, but instead possessed by Beelzebub. This was the ground on which the Pharisees rejected the messiahship of Yeshua.

The Messiah responded to this accusation by telling them that their statement could not be true because it would mean that Satan's kingdom was divided against itself (vv. 25–29). And he pronounced judgment on the generation of that day in verses 31–37:

> Therefore I say unto you, every sin and blasphemy shall be forgiven unto men; but the blasphemy against the Spirit shall not be forgiven. And whosoever shall speak a word against the Son of man, it shall be forgiven him; but whosoever shall speak against the Holy Spirit, it shall not be forgiven him, neither in this world, nor in that which is to come. . . . And I say unto you, that every idle word that men shall speak, they shall give account thereof in the day of judgment. For by your words you shall be justified, and by your words you shall be condemned. (ASV)

According to verse 31, that generation had committed the unpardonable sin: blasphemy of the Holy Spirit. This is the only context in which the unpardonable sin is found, and it must be interpreted accordingly. The unpardonable sin is not an individual sin, but a national sin. It was committed by that generation of Israel in Jesus' day and cannot be applied to subsequent Jewish generations. The content of the unpardonable sin was the national rejection of the messiahship of Yeshua, based on the grounds that he was demon possessed, while he was physically present. This sin was unpardonable, and judgment was set. The judgment came forty years later in A.D. 70 with the destruction of Jerusalem and the Temple, and the worldwide dispersion of the Jewish people. This does not mean that individual members of that generation could not be saved, for many were. It did mean, however, that henceforth nothing could avert the coming destruction of Jerusalem.

In summary, four things must be said about the unpardonable sin. First, this is a national sin and not an individual one. Even for individual members of that generation it was possible to escape the judgment for the unpardonable sin by repenting—changing their minds about Jesus. No individual can commit this sin today for two reasons: it was not an individual sin to begin with, and all sins are forgivable to that individual who comes to God through Jesus the Messiah. But for the nation as a nation, it was unpardonable. Second, the unpardonable sin was a sin limited to that generation. Note the emphasis in the Gospels on the guilt of *this generation.* Third, this is not a sin that any nation can commit today because the Messiah is not now physically and visibly present with any nation, offering himself as that nation's Messiah. This was unique to his relationship to Israel and to no other. And finally, the committal of the unpardonable sin by that generation had two ramifications for that generation. The first is that the offer of the kingdom to that generation was rescinded; instead, it will be reoffered to a later Jewish generation that will accept it, the Jewish generation of the Great Tribulation introduced in Matthew 24–25. The second is that divine judgment fell upon that generation, the physical judgment of the destruction of Jerusalem and the Temple in A.D. 70.

The Sign of the Resurrection: Matthew 12:38–40

> Then certain of the scribes and Pharisees answered him saying, Teacher, we would see a sign from you. But he answered and said unto them, An evil and adulterous generation seeks after a sign; and there shall no sign be given it but the sign of Jonah the prophet: for as Jonah was three days and three nights in the belly of the whale; so shall the Son of man be three days and three nights in the heart of the earth. (ASV)

The Pharisees were stunned by Jesus' pronouncement of judgment. They tried to retake the offensive by demanding a sign (v. 38), as though the Messiah had done nothing thus far to substantiate his messiahship! But there was now a change of policy regarding his signs (v. 39): from now on, there would be no more signs for the nation, except one. While the Messiah would continue (after Matt. 12) to perform miracles, the purpose of his miracles had changed. No longer would they be performed for the purpose of authenticating his person and his message in order to get the nation to come to a decision. That decision had already been made. Rather, his miracles would be for the purpose of training the Twelve for the new kind of ministry that they would need to conduct as the result of his rejection. The apostles performed this ministry in the Book of Acts.

For that generation, though, there would be no further signs but one: the sign of Jonah, the sign of resurrection. It is a sign that would come for Israel on three occasions: at the resurrection of Lazarus (John 11:1-46); at his own resurrection (Matt. 16:1–4); and at the resurrection of the two witnesses in the tribulation (Rev. 11:3–13).

The first two signs were rejected. The third will be accepted, for the resurrection of the two witnesses will lead to the salvation of the Jews of Jerusalem.

Swept, Garnished, and Empty: Matthew 12:41–45

> The men of Nineveh shall stand up in the judgment with this generation, and shall condemn it: for they repented at the preaching of Jonah; and behold, a greater than Jonah is here. The queen of the south shall rise up in the judgment with this generation, and shall condemn it: for she came from the ends of the earth to hear the wisdom of Solomon; and behold, a greater than Solomon is here. But the unclean spirit, when he is gone out of the man, passes through waterless places, seeking rest, and finds it not. Then he says, I will return into my house whence I came out; and when he is come, he finds it empty, swept, and garnished. Then goes he, and takes with himself seven other spirits more evil than himself, and they enter in and dwell there: and the last state of that man becomes worse than the first. Even so shall it be also unto this evil generation. (ASV)

This passage concludes with more words of judgment from Yeshua for that generation. Notice how often the phrase *this generation* appears in this passage. In the final judgment, Nineveh and the Queen of Sheba—Gentiles both—will stand in judgment of this generation. Without verbal revelation or miracles, they responded to God. But this generation did not.

To illustrate the final outcome of that generation, the proclamation of judgment concludes with a story about a demon (v. 43–45). Jesus related the account of a demon who, on his own volition, left a man whom he had possessed. But when he was unable to find a new body to indwell and control, he returned to his original abode. Although he found it swept and garnished, he also found it still empty. The individual never took the opportunity to fill his life with the Holy Spirit. Nor had another demon entered him. So the demon re-entered the man he originally possessed and invited seven other demons to join him. The outcome was that the last state of the man had become worse than the first, because now he was possessed by eight demons.

The point of this story is often missed. The Messiah closed the story with the point that what was true of the man was also true of that particular evil generation. When that generation began, it began with the preaching of John the Baptist. John's ministry was to prepare the people for the reception of the Messiah. By means of the preaching of John, that generation was swept and garnished. But now that the Messiah had come, they rejected him on the basis of demon possession. The nation that was swept and garnished now remained empty on account of the rejection of the messiahship of Yeshua. And because it remained empty, the last state of that generation was to be worse than the first.

When that generation began, though it was under Roman domination, it had a national entity. It had a semi-autonomous form of government in the Sanhedrin. Jerusalem stood in all its Herodian glory, and the religious worship system in the Temple remained intact. But later, as a result of the rejection and judgment, in A.D. 70 the national entity of Israel ceased to exist. In the place of bondage, they were dispersed by the Roman armies. The Temple, the center of Judaism, was destroyed so that not one stone stood upon another. Eventually, the Jews were dispersed all over the world. So, indeed, the last state of that generation became worse than the first. They went from bondage to worldwide dispersion.

The Sign of Jonah: John 11:1–57

Even after the events of Matthew 12, the Pharisees approached Messiah demanding a sign to authenticate his person and his message (Matt. 16:1-4). But again Christ refused to give them any more signs and promised them only the sign of Jonah, which is the sign of resurrection.

The resurrection of Lazarus, recorded in John 11:1–44, is the presentation of the first sign of Jonah. The Messiah had raised others from the dead, yet all of the other resurrections are covered in just a few verses. But here, John the apostle uses 44 verses to give great detail about the resurrection of Lazarus. Why? This is the sign of Jonah that Yeshua had promised. In verse 42, Jesus makes it very clear for whom Lazarus was raised, namely, the Jewish multitudes:

> And I knew that you heard me always: but because of the multitude that stands around I said it, that they may believe that you did send me. (ASV)

The response of the Jews follows in verses 45–46: "Many therefore of the Jews, who came to Mary and beheld that which he did, believed on him. But some of them went away to the Pharisees, and told them the things which Jesus had done."

Some of the Jews responded correctly to this first sign of Jonah and believed that Yeshua was who he claimed to be. But others still wanted some kind of word or judgment from their leaders, and so they reported to the Pharisees what Jesus had done. Since this was the sign the Messiah had promised them, they must respond in some way or another.

The Sanhedrin's Verdict: John 11:47–50, 53

> The chief priests therefore and the Pharisees gathered a council, and said, What do we? for this man does many signs. If we let him thus alone, all men will believe on him: and the Romans will come and take away both our place and our nation. But a certain one of them, Caiaphas, being high priest that year, said unto them. Ye know nothing at all, nor do ye take account that it is expedient for

you that one man should die for the people, and that the whole nation perish not. . . . So from that day forth they took counsel that
they might put him to death. (ASV)

The Pharisees responded in keeping with their original verdict
of Matthew 12. The Sanhedrin gathered together to make a decision
as to how to respond to the sign of Jonah given in the resurrection of
Lazarus. They issued a decree of rejection and sought an opportunity
to put Jesus to death. The rejection of the messiahship of Yeshua was
now complete. Going beyond the rejection of his messiahship, they
now condemned him to death.

The results of the Sanhedrin's verdict are threefold: first, the
Messiah went into hiding for a short period of time, because the hour
of his death was not yet come (v. 54); second, the people still raised
questions concerning his person, a logical thing for them to do in light
of the resurrection of Lazarus (v. 55–56); third, the Sanhedrin's verdict filtered down to the masses (v. 57):

> Now the chief priests and the Pharisees had given commandment
> that, if any man knew where he was, he should show it, that they
> might take him. (ASV)

They sought an opportunity to put him to death. The rejection
that had occurred in Matthew 12 culminated in John 11 with a decree
of death hanging over the person of the Messiah. The first sign of
Jonah, the resurrection of Lazarus, was rejected.

The Triumphal Entry: Luke 19:41–44

> And when he drew nigh, he saw the city and wept over it, saying, If
> you had known in this day, even you, the things which belong unto
> peace! but now they are hid from your eyes. For the days shall come
> upon you, when your enemies shall cast up a bank about you, and
> compass you round, and keep you in on every side, and shall dash
> you to the ground, and your children within you; and they shall not
> leave in you one stone upon another; because you knew not the
> time of your visitation. (ASV)

Thousands of Jews cried out, "Blessed is the King that comes in the name of the Lord," an official messianic greeting based on the messianic context of Psalm 118:26. The Jewish masses proclaimed Jesus' messiahship as he approached Jerusalem. But the Jewish leaders had already committed the unpardonable sin. Judgment had already been set on that generation. Since the sin as unforgivable, there was no way of alleviating that judgment. So in spite of the masses' proclaiming him to be the Messiah, Jesus pronounced words of judgment upon the city of Jerusalem.

The Pharisees Denounced: Matthew 23:1–36

This entire chapter is devoted to a condemnation of Israel's leaders, the scribes and the Pharisees, for various sins. They are condemned for their hypocrisy (vv. 1–12). They are condemned for leading the nation in the rejection of Yeshua's messiahship (vv. 13–14). They are condemned for corrupting the proselytes (v. 15). They are condemned for making the Mosaic Law ineffectual through Pharisaic traditions (vv. 16–22). They are condemned for majoring on minor matters (vv. 23–24). They are condemned for being concerned with externals only (vv. 25–28). And they are condemned for rejecting the prophets (vv. 29–36).

Two condemnations are especially relevant to this study. In 23:13, the Pharisees are held accountable not only for their rejection of the messiahship of Jesus, but also for leading the entire nation to reject his messiahship: "Ye enter not in yourselves, neither suffer ye them that are entering in to enter." This is an important component of the pillar that forms the basis of the second coming of the Messiah.

The other especially relevant condemnation, 23:29–36, emphasizes the severity of the judgment on that generation:

Woe unto you, scribes and Pharisees, hypocrites! for ye build the sepulchers of the prophets, and garnish the tombs of the righteous, and say, If we had been in the days of our fathers, we should not have been partakers with them in the blood of the prophets. Wherefore ye witness to yourselves, that ye are sons of them that slew the prophets. Fill ye up then the measure of your fathers. Ye serpents, ye offspring of vipers, how shall ye escape the judgment of hell? Therefore, behold, I send unto you prophets, and wise men, and scribes: some of them shall ye kill and crucify; and some of them shall ye scourge in your synagogues, and persecute from city to city: that upon you may come all the righteous blood shed on the earth, from the blood of Abel the righteous unto the blood of Zachariah son of Barachiah, whom ye slew between the sanctuary and the altar. Verily I say unto you, All these things shall come upon this generation. (ASV)

The judgment falls primarily upon the leaders of that generation, but it also falls upon the nation whom the leaders led in the rejection of his messiahship. Yeshua stated that they were to be held accountable not only for the rejection of his messiahship; they were also to be held accountable for the blood of all the Old Testament prophets. In the Jewish order of the books of the Old Testament, which Yeshua used, the first book is Genesis, where Abel is mentioned. The last book is 2 Chronicles, where Zechariah is mentioned. Yeshua declared that they were guilty of all the blood from Genesis to 2 Chronicles, much as someone today would say, "from Genesis to Revelation." So that generation was guilty of the blood of all the prophets.

Why? Because everything God intended to say concerning the Messiah had already been said by the Jewish prophets. That generation possessed in their hands the entire Old Testament canon. Further, they had the preaching of John the Baptist announcing the soon coming of the Lord. Finally, they had the physical manifestation and presence of Jesus the Messiah, who came with authenticating signs. Yet, following their leaders, they rejected his messiahship. For this reason, they would be held accountable for the blood of all the prophets who spoke about the Messiah.

The point made in this study thus far is that the messiahship of Yeshua was rejected by the Jewish leadership, and they led the nation to the rejection of his messiahship. This was the unique sin of that generation, as verse 36 indicates: "Verily I say unto you, All these things shall come upon this generation" (ASV). It is the judgment of the unpardonable sin.

A few days after Jesus spoke these words of judgment, the second sign of Jonah was given: the resurrection of the Messiah. Israel again followed her leaders in rejecting this second sign of Jonah, as Luke records in Acts 1–7. The stoning of Stephen by the Sanhedrin in Acts

7 marked the official and final rejection of the second sign of Jonah. That is why not until Acts 8 does the gospel go out to the non-Jewish world.[5]

The Change in Jesus' Ministry: Matthew 13

After the rejection in Matthew 12 because of the unpardonable sin the ministry of Jesus changed radically in four ways. First, the purpose of his miracles changed. No longer were they for the purpose of serving as signs of his messiahship to Israel. Now they were for the purpose of training the apostles for their ministry (Matt. 16:1-4).

The second change was the change of audience for whom Jesus performed his miracles. Until the events of Matthew 12, Jesus performed miracles for the benefit of the masses without requiring them to have faith first. After Matthew 12, he performed miracles only in response to needs of individuals who had faith in him. Furthermore, before Matthew 12, those he healed were free to proclaim what had been done for them, but after Matthew 12, Jesus initiated a policy of silence and forbade those he healed to tell anyone about it (Mark 7:36; Luke 8:56, et al.)

The third change was in the message that Jesus and the apostles now proclaimed. Until Matthew 12 both he and they went throughout the land of Israel proclaiming Jesus to be the Messiah. In Matthew 10 the apostles were sent out two by two to do just that. But after

---

5. When Jesus was rejected, the offer of the messianic kingdom was rescinded and the mystery kingdom replaced it. It is this concept that is so often ridiculed by covenant theologians and is the basis of their claim that dispensationalism minimizes the cross and makes it an afterthought in the plan of God. This is far from the truth. Dispensationalism strongly believes that the death of Messiah was inevitable, for it was absolutely necessary for the atonement. Yeshua would have died even if Israel had accepted him. The nation would have proclaimed Yeshua as their King, which would have been viewed by Rome as a rebellion against Caesar. Yeshua would then have been arrested, tried, and crucified for treason against Rome, as was the case anyway. Three days later, following his resurrection, he would have dispensed with Rome and set up the Messianic kingdom. His death would have occurred regardless of what Israel did. However, it was already known, on the basis of Old Testament prophecy, that Israel would reject his messiahship. The simple fact is that Israel could not reject that which was not offered. In the plan of God, it was by means of the rejection of the messiahship of Jesus that the death of the Messiah was accomplished. As all good Calvinists know, God ordains both the end and the means.

Matthew 12, the apostles were ordered to follow the new policy of silence, and they were forbidden to tell anyone that Jesus was the Messiah. In Matthew 16, after Peter made his famous confession, "You are the Christ [Messiah] the Son of the living God," Jesus ordered Peter to tell no one that He was the Messiah (Matt. 16:20). They were to follow the policy of silence (Matt. 17:9) until it was rescinded with the Great Commission (Matt. 28:18–20).

The fourth change was the change of teaching method. Until Matthew 12, Jesus taught the people in terms that they could and did understand. For example, Matthew states at the close of the Sermon on the Mount (Matt. 5–7), the people understood not only what he was saying, but where it differed from the teaching of the scribes and Pharisees. But in Matthew 13, Jesus began teaching with a new method, the parabolic method, the purpose of which was to hide the truth from the masses. The very act of teaching in parables was a sign of judgment against Israel. And the first series of parables Jesus spoke introduced the mystery kingdom, the stage of God's kingdom program that was inaugurated as a result of the rejection of the messiahship of Jesus and the rescinding of the offer of the messianic kingdom.

In summary, to clearly comprehend what is happening in Matthew 13, one must understand the relationship between Matthew 12 and 13. Matthew 12 records the national rejection of the messiahship of Jesus. Jesus was officially rejected by the leadership of Israel. By so doing they were guilty of the unpardonable sin. From that point on they were condemned to the judgment that fell in A.D. 70, the destruction of Jerusalem and the Temple. In Matthew 13, Jesus taught a series of parables. These parables were spoken on the very same day of the occurrence of the rejection by the nation of the messiahship of Jesus (Matt. 13:1-3). On that same day the parabolic method of teaching began as a result of the rejection of the messiahship of Jesus.

Matthew 13:10–18 states the purpose of these parables.

> And the disciples came, and said unto him, Why speakest thou unto them in parables? And he answered and said unto them, Unto you it is given to know the mysteries of the kingdom of heaven, but to them it is not given. For whosoever hath, to him shall be given, and he shall have abundance: but whosoever hath not, from him shall be taken

away even that which he hath. Therefore speak I to them in parables; because seeing they see not and hearing they hear not, neither do they understand. And unto them is fulfilled the prophecy of Isaiah. (ASV)

This was the beginning of the parabolic method of teaching, and the disciples, surprised that Jesus was no longer teaching the people in straightforward, clear language, wanted to know the reason why. In verses 11–14 Jesus said there were three reasons for the parabolic method of teaching. First, it would illustrate the truth for the disciples. Second, it would hide the truth from the masses. Third, it would fulfill prophecy that the Messiah would deliberately speak to the Jewish people in such a way that they would not be able to understand.

The summary in Matthew 13:34–35 reiterates the second and third purposes: All these things spake Jesus in parables unto the multitudes; and without a parable spake he nothing unto them: that it might be fulfilled which was spoken through the prophet, saying, I will open my mouth in parables; I will utter things hidden from the foundation of the world. (ASV)

Understanding that God's kingdom program has different facets is essential to understanding that one facet of that kingdom could be offered to Israel and be rejected, while another facet could then temporarily take its place. That is exactly what has happened. And this leads directly to the question of the prerequisite to the second coming and the establishment of the messianic kingdom.

THE PREREQUISITE TO THE SECOND COMING

The prerequisite, or second pillar of the basis of the second coming, is discovered by examining five passages of Scripture.

Leviticus 26:40–42

And they shall confess their iniquity, and the iniquity of their fathers, in their trespass which they trespassed against me, and also that, because they walked contrary unto me, I also walked contrary unto them, and brought them into the land of their enemies: if then their uncircumcised heart be humbled, and they then accept of the punishment of their iniquity; then will I remember my covenant with Jacob; and also my covenant with Isaac, and also my covenant with Abraham will I remember; and I will remember the land. (ASV)

In Leviticus 26, Moses predicts that the Jews will be scattered over the world because of their disobedience to God's revealed will. According to the New Testament, this came as a direct result of the rejection of the messiahship of Yeshua. At the end of Leviticus 26:39, the worldwide dispersion is a fact. And up to this point, Leviticus 26 has been fulfilled today.

In verse 42, Moses states that God has every intention to give Israel all the blessings and promises of the Abrahamic covenant, especially the land promise. But before they can begin to enjoy these blessings during the messianic age, it is first necessary for them to fulfill the condition of verse 40: they shall confess their iniquity, and the iniquity of their fathers. Notice that the word *iniquity* is singular and that it is specific. There is one specific iniquity that Israel must confess before she can begin to enjoy all of the benefits of the Abrahamic covenant. This iniquity was committed by their fathers or ancestors, but now must be confessed by a subsequent generation.

Jeremiah 3:11–18

And Jehovah said unto me, Backsliding Israel has showed herself more righteous than treacherous Judah. 'Go, and proclaim these words toward the north, and say, Return, you backsliding Israel, says Jehovah; I will not look in anger upon you; for I am merciful, says Jehovah, I will not keep anger for ever. Only acknowledge your iniquity, that you have transgressed against Jehovah your God, and have scattered your ways to the strangers under every green tree, and ye have not obeyed my voice, says Jehovah. Return, O backsliding children, says Jehovah; for I am a husband unto you: and I will take you one of a city, and two of a family, and I will bring you to Zion: and I will give you shepherds according to my heart, who shall feed you with knowledge and understanding. And it shall come to pass, when ye are multiplied and increased in the land, in those days, says Jehovah, they shall say no more, The ark of the covenant of Jehovah; neither shall it come to mind; neither shall they remember it; neither shall they miss it; neither shall it be made any more. At that time they shall call Jerusalem the throne of Jehovah; and all the nations shall be gathered unto it, to the name of Jehovah, to Jerusalem: neither shall they walk any more after the stubbornness of their evil heart. In those days the house of Judah shall walk with the house of Israel, and they shall come together out of the land of the north to the land that I gave for an inheritance unto your fathers. (ASV)

In verses 14–18, Jeremiah begins to describe the blessings that God has in store for Israel in the messianic kingdom. It will be a time of tremendous blessing and restoration for the Jewish people when the kingdom is established by their Messiah. But all these blessings are conditioned (v. 13) upon their acknowledgment, or confession, of the one specific iniquity that they committed against Jehovah their God.

Zechariah 12:10

Zechariah 12, 13, and 14 are one prophetic revelation, a unit of thought that develops one theme. Chapter 13 speaks of the national cleansing of Israel from their sin. Chapter 14 describes the second corning of the Messiah and the establishment of the Kingdom.

But the cleansing of Israel followed by the second coming of the Messiah and the messianic kingdom are all conditioned on something, according to Zechariah 12:10:

And I will pour upon the house of David, and upon the inhabitants of Jerusalem, the spirit of grace and of supplication; and they shall look unto me whom they have pierced; and they shall mourn for him, as one mourns for his only son, and shall be in bitterness for him, as one that is in bitterness for his first-born. (ASV)

Before Israel will receive the cleansing of her sin and before the Messiah will return to establish his Kingdom, Israel must first look unto (not upon as in the KJV) the One whom they have pierced and plead for his return. Then, and only then, will they receive their cleansing and begin to enjoy the blessings of the messianic age.

Hosea 5:15

> I will go and return to my place, until they acknowledge their offence, and seek my face: in their affliction they will seek me earnestly. (ASV)

The One who is speaking throughout this chapter is God himself. In this passage, God states that he is returning to his place. God's place is heaven. Before God can go back to heaven, he must first leave it. When did God ever leave heaven? God left heaven at the incarnation, when he came to earth in the person of Jesus of Nazareth. Then, because of one specific offense committed against him, he returned to heaven upon his ascension from the Mount of Olives.

This verse further states that he will not come back to the earth until the offense that caused him to return to heaven is acknowledged or confessed. What is that Jewish national offense committed against the person of Yeshua? It is not, as many believe, the act of killing him. The actual killing of the Messiah was done by Gentile, not Jewish, hands. He was condemned and sentenced by a Gentile judge. He was crucified by Gentile soldiers. And regardless of Jewish acceptance or rejection, Jesus would have to die anyway to become the sacrifice for sin. No, the national offense of Israel was their rejection of his messiahship. According to this verse, only when this offense is acknowledged or confessed will the Messiah return to the earth.

Matthew 23:37–39

> O Jerusalem, Jerusalem, that killed the prophets, and stoned them that are sent unto her! how often would I have gathered your children together, even as a hen gathers her chickens under her wings, and ye would not! Behold, your house is left unto you desolate. For I say unto you, Ye shall not see me henceforth, till ye shall say, Blessed is he that comes in the name of the Lord. (ASV)

As mentioned earlier, this chapter contains the Messiah's denunciation of the scribes and Pharisees, the Jewish leadership of that day, for leading the nation to the rejection of his messiahship. Still speaking to the Jewish leadership, Yeshua declares in verse 37 his original desire to gather them to himself, if only they would accept him. Because of their rejection of his messiahship, they will be scattered instead of being gathered.

In verse 38, their house, the Jewish Temple, will be left desolate and will be destroyed, with nothing remaining. But then he declares that they will not see him again until they say, "Blessed is he that comes in the name of the Lord." This is a messianic greeting, and it will signify their acceptance of his messiahship.

So Yeshua will not return to the earth until the Jews and the Jewish leaders ask him to come back. For just as the Jewish leaders once led the nation to the rejection of his messiahship, they must some day lead the nation to the acceptance of his messiahship.

This, then, is the twofold prerequisite to the second coming of the Messiah: first, Israel must confess her national sin; second, Israel must then plead for Messiah to return, to mourn for him as one mourns for an only son.

LESSONS AND APPLICATIONS

This study is relevant to Jewish evangelism in three important ways. First, it helps to understand the biblical foundations of anti-Semitism, and why Satan has had this long unending war against the Jews so as to destroy them at every opportunity. Satan knows that once the second coming occurs his career is over, but he also knows there will be no second coming apart from the Jewish request for it to happen. So if he can succeed in destroying the Jews once and for all, before they have a chance to plead for the Messiah to return, then there will be no second coming, and Satan's career will be safe forever.

This is the reason Satan has waged a perpetual war against the Jews throughout history, from the time of Abraham to the present. This is the why the Crusades occurred, and the Russian pogroms, and the Nazi Holocaust. And this is why today it is the declared goal of Islam masses to annihilate Israel. Knowing his time is short, Satan expends all of his energies to try to destroy the Jews once and for all. Anti-Semitism in any form, active or passive, be it racial, ethnic, national, economic, political, religious, or theological, is all part of the satanic strategy to avoid the second coming.

Second, this study helps to explain why Satan has used one name more than any other name to persecute Jews. Since the fourth century, more than 90 percent of all persecutions against the Jews have been done in the name of Christ. Satan knows the one name they need to call upon for national salvation and the second coming, so he mapped out a strategy to make that name odious in the Jewish community, and indeed it has become odious. The vast majority of Jewish reaction to Jesus today is not based upon a knowledge of the Yeshua of the New Testament, but based upon the Jesus of Jewish and church history, which is not the biblical Jesus at all. Because of such massive persecution in that one name, Jewish reaction toward a Jew who believes in Jesus is much more hostile than to the Jew who accepts Buddhism or even atheism.

This subject of hostility brings us to the third and final point: the need for Jewish evangelism today. Because of Jewish hostility toward the name of Christ, some evangelical groups have adopted the misguided policy of simply being nice to Jewish people but never sharing the gospel with them, under the faulty premise that they have lost the right to do so. There is nothing wrong in being nice to Jewish people and helping Jews move to Israel, but there is everything wrong if these are done at the sacrifice of sharing the gospel. The call of the church is not to help Jews move anywhere, but to present the gospel to the Jew first and also to the Greek.

When Peter declared there was no other name given under heaven whereby one could be saved (Acts 4:12), he was speaking to a Jewish audience—not a Gentile one. Furthermore, he was speaking to Orthodox Jews and not secular Jews. Even the most Orthodox Jews, therefore, will not find salvation apart from conscious faith in the messiahship of Yeshua, who died for their sins and rose again. The Scripture promises there always was and still is a remnant of Israel coming to faith today, but the remnant comes to faith only when they hear and believe the gospel. So at the present time, Jewish evangelism is essential for the sake of building up the remnant of Israel. Seeds planted now may bear fruit used by God to bring the Jewish people as a nation to himself, which is prerequisite to bringing about both the second coming and the messianic kingdom. If the basis of the second coming of the Messiah teaches anything, it teaches the importance of Jewish evangelism both for the present and the future.

12

EVANGELISM AND THE FUTURE OF ISRAEL

BARRY E. HORNER

T he motivation to Jewish evangelism affects the actual fruitful gospel outreach to the Jewish people. Not all such motivation has proved to be legitimate—according to biblical standards. The history of the Christian church is full of declarations of interest in the conversion of the Jews. Yet much of this thrust has been under girded by anti-Judaic presuppositions that, following the conversion of a Jew to saving faith in Jesus Christ as his Messiah, have led to his ongoing humiliation and the eradication of any future Jewish identity. The exception to such eradication of identity would be the use of broad and abstract Judaic terms that apply equally to the converted Gentile as well as the Jew.

Consider the infamous forced conversion of Jews, on pain of death, in Spain and Portugal during the inquisitorial fifteenth century, resulting in *conversos*, or derogatively speaking, *marranos*, that is "pigs," who continued to be humiliated.[1] Was this not motivated by a spirit of evangelism? Note, too, the concern of Napoleon whereby he proposed that the remedy concerning the existence of objectionable Jewry within Europe lay in it being dissolved into Christianity.[2]

In other words, through evangelism, Jewish conversion to Christianity would result in absorption of the Jew into the Christian church and consequently the elimination of Jewish ethnicity, nationality, and territory according to divine covenantal recognition. The end result would then be said to be one homogenous people of God.

Even today those who lean toward favoring absorption would strenuously claim that they believe in Jewish evangelism. They would also assert, somewhat conciliatorily, that while they differ with the eschatology of other Christians—especially those who believe that God has a present and future regard for the Jew ethnically, nationally, and territorially—these differing concerns should not detract from the fulfillment of a common and higher purpose. The proclamation of the gospel to the Jewish people, however one defines this nomination, ought to prevail over eschatological differences. In other words, Christians who subscribe to Augustinian replacement or supersessionist theology, with its inherent denial of divine Jewish ethnicity, nationality, and territory, would nevertheless maintain evangelistic concern for the contemporary unbelieving Jew, however ambiguously or abstractly they might employ this term. Consequently, with a call also being given for the priority of this evangelistic concern, the pro-absorption evangelists would suggest, along with such an overture, the need for a truce over eschatological differences concerning Israel so that first place might be given to the proclamation of Jesus as the Christ to the Jewish people.

Such a conciliatory appeal is, in the main, both sincere and well intentioned. Marten Woudstra, for instance, firmly committed to the Augustinian Reformed tradition, declares that "[t]he church-and-Israel

---

1. Robert S. Wistrich, *Antisemitism: The Longest Hatred* (New York: Pantheon Books, 1991), 35–36, 314.
2. Dan Cohn-Sherbok, *Anti-Semitism: A History* (Sutton, England: Thrupp, Stroud, Gloucestershire, 2002), 182.

question presents all evangelicals, regardless of where they stand with regard to any of the . . . [divergent eschatological] questions, with the challenge to preach the gospel to the Jews."[3]

Such, it seems, was the purpose of the *Willowbank Declaration on the Christian Gospel and the Jewish People*, developed and adopted on April 29, 1989, through the sponsorship of the World Evangelical Fellowship (WEF). Contributing and commending participants represented a broad spectrum of eschatological perspectives. Without doubt all had a genuine interest in proclamation of the gospel to the Jew. As a consequence they attempted to articulate a concerted interest that would necessarily transcend a too precise eschatological estimate of Israel, ethnically, nationally, and territorially, with regard to the present and the future. Some examples from the text make this approach quite obvious, notwithstanding other excellent affirmations and denials.

ARTICLE II.9

> WE AFFIRM THAT the profession of continuing Jewish identity, for which Hebrew Christians have in the past suffered at the hands of both their fellow Jews and Gentile church leaders, was consistent with the Christian Scriptures and with the nature of the church as one body in Jesus Christ in which Jews and non-Jews are united.

> WE DENY THAT it is necessary for the Jewish Christians to repudiate their Jewish heritage.

ARTICLE III.12

> WE AFFIRM THAT Jewish people have an ongoing part in God's plan.

> WE DENY THAT indifference to the future of the Jewish people on the part of Christians can ever be justified.

---

3. Marten H. Woudstra, "Israel and the Church: A Case for Continuity," in *Continuity and Discontinuity: Perspectives on the Relationship Between the Old and New Testaments*, ed. John S. Feinberg (Westchester, IL: Crossway, 1988), 237.

ARTICLE III.16

WE AFFIRM THAT the Bible promises that large numbers of Jews will turn to Christ through God's sovereign grace.

WE DENY THAT this prospect renders needless the active proclamation of the gospel to Jewish people in this and every age.

ARTICLE IV.20

WE AFFIRM THAT the church's obligation to share saving knowledge of Christ with the whole human race includes the evangelizing of Jewish people as a priority: "To the Jew first" (Rom. 1:16).

WE DENY THAT dialogue with Jewish people that aims at nothing more than mutual understanding constitutes fulfillment of this obligation.

ARTICLE V.27

WE AFFIRM THAT the Jewish quest for a homeland with secure borders and a just peace has our support.

WE DENY THAT any biblical link between the Jewish people and the land of Israel justifies actions that contradict biblical ethics and constitute oppression of people-groups or individuals.[4]

That the language here endeavors to navigate safely between Scylla and Charybdis is not difficult to discern. In Article 11.9, "Jewish identity" and "Jewish heritage" are not clearly defined, especially with regard to divine covenantal intent. The language here purposely avoids specific certitude. Likewise in Article III.12 there is no specificity concerning how "Jewish people have a part in God's plan." The vagueness satisfies no one who studies Scripture in detail.

---

4. Lausanne Committee for World Evangelization, "The Willowbank Declaration" (1989), http://www.lcje.net/ willowbank.html.

So in Article III.16, allusion to Romans 11 yet leads one to conclude that the details of Paul's passionate eschatological hope need not be regarded as vital in evangelistic proclamation. Even while Article IV.20 gives right emphasis to the priority of Jewish evangelism, the understanding and implications of Romans 1:16 receive no clarification in this regard. Further, the jibe at those who lopsidedly focus on Jewish/Christian understanding at the expense of evangelism makes no mention of those who stress evangelism of the Jews and shy away from compassion for Israel at a social and national level. Then Article V.27 is obviously crafted so as to avoid any specific reference to the land of Israel. The meaning of "homeland" could refer to any parcel of land on planet earth, while there is no indication as to whether the parameters of this territory are determined by Scripture or the United Nations. Further, the negative qualification is subtly slanted so that while "unbiblical actions" are left undefined, the slant intimates allegedly downtrodden Palestinians rather than the unceasing pan-Arab aggression that Israel has endured. Consequently, we question whether in fact such a middle ground best accomplishes the evangelistic purposes of the New Testament, and especially those of Paul. We further question whether church history indicates that this type of evangelical ecumenicity really accomplishes the desired end.

Moreover, has this reductionist approach, while doubtless well intentioned, resulted in a hoped-for awakening, a surge in the realm of Jewish evangelism since *The Willowbank Declaration* was composed. I am not convinced that this is so, and I propose that the desired authentic evangelistic enthusiasm concerning the Jews be rooted in a right understanding of the present and future status of Israel that is necessarily in ethnic, national, and territorial terms. Granted, this conviction resurrects rather than sublimates eschatological differences. Nevertheless, the Judeo-centricity of all of Scripture, and the awakening to Jewish evangelism during the nineteenth and twentieth centuries, provide substantial evidence of what ought to be followed in this twenty-first century. Broadly speaking, and allowing for notable exceptions, the dominant shameful approach toward Jewish evangelism employed during the second through the eighteenth centuries only adds further proof of the present need for Jewish evangelism that acknowledges an authentic regard for Israel, present and future.

HISTORIC MOTIVES

When speaking of enthusiasm for evangelistic outreach toward the Jewish people, exactly what does that mean? As already indicated, the likes of Ambrose, Augustine, Chrysostom, Luther, and others expressed a personal desire for the conversion of the Jews, yet their writing in this regard was filtered through a decidedly shameful anti-Judaic grid. So, too, today those who are still related to this historic tradition want to see the modern Jew saved, and in large numbers, yet at the same time manifest an aversion to things Jewish. The desire of these evangelists is for absorption of Jews into the Christian church, the result being absolution from Jewish identity in any distinctive sense. This absorption is, however, far removed from the passion of Paul. His enthusiasm was born of a Judeo-centric perspective that he did not regard as divinely passé.

Emphasis upon evangelistic outreach toward the Jew has not followed a consistent pattern over the centuries of church history. King Edward I expelled all Jews from England in A.D. 1290, a policy continued until 1655, when a Jewish scholar in Amsterdam, Manasseh Ben Israel, prompted by European persecution, successfully petitioned Oliver Cromwell concerning the Jews' eventual return at a time of great Puritan ferment. Not that all nonconformists were happy with this return of the Jews. British Puritan statesman William Prynne (1600–1669) "stated that the readmission of the Jews to England was against law and public welfare. Prynne also declared that the Jews were the enemies of Christ, usurers, coin clippers, murderers, and crucifiers of children, 'not fit for our land nor yet for our dung hills.'"[5] Because of the persistence of this latent anti-Judaic attitude, "[n]ot until 1858 could a Jew sit in the House of Commons."[6]

At the same time, the seventeenth century Puritan era also witnessed an increased tolerance toward the influx of Jews returning to England. Surely, though, that stimulation of interest was especially concerned with the destiny of the Jewish people from a biblical perspective. Furthermore, there was also a sudden surge in the publi-

---

5. Paul E. Grosser and Edwin G. Halperin, *The Causes and Effects of Anti-Semitism: The Dimensions of Prejudice* (New York: Philosophical Library, 1978), 185.
6. A. E. Thompson, *A Century of Jewish Missions* (New York: Fleming Revell, 1902), 67–68.

cation of biblical writings that included enthusiasm for and criticism of all three of the major millennial opinions. Crawford Gribben enlightens us in this regard as follows:

> If, as [Christopher] Hill claims, English Calvinism was crumbling in the 1590s, then after the 1640s both strict church discipline and Calvinist theology finally "lost their grip": "Calvinism broke down when the Revolution established freedom of discussion." . . . The revolution's literary implications were also enormous. . . . As Thomas Manton noted in 1655, "The press is an excellent means to scatter knowledge, were it not so often abused. All complain there is enough written, and think that now there should be a stop. Indeed, it were well if in this scribbling age there were some restraint. Useless pamphlets are grown almost as great a mischief as the erroneous and profane." Hill has noted, "The collapse of censorship saw a fantastic outpouring of books, pamphlets and newspapers. Before 1640, newspapers were illegal; by 1645 there were 722. Twenty-two books were published in 1640; over 2,000 in 1642. As both sides in the Civil War appealed for support from the ordinary people, the issues at stake had to be discussed. But it went farther than that . . . No old shibboleths were left unchallenged in this unprecedented freedom." Perhaps Owen had been right in hoping "we might have less writing, and more praying."[7]

Thus, from the days of Augustine until the mid-seventeenth century, such freedom of expression was not tolerated, and for this reason the eschatology of Augustine, with its inherent promotion of Jewish humiliation, remained dominant, and the Roman Catholic Church loved to have it so. Consequently the legacy of the Reformation of free Bible enquiry led to subsequent centuries where the Augustinian eschatology still prevailed, yet there developed a consideration of other perspectives. Such was the case with the Pietistic reaction toward cool Lutheran orthodoxy. As a result of Philipp Jakob Spener (1635–1705), a German theologian of Halle, calling for experiential Christianity, an openness to

---

7. Crawford Gribben, *The Puritan Millennium: Literature and Theology, 1550–1682* (Portland, OR: Four Courts Press, 2000), 194–95.

millennialism spread, the result being a more tolerant, indeed loving, attitude toward the Jews.[8] In a similar vein was the esteemed Wilhelmus à Brakel (1635–1711), a Dutch Reformed theologian of Rotterdam, whose philo-Semitism contrasted with the prevailing Dutch Reformed Augustinianism.[9]

Yet while acknowledging these exceptional, more biblical responses to the Jewish people, "It can be demonstrated," William Bjoraker has indicated, "that the last two [nineteenth and twentieth] centuries have witnessed the greatest growth and success of Jewish missions since the first century A.D."[10] Hence we would do well to consider the reasons for this awakening, especially the motivation. In general, Augustinian supersessionist eschatology, by its very nature, did not contribute toward this awakening. Rather, two essential elements were redempto-centric and Judeo-centric perspectives.

REDEMPTO-CENTRIC MOTIVES

A recent volume titled *Standing with Israel* is authored by David Brog, a Jew who writes in defense of contemporary Christian Zionism. As a lawyer, former chief of staff to Senator Arlen Specter, and later staff director of the Senate Judiciary Committee, he encourages skeptical Jews to rethink their doubts about philo-Semitic Christians. There is much in this book that calls for high commendation. One chapter is titled "Motives," in which is described the driving concern whereby so many evangelical believers in Jesus Christ are passionately interested in the Jewish people and their modern rise to national prominence. Brog's estimate of these evangelicals is directed by an understanding of Pat Robertson, Jerry Falwell, John Hagee, Gary Bauer, Ralph Reed, Tom DeLay, Tim LaHaye, Hal Lindsey, as well as such agencies as Bridges for Peace and Moral Majority. It is significant, however, that Brog makes no mention of well-known evangelistic agencies such as

---

8. K. James Stein, *Philipp Jakob Spener, Pietist Patriarch* (Chicago: Convenant Press, 1986), 246–47, 264–65.

9. Wilhelmus à Brakel, *The Christian's Reasonable Service*, 4 vols., trans. Bartel Elshout (Morgan, PA: Soli Deo Gloria Publications, 1992), 4:530–31, 534–35.

10. William Bjoraker, "The Beginning of Modern Jewish Missions in the English-Speaking World," *Mishkan* 1, no. 16 (1992): 60. A. E. Thompson is of a similar opinion (*A Century of Jewish Missions*, 86).

Christian Witness to Israel, The Friends of Israel Gospel Ministry, and Jews for Jesus.

More to the point, it becomes plain that this author seems unconscious of the deepest of all motivations that has driven so many Christians with unapologetic, fervent evangelistic concern, to support the national cause of Israel and individual Jews wherever they are encountered. It is that supreme desire that the Jew might savingly believe in the Lord Jesus as her Messiah, her Savior from sin and wrath, that she might, through faith in Jesus' atoning blood and substitute righteousness, discover the fulfillment of her Jewish heritage in being joined to him and as a result live for him. Perhaps not unexpectedly, Brog has no real conception of this essential, driving passion such as that possessed by the apostle Paul (Rom. 9:3; 2 Cor. 5:14). Concerning Christian philo-Semitism Brog writes, "[F]or most Christian Zionists, no one motive stands alone. Each individual combines these motives—the theological, the moral, and the strategic—in a personal mix with their own particular emphasis."[11] And sad to say, the reason for this lack of discernment here may not be Brog's alone. He frankly understands "that most evangelical Christians *do*, in their heart of hearts, want to see Jews accept Christ."[12] Nevertheless, he seems to be employing "acceptance of Christ" according to that loose, cliché terminology to which he has been exposed and that has become endemic within modern evangelicalism. Then he makes an astonishing comment that ought to be cause for serious thinking among earnest Christians:

Not one of the Jewish leaders interviewed for this book can remember a time when one of their Christian allies attempted to convert them. . . . [A]fter more than three years of attendance at evangelical churches and conferences as an open Jew, I have yet to be subjected to a serious effort to convert me to Christianity.[13]

This honest comment is tragic in its implications. Let me be crystal clear—I do not countenance social indifference toward the modern

---

11. David Brog, *Standing with Israel: Why Christians Support Israel* (Baltimore: Frontline, 2006), 188.
12. Ibid.
13. Ibid., 67–68.

travail of the Jew, whether as Diaspora or the nation of Israel. I spurn that bifurcated approach that separates merciful, material interest in the Jew and his national status from spiritual interest in the saving of his soul. But I also spurn that reverse bifurcated approach that here appears to separate spiritual interest in the saving of a Jew's soul from merciful, material interest in his individual and national status. This being the case, what causes evangelicals in Brog's scenario to be primarily concerned about the Jewish body rather than the Jewish soul? Surely if David Brog had met the apostle Paul in our contemporary situation, it is inconceivable that he would not have been seriously confronted with the gospel through the instrumentality of Scripture. Two vital matters address this most vociferous professed love for Israel yet nevertheless restrict biblical gospel witness to at best a muted whisper. Both matters are derived from Paul's Epistle to the Romans, and provide the answers to the above question.

The Gospel Factor of Romans 3:9–26

Make no mistake—Paul desires the salvation of the Jews. Apostle to the Gentiles though he was, yet on every occasion when he evangelized Gentile territory, he first declared the gospel in the local Jewish synagogue. He never retreated from this priority. So to the church at Rome he expresses the desire that they, together with him, might "move to jealousy my fellow countrymen and save some of them" (Rom. 11:14 NASB). But how are the Jews to be saved? The answer is not difficult to discover, since in Romans 3:9–26 we have the definitive gospel declaration. It is based upon the most devastating revelation of the sinful human predicament in all of Scripture that concerns "both Jews and Greeks" (v. 9). They are all sinners, extensively, without exception (v. 10–12), and at the same time they are all sinners individually, thoroughly, in every part of their being, vs. 13–18. So both Jew and Gentile "are all under sin" (v. 9), that is hopelessly captive to thorough corruption and consequent condemnation.

If Gentiles find it disturbing to hear of this bad news, then it is to be expected that Jews will respond with no less a degree of aggravation. Surely it is for this reason that Paul repeatedly came under physical assault by his Jewish audiences. So today the Jew also needs to learn of his fundamental alienation from God (Isa. 59:2), even if he finds this message offensive (Rom. 9:33). Such an approach is of the very essence of the prophets, and they were killed for it (Matt. 23:37). This aggravation on the part of the Jew in no way means that we should oppose support for Israel at a material and national level, any more than in witnessing to a neighbor who becomes offended by the gospel would we refuse to care for their property and continue to be socially compassionate.

In Romans 3:21–26, Paul continues, based upon the inclusive and individual terms of verses 10–18, to declare the gospel of free justification, which is applicable to "all [who] have sinned," obviously both Jews and Gentiles. Here, then, is the gospel that the Jew needs to hear; it is the gospel by which he may be saved (Rom. 11:14) through faith alone in Jesus as "the hope of Israel" (Acts 28:20). It is the gospel that David Brog has not heard from multitudes of Christians with whom he has interacted. One wonders, then, to what extent this gospel, which these Christians nevertheless personally profess—that of "accepting Christ" as Brog perceives it—reflects Romans 3:9–26. For if those who proclaim a gospel of "accepting Christ" understood this to be the glorious saving message of Romans 3:9–26, then is it likely that they would refrain from commending it to a friendly Jew?

In such a situation, Paul's passion for the gospel would not allow him to contain himself. Here, his gospel message is essentially about the righteousness of God that not only condemns men based upon holy wrath, but also saves them with integrity according to pure grace through the blood atonement of Jesus, the Christ. Yes, this gospel does bring about intimacy of relationship between God and the alienated sinner, but only through terms of reconciliation established through redemption provided by the Lamb of God.

Hence in reaching out to the Jew, the gospel must constrain after the apostolic model, for as Peter and John replied to their captors, "We cannot stop speaking about what we have seen and heard" (Acts 4:20). They were men driven by the power of the gospel, come what may. If this unstoppable, burning desire is not present in a Christian, then there is something lacking in her comprehension of the gospel. It would be unthinkable for Paul to withhold the gospel from Jewish acquaintances because it might offend them and spoil a beautiful friendship. Rather, he would fervently commend the truth of salvation through faith in Jesus, the Messiah, so that fulfilled Jewishness might result. Here, then, is biblical dynamic that thrusts the Christian forth and at the same time, for all of its offensiveness (1 Peter 2:7–8), has an engaging savor about it (2 Cor. 2:14) that is designed to arouse jealousy in the heart of the Jew.

The Jealousy Factor of Romans 11:11, 14

Consider an expanded translation of Romans 11:11. "Therefore I [Paul] raise a further critical question in the light of such ongoing abject unbelief [10:21]. National Israel did not trip or stumble in its earthly pilgrimage so that a fatal, irrevocable fall eventually resulted, did it? Surely not! No, a thousand times, no! Bur rather through their transgression and unbelief salvation has come to the Gentiles for the purpose that the Jews be made jealous [10:19]." But specifically, how are the Gentiles intended to provoke jealousy among the Jews? The intensive *parazēloō* describes aroused jealous desire on account of acknowledged personal poverty, so that "I will make them [Jews of the synagogue of Satan] come and bow down at your feet, and make them know that I have loved you [Philadelphia Gentiles]" (Rev. 3:9). Clearly Paul feels a compulsion to contribute toward this process (vv. 13–14); he must proclaim and demonstrate that with "a [foolish] nation without understanding will I anger you" (10:19; cf. Deut. 32:21), in a way similar to that of the elder brother becoming jealous at the rich grace being poured out upon the repentant prodigal (Luke 15:25–32). Thus the Jews are to become desirous of God's evident blessing poured out upon the Gentiles, not that they might become Gentiles, but fulfilled Jews under their covenant head and Messiah.

What, then, is the record of Christianity over the centuries in witnessing to the Jew? The Augustinian heritage of enforced humiliation, even until today, is largely one of shame, which has resulted in a response of understandable fear on the part of most Jews, and not jealousy. David Larsen comments, "Christian love, instead of arrogance [cf. Rom. 11:11, 18, 31], ought to foster envy or jealousy among the Jews for what Christians possess in [gracious favor from God through] Christ (Rom. 11:11). How frequently has this gracious virtue been in evidence in Christian history or even now?"[14] It will not do for the

---

14. David L. Larsen, "A Celebration of the Lord Our God's Role in the Future of

esteemed Martyn Lloyd-Jones to evade responsibility in history and the present when he comments on Romans 11:11:

> Seeing the blessings of the Gentiles it will create in the Jews a spirit which will make them say 'Well, why are we not getting this blessing?' and that will make them examine the whole question over again and eventually it will bring them back. This had happened, of course, to certain individuals at that time. It has also been happening ever since. But the Apostle's point here is, that a day is coming when it will happen to the Jewish nation as a whole. He is not saying that they [the Jews] were being provoked to jealousy or to emulation there and then, except in the case of individuals. But he is already introducing the big idea that a day is coming when the nation of Israel as a whole will be provoked to jealousy and emulation when they see the blessing of the Gentiles, and that will be the means of bringing them back.[15]

The eschatological emphasis here, which God in his sovereignty will certainly accomplish, is no excuse for broad historic shame and irresponsibility on the part of Gentiles up to the present. When Paul exhorted these Gentile Christians at Rome, "Do not be arrogant toward the [severed] branches" (Rom. 11:18), obviously he was urging compassionate concern for the Jew, both his body and soul, even when confronted with his inveterate unbelief. Why should he do this? Because the God of Abraham, while declaring the Jews to be his enemies for the sake of the Gentiles, yet continues to unshakably and perpetually regard them as "beloved for the sake of the fathers" (Rom. 11:28).

JUDEO-CENTRIC MOTIVES

Concerning the lively topic of the present status of the Jews and the State of Israel, a variety of strong convictions are held among evangelical Christians. Broadly speaking, two perspectives are fiercely debated. First is the Augustinian viewpoint, which has flowed on through

---

Israel," in *Israel: The Land and the People*, ed. H. Wayne House (Grand Rapids: Kregel, 1998), 319.

15. D. Martyn Lloyd-Jones, *Romans, Exposition of Chapter 11 to God's Glory* (Carlisle, PA: Banner of Truth, 1999), 60–61.

centuries of Roman Catholic dominance, the Reformation era, and on to the present day. In this viewpoint, Israel has become superseded or replaced by the Christian church. Some of this persuasion prefer the terminology of *fulfillment* or *absorption*. Nevertheless, all holding this viewpoint agree that national Israel, according to its Old Testament historic status, has become passé in the New Testament era. The church, although inheriting ancient Hebrew imagery, is wholly comprised of spiritual Israelites who are divested of divine Jewish identity that is distinct from Gentile identity. Thus, the modern State of Israel is covenantally not of God. Hence, those of this conviction, while accepting the term *Jew* and *Israel* as acceptable terms for practical purposes in this present turbulent world, nevertheless reject divine recognition of Israel. The most honest of this viewpoint will declare that God is finished with the ethnic Jew forever. Some attempt to believe a divine recognition of ethnicity, but not nationality or territory. Others believe that an eschatological mass conversion of Jews at the end of this age will result in their incorporation into the one redeemed people of God, which will then totally exclude any distinction between Jew and Gentile.

The other major perspective—even older than the Augustinian legacy though not as dominant through the centuries—is the millennial or Jewish restorationist viewpoint. It has been perpetuated by postmillennialism, but chiefly by premillennialism and its subset of dispensationalism. Under this viewpoint, Old Testament definitions of ethnicity, nationality, and territory are perpetuated through the New Testament age and—notwithstanding present rejection of Jesus as the Messiah—the converted nation of Israel will be central in the coming messianic age upon earth when Jesus will be acknowledged as "king over all the earth" (Zech. 14:9). Further, as this present age draws to a close, it will also witness the dispersed Jews' restoration to the land as inviolately covenanted by God to Israel.

Hence, in regard to evangelistic outreach to the Jews, the panorama of Scripture upholds not the disenfranchisement of Augustinianism but the divine perpetuation of the Jewish people and their promised land in the present and on into the future. This perspective is of fundamental importance where evangelistic outreach toward the Jew is concerned. Thus, any attempt at synthesis based upon ambiguous language and avoidance of definition is not a viable or, indeed, a fruitful option.

The Importance of Ethnicity, Nationality, and Territory

That the Augustinian viewpoint faces a problem in the realm of Jewish evangelism is not difficult to grasp considering its belief that God has permanently cast aside all Jews, and thus invalidated his promise of "a land" in which the Jews would dwell as "a great nation" (Gen. 12:1–2). The difficulty arises as to how, in all honesty, he can declare to a Jew, "Let me tell you about the good news of how your believing that Jesus is your personal Messiah will result in your absorption into Christian fellowship that will eliminate any ethnic Jewish identity in the sight of God, both now and forever more." Paul was obviously never faced with such a dilemma in his numerous confrontations with the Jews, and herein is an indication that, as a converted Jewish rabbi, he never for a moment considered that he had forfeited his Jewishness. Rather, he confessed it quite often as a present reality (Acts 21:39; 22:3; Rom. 9:3; 11:1).

A vivid illustration of the problem inherent in Augustinianism is revealed in a recording of a recent Baptist conference speaker who was responding during a question-and-answer segment. This scholar, of obvious Augustinian Reformed convictions, had been asked, "Is there a future for national Israel, as national Israel?" His verbatim response included the following:

> I spent a month in Israel a couple of years ago and it was very interesting to see how the Jewish Reformed Baptists have a consciousness of their role as Israel, as ethnic Jews, and they view themselves differently from all of the rest of us Gentiles in a very interesting way. I couldn't exactly put my finger on it. I had some interesting discussions. I remember one young lady was shocked that I didn't think that there was a specific place for the future of national Israel. It just took her off guard that I could possibly even think that. But I am just a dumb Gentile, you know, reading the Bible here in the United States.[16]

How is it conceivable that Christians could attempt church planting in Israel while declaring to the resident Jews that to become a Christian

---

16. The scholar was approached for his approval to reference his name in this incident. He requested, however, that his name not be mentioned.

would involve the loss of their covenanted Jewish identity? Yes, there are Christian churches in Palestine that follow an Augustinian eschatology. They are mainly Palestinian Christians, however, with Eastern Orthodox roots. So Father George Makhlouf, a parish priest of St. George's Greek Orthodox Church in Ramallah, Israel, was asked,

> "How can you argue with the Israeli claim to own this land since God gave it to the Jews in the Old Testament? Israeli Jews have inherited the promises to Abraham, have they not?" He responded, "The church has inherited the promises of Israel. The church is actually the new Israel. What Abraham was promised, Christians now possess because they are Abraham's true spiritual children just as the New Testament teaches."[17]

This stance is classic Augustinianism, which I doubt makes the Israelis jealous. Not surprisingly, they are repulsed by this nullification of what they believe to be their ongoing biblical status.

For all of the difficulties that Christian Zionism has encountered in its support of the Jew, David Brog nevertheless makes a powerful point at the conclusion of *Standing with Israel* when he describes "three vignettes [that] capture the true depth of . . . Christian-Jewish relationships. . . . [The first concerns when] Theodore Herzl, the father of modern Zionism, lay dying. . . . As he lay on his deathbed, Herzl permitted only one visitor from outside of his immediate family. This visitor was William Hechler, Herzl's first Christian ally."[18] It should also be pointed out that when Herzl had been granted an audience with Pope Pius X so that he might obtain support for the cause of a national home for the Jews in Israel, he received an arrogant rebuff and was obviously not made to feel jealous of the pontiff's faith![19]

The second incident concerns Lord Arthur Balfour, the author of the Balfour Declaration, when he also lay on his deathbed. Brog continues,

---

17. Gary M. Burge, *Whose Land? Whose Promise? What Christians Are Not Being Told About Israel and the Palestinians* (Cleveland: Pilgrim Press, 2003), 167.
18. Brog, *Standing with Israel*, 254.
19. Marvin Lowenthal, *Diaries of Theodor Herzl* (New York: Grosset & Dunlap, 1962), 427–30.

Like Herzl, Balfour limited his visitors to his immediate family, but he made one exception. He called for Chaim Weizmann, the Zionist leader who helped persuade Balfour to embrace the Zionist cause. According to Balfour's niece, . . . "No words passed before them, or could pass, for Balfour was very weak, and Dr. Weizmann much overcome."[20]

The third incident takes place in Jerusalem in 1983. Former Prime Minister of Israel, Menachem Begin, had been in seclusion for nine years until the onset of his death in 1992. "During this entire period, Begin allowed only his children, grandchildren, and old comrades from his underground days to visit him. With, of course, one exception: the Reverend Jerry Falwell."[21] However imperfect the witness to Jesus of Nazareth as the Christ may have been represented in all three of these instances, yet here were Christians with warm relationships involving significant Jews, relationships that drew closer by far to the spirit of Romans 11:11, 18, 31 than ever did the disenfranchising and belittling heritage of Augustinianism. The fact that all three professing Christians here were restorationist in their theology only reinforces the biblical connection between compassion for the Jew and the underpinning of belief in his divine ethnicity, nationality, and territory. Certainly history indicates that to deny this theology in no way has been a stimulus for warm, biblical, fruitful evangelistic outreach toward the Jewish people.

The Importance of Future Destiny in Jewish Evangelism

Charles Haddon Spurgeon, the most published and celebrated preacher of this church age, was not only premillennial in his eschatology[22] but also restorationist with regard to the Jews.[23] His message titled "The Restoration and Conversion of the Jews" based upon Ezekiel 37:1–10 was delivered at the Metropolitan Tabernacle, London, 1864,

---

20. Brog, *Standing with Israel*, 254
21. Ibid., 255.
22. Refer to Dennis Michael Swanson, *Charles H. Spurgeon and Eschatology: Did He Have a Discernable Millennial Position?* http://www.spurgeon.org/eschat.htm (December 2006).
23. C. H. Spurgeon, *Metropolitan Tabernacle Pulpit*, Sermons, Ages Software 10:582; 18:1050; 23:1362; 30:1805; 33:1954; 34:2036; 2046; 50:2910.

in aid of the British Society for the Propagation of the Gospel Amongst the Jews. It is straightforward, unapologetic, and evangelistic in tone. In terms of making a winsome approach toward the Jew, Spurgeon declares,

> The text says we are to prophesy, and assuredly every missionary to the Jews should especially keep God's prophecies very prominently before the public eye. It seems to me that one way in which the Jewish mind might be laid hold of, would be to remind the Jews right often of that splendid future which both the Old and the New Testaments predict for Israel. Every man has a tender side and a warm heart towards his own nation, and if you tell him that in your standard book there is a revelation made that that nation is to act a grand part in human history, and is, indeed, to take the very highest place in the parliament of nations, then the man's prejudice is on your side, and he listens to you with the greater attention.
>
> But still, the main thing which we have to preach about is Christ. Depend upon it, dear brethren, the best sermons which we ever preach are those which are fullest of Christ Jesus the Son of David and the Son of God; Jesus the suffering Savior by whose stripes we are healed; Jesus able to save unto the uttermost—here is the most suitable subject for Gentiles, and God has fashioned all hearts alike, and therefore, this is also the noblest theme for Jews.[24]

Much later, on a Sunday morning in 1888, Spurgeon preached on Jeremiah 32:41: "Yea, I will rejoice over them to do them good, and I will plant them in this land assuredly with my whole heart and with my whole soul" (KJV). Here, the same point is emphasized that a restorationist understanding of Scripture is an encouragement to Jewish evangelism. Further is the intimation that those who reject this specific eschatological hope ought not to attempt such a hopeless endeavor as witnessing to the Jews while believing that their Jewishness has become invalid!

> We cannot help looking for the restoration of the scattered Israelites to the land which God has given to them by a covenant of salt: we

---

24. Ibid., 10:582, 540.

also look for the time when they shall believe in the Messiah whom they have rejected, and shall rejoice in Jesus of Nazareth, whom to-day they despise. There is great encouragement in prophecy to those who work among the seed of Israel; and it is greatly needed, for of all mission fields it has been commonly represented to be one of the most barren, and upon the work the utmost ridicule has been poured. God has, therefore, supplied our faith with encouragements larger than we have in almost any other direction of service. Let those who believe work on! Those who believe not may give it up. They shall not have the honor of having helped to gather together the ancient nation to which our Lord himself belonged; for be it never forgotten that Jesus was a Jew.[25]

Here then we are introduced to the character of that fervent awakening to evangelistic witness to the Jews, which was earlier identified by William Bjoraker as erupting during the nineteenth and twentieth centuries. Bjoraker rightly makes the point concerning modern Jewish missions when he writes,

Premillennial eschatology asserted that the Jewish people would be restored to the Land of Israel, and there, turn to Messiah. Such a view naturally assures an ongoing concern for the Jews. Its appreciation for Jewish heritage and its support for the state of Israel brings Jews and Christians closer. It reminds the Church of her Jewish roots and prevents anti-Semitism. Relationships can lead to witness and evangelism.[26]

This author provides not the slightest suggestion that Augustinian eschatology made any substantial, enthusiastic contribution during this period. He does point out that a distorted premillennial, restorationist view can hinder evangelism. Nevertheless, for all of the weaknesses that attached to this broad movement, indeed to any evangelistic enterprise, it remains true today that the present investment in Jewish

---

25. Ibid., 34:2036, 545.
26. Bjoraker, "The Beginning of Modern Jewish Missions in the English-Speaking World," *Mishkan* 1, no. 16 (1992): 66.

missions is rooted in the nineteenth century and a definite eschatological slant that was millennial and restorationist. What initiating
Augustinian agencies arose during this same twentieth-century period
resulted in comparable, distinctive enthusiasm, quite apart from mere
creedal affirmation, for the conversion of the Jewish people? Some
Augustianians did become involved in Jewish missions, though not
without voicing their disdain for "foolish and Utopian expectations,"[27]
particularly prompted by the rise of distinctive Plymouth Brethren
eschatology. Bishop Samuel Wadegrave's Bampton Lectures of 1855
titled "New Testament Millennialism" were pointedly of this same critical character, especially since he confessed that the most prominent
subject in his published eschatology, it obviously being Augustinian in
tone, was with regard to the status of "literal Israel."[28]

Rather, time after time it was converted Jews, certainly not eschatological Augustinians, who became founders of such a burgeoning
evangelistic movement. To summarize this involvement, consider
that at the commencement of the nineteenth century, "there was not
a Jewish Mission in existence,"[29] that is until the arrival in England
of Joseph Frey from Germany in 1801. As a Hebrew Christian he is
considered to be the father of modern Jewish missions, and in particular The London Society for Promoting Christianity Amongst the
Jews, or The London Jews Society [LJS], known today as the Church's
Ministry Among the Jews [CMJ], which eventually became an agency
of the Anglican Church. By the end of the nineteenth century, Jewish
mission societies numbered thirty-two in the United States, twenty-
eight in the British Isles, and twenty-one in Europe.[30] A notable feature about this movement is that most of the resultant missionaries
were Hebrew Christians who passionately evangelized their Hebrew
kinsmen.[31] Further, and this we consider to be a most vital matter, they
were in most instances millennial and restorationist in their escha-

---

27. W. T. Gidney, *The History for the London Society for Promoting Christianity Amongst
the Jews, From 1809 to 1908* (London: Palestine House, 1908), 35.
28. Samuel Waldegrave, *New Testament Millennialism* (London: Hamilton, Adams,
and Co., 1855), 547.
29. Thompson, *A Century of Jewish Missions*, 263.
30. Ibid., 277–81.
31. Jacob Gartenhouse, *Famous Hebrew Christians*, rev. ed. (Chattanooga, TN: International Board of Jewish Missions, 1998), 207; Louis Meyer, *Eminent Hebrew*

tology.[32] This was also the case even where Gentile Christians were involved in this same Jewish evangelism. So Robert Murray M'Cheyne, in commenting on Isaiah 62:4 concerning Israel being restored from desolation, declares "that it is literal Israel that is spoken of, for there is a sweet promise to their land."[33] So with regard to the nineteenth century, Kelvin Crombie states,

> [T]here seems little doubt that the awakened evangelical interest and concern for the Jewish people was strongly attached to the concept of Israel's restoration. . . . [Concerning the London Jews Society, it] quickly developed into a major institution. I propose this was due to the strong interest then prevalent in evangelical circles pertaining to the return of Israel to its land. . . . The LJS/CMJ clearly viewed the new Zionist movement in a positive light. . . . [As at 1948], there is much within the previous 140–year period to reveal that this Society had established a very clear, uncompromising attitude toward the connection between the Jewish people and their restoration to Eretz Israel.[34]

George Peters, an American Lutheran, makes the same observation, not only concerning the evangelistic and restorationist convictions of Frey, but also the millenarian character of this movement as a whole. So, according

> to our Pre-Millennarian views, the Jews are more accessible, as evidenced by the conversions of Jews, and the numerous Jewish Pre-Millennarian writers in Europe and this country. Lederer, formerly editor of the *Israelite Indeed* (vol. 8, p. 82), and a missionary among the Jews, after delineating our [premillennarian] doctrine as particularly adapted to reach the Jews, declares that, "Indeed,

---

Christians of the Nineteenth Century: Brief Biographical Sketches, ed. David A. Rausch (New York: Edwin Mellen Press, 1983), 113–19.

32. David A. Rausch, introduction to *Eminent Hebrew Christians of the Nineteenth Century: Brief Biographical Sketches*, by Louis Meyer (New York: Edwin Mellen Press, 1983), xiv–xvi.

33. Andrew Bonar, *Memoir and Remains of Robert Murray M'Cheyne* (Edinburgh: Oliphant, Anderson & Ferrier, 1883), 292.

34. Kelvin Crombie, "Early Christian Zionists: The London Jews Society and the Return to the Land," *Mishkan* 26 (1997): 44, 46, 55.

by the preaching of a full Gospel to the Jews, there have been more Jews converted in the last twenty-five years, than during seventeen centuries of the Christian era. All converted Jews, therefore, with but few exceptions, are Premillenarian." Our most bitter opponents concede that converted Jews are almost exclusively Millenarian.[35]

The question, then, is obvious: Why, according to history, is this eschatological predisposition so evidently fruitful? The answer is abundantly clear in Romans 9–11. Paul, without the slightest equivocation, declares in Romans 9:4 that his brethren, even in unbelief, "are Israelites, to whom belongs the adoption as sons, and the glory and the covenants and the giving of the Law and the temple service and the promises." Thomas Schreiner stresses a crucial point here: "The present tense verb (*eisin*, they are) indicates that the Jews still 'are' Israelites and that all the blessings named still belong to them."[36] In Romans 11:1, Paul makes a related personal point: "I too am an Israelite, a descendant of Abraham, of the tribe of Benjamin." Again he writes in the present tense and here claims his national and territorial inheritance. Then, climactically, in Romans 11:28, the apostle declares that unbelieving national Israel, notwithstanding its present enemy status, remains "beloved for the sake of the fathers," which verse 31 also confirms is a present tense declaration. Here the doctrine of the triumphant sovereignty of covenant grace rings the death knell of Augustinian supersessionism. Here also is the ground of nineteenth-century Jewish evangelism that was motivated by distinctive eschatological conviction about ongoing, valid Judaism. Hence, evangelism cannot be divorced from eschatology, especially with regard to the Jew, for the two elements are interconnected. And when Jews for Jesus erupted onto the twentieth-century scene, this connection was both evident and also fruitful through the ministry of its founder Moishe Rosen. If this linkage between evangelism and eschatology is broken, then life will go out of this movement. If the union remains healthy, then the same abundant increase that broke forth at

---

35. George N. H. Peters, *The Theocratic Kingdom*, 3 vols. (New York: Funk & Wagnalls, 1884), 3:148, 408–9.

36. Thomas R. Schreiner, *Romans*, Baker Exegetical Commentary on the New Testament (Grand Rapids: Baker, 1988), 485.

the commencement of the nineteenth century will follow on into the twenty-first century.

Should the Augustinian object to this claim, then we simply invite him to look at the record of church history. Where has Augustinian eschatology biblically, fervently, lovingly, distinctively, fruitfully initiated gospel witness toward the Jewish people? Quite to the contrary, its record in this regard is one of centuries of shame. Consider, however, the repentance of Professor C. E. B. Cranfield in this regard:

> I confess with shame to having also myself used in print on more than one occasion this language of the replacement of Israel by the Church.
>
> It is only where the church persists in refusing to learn this message [of Romans 9–11], where it secretly—perhaps unconsciously—believes that its own existence is based on human achievement, and so fails to understand God's mercy to itself, that it is unable to believe in God's mercy for still unbelieving Israel, and so entertains the ugly and unscriptural notion that God has cast off His people Israel and simply replaced it by the Christian Church. These three chapters emphatically forbid us to speak of the Church as having once and for all taken the place of the Jewish people.[37]

If such an esteemed scholar can humble himself and change at this point, then we invite others to consider similar eschatological repentance.

---

37. C. E. B. Cranfield, *The Epistle to the Romans*, *II* (Edinburgh: T & T Clark, 1979) 2:448, 448n. 2.

13

THE EVANGELIZATION AND CONVERSION OF THE JEWS IN THE TRIBULATION

An Inquiry and a Proposal

DAVID L. LARSEN

The ongoing of Jewish evangelization and its priority ("to the Jew first," Rom. 1:16) are imperative in the church age in which we live. Few in our times have seen this more clearly than my beloved friend, Moishe Rosen. In modern times, no one has championed such creative and effective ways of winning Jewish people to Christ as has our brother, as he has founded and for so many years directed the unique ministry called Jews for Jesus. It is a privilege to add to this tribute to Moishe.

I foresee a great people-movement to Jesus the Messiah at the end of the age during the eschatological "Messianic woes" or tribulation period, and propose that there is significant biblical evidence to support my proposal. As I lay the evidence before you, it is to recognize and honor the continuity of God's gracious intentions for his ancient covenant people Israel, in contradistinction to the replacement theology and supersessionism, which are increasingly rampant in our time.

JEWISH EVANGELIZATION AND CONVERSION IN THE TRIBULATION: PREDICTIONS IN THE OLD TESTAMENT

The gracious and loving heart of God for all of fallen humankind is clear in Genesis 12:1–3, in what some have called "The Great Commission of the Old Testament," wherein God promises Abraham that "all peoples on earth will be blessed through you" (NIV). Thus, God sovereignly elected Israel as a unique and distinct people, that through them the Savior and sin-bearer would come, the Scriptures would be entrusted, and the task of worldwide witness would be achieved (his witnesses, Isa. 43:10, 12; 44:8).

From Genesis, the growing corpus of predictive messianic prophecy in the Old Testament begins to fill and in and make clear the redeeming and reconciling work of the Messiah to come. The sacrificial system given to Israel underscored the mediation of shed blood as necessary for estranged sinners—both Jews and non-Jews—to enter into fellowship with God. That a merciful God had all of the world in his purview of salvation is obvious in the Old Testament (2 Sam. 22:50; Pss. 18:49; 117:1; Deut. 32:43; Isa. 11:10; Mal. 1:11, etc.). Thus, three-quarters of our Bible focuses on the preparation for Messiah and that unique ethnic instrument God chose.

Israel itself needed salvation and individual forgiveness, although how much an average Israelite understood of the soteriological plan is not altogether clear. Still, Abraham was justified (Gen. 15:6) and saw Messiah's day (John 8:56), King David was forgiven (Pss. 32, 51), and in some sense believing Jews were saved (Rom. 3:25–26). Despite her national failure and rejection of Messiah (John 1:10–11), Israel was not cast on the slag heap of history in final disapprobation. God would keep his unconditional promises to his people. The judgments on Israel have been literal and historical, and so must be the promises.

Supersessionism, the idea that Israel's promised blessings have been transferred to the church, involves us in a most egregious violation of historical-grammatical exegesis. Nothing less than the character of God is involved in the supersessionist theory. The Pauline answer to this canard is clear: "God did not reject his people, whom he foreknew" (Rom. 11:2 NIV [throughout this chapter, unless otherwise specified]). While individual Jews have been converted through the ages (all praise be to God!), there will be a restoration of this people physically to their land, and spiritually to faith in the Messiah in huge numbers in the wrap-up of time-space history. Israel will ultimately fulfill her divine appointment as the worldwide witness to the true and living God and to his Son; the Old Testament predicts this with unequivocal clarity.

We can examine a few of these predictions. One such prediction speaks of the restoration of Israel. It is true that the actual possession of the full promise of landedness (Gen. 17:8) and prosperity in the land are contingent on obedience (Lev. 26:14ff.), and that punishment for disobedience to God is explicit, eventuating in expulsion from the land. But the possibility of forgiveness and restoration for the Diaspora is also clear: "I will not reject them or abhor them so as to destroy them completely, breaking my covenant with them" (Lev. 26:44). Even the pagan seer Balaam in his third oracle saw a restoration and recovery for this people (Num. 24:5–9). Similarly, the Deuteronomic covenant in Deuteronomy 28 traces the anguish of dispersion among the nations but predicts there *will be*—not *may be*—a dramatic reversal, that Israel will return to the Lord and obey him. In the glorious triumph of divine grace, God will restore them and "circumcise their hearts" (Deut. 30:1–10).

To God's covenant people in rebellion, God extends the invitation to come for cleansing and forgiveness (Isa. 1:18), and extends, too, the promise that "in the last days" will come a restoration of the Lord's Temple, and "all nations will stream to it" (Isa. 2:1ff.). Here is a prediction of physical and spiritual restoration set in the context of the apocalyptic "Day of the Lord," that final epoch of divine wrath and judgment of which virtually every prophet speaks (Isa. 2:6ff.). It is my argument that the divided seven years of Daniel 9:24–27 is the yet-to-be experienced final outpouring of "the wrath of the Lamb" upon the inhabitants of the earth in the consummation of the age. But involved in that complex of end-time events is the physical and spiritual recovery of Israel, and all of this in the economy of the undeserved grace of God.

The prophet Jeremiah graphically predicts the physical return to the land (16:14ff.) and the perpetuity of the life of geopolitical Israel (31:35–37). But he also speaks of God's "everlasting love" for his people (31:3–31) and his resultant "new covenant" with those brought back from captivity (31:31–34). This is a radical spiritual renewal, not yet experienced, but one in which the church itself has become a beneficiary (cf. 2 Cor. 3:7ff.; 1 Cor. 11:25, "the new covenant in [his] blood").

The prophet Ezekiel speaks of a great return to the land (36:8ff.) and a spiritual recrudescence of gigantic proportions—sprinkling, cleansing, a new heart, and the Holy Spirit (36:24–27). The vision of life in the death valley (Ezek. 37) is not only national resuscitation but spiritual regeneration: "Then you, my people, will know that I am the Lord. . . . I will put my Spirit in you and you will live" (37:13–14 NIV). The dry bones will live again. This is nothing less than national resurrection.

In Daniel 9:24–27, the prophet describes "the end that is decreed." He predicts that "the ruler who will come" will make a seven-year covenant. But with whom will he make that covenant—unless it be the Jews restored to their land and in a rebuilt Temple, since Daniel decrees "an end to sacrifice and offering" (9:27)? Indeed, when Daniel describes Michael as "the great prince who protects your people," those people can only be the Jews, who rise in "a time of distress such as has not happened from the beginning of the nations until then." This time of distress is most certainly the great tribulation, but, says Daniel, "everyone whose name is found written in the book will be delivered" (Dan. 12:1–3). The evidence that many are led to righteousness in this spiritual revival is difficult to avoid (v. 3).

The prophet Hosea predicts that "in the last days," after extended deprivation, "The Israelites will return and seek the LORD their God and David their king. They will come trembling to the LORD and to his blessings" (Hos. 3:4–5).

This sampling of predictions points to something far more epochal than the return of a meager band of exiles in 539 B.C. The prophet Zechariah, writing after the exile, was still expecting something on a grander scale—a return from "distant lands" with a spiritual remnant (10:9–12). In connection with a final outbreak of anti-Semitism— often the focus of Satan's antipathy to God's great plan of reconciliation in which Israel has been so pivotal—Zechariah sees an outpouring of "a spirit of grace and supplication" upon "the house of David and the inhabitants of Jerusalem" (12:10ff., 13:1ff.). He sees, too, an extraordinary experience of repentance and cleansing, when Israel "looks on me, the one they have pierced" (12:10b; cf. John 19:37).

To detach all of the above promises from the nation Israel and to assign them instead to the experience of the church is to jettison any reasonable notion of authorial intent and a historical-grammatical hermeneutic. These passages must be understood to speak of a great future of turning to Christ by ethnic Israel during a time of acute stress and unparalleled persecution (Zech. 13:8–9). Just how this people-movement to Messiah is brought to pass is not sketched fully, other than the prediction that there will be a witness given to Israel to which she will respond, as Malachi writes in the concluding promise of the Old Testament: "See, I will send you the prophet Elijah before that great and dreadful day of the LORD comes. He will turn the hearts of the fathers to their children, and the hearts of the children to their fathers" (Mal. 4:5–6). Thus it would seem that a solid foundation is laid in the Old Testament for a great future evangelization and conversion of the Jews. But when and how?

JEWISH EVANGELIZATION AND CONVERSION IN THE TRIBULATION: INTIMATIONS IN THE NEW TESTAMENT

As we move into the New Testament, the pressing issue for the matter at hand is the hermeneutic of the writers under the guidance of the Holy Spirit. Do these writers nullify the promises of the perpetuation of Israel as a special ethnic entity and do they revoke the land promises? This is a vital question for all believers in Christ because our own future hope rests on a promise of God. He has given "eternal life" and has promised that it is ours (John 3:16; 3:36). Is this something we can count on, or can the promise of God be abrogated and transferred to someone else? Much is at stake in this investigation.

That God's great redeeming love in Christ reaches out to all humankind is crystal clear (1 Tim. 2:3–6; 2 Peter 3:9; 1 John 2:2). In the church "there is neither Jew nor Greek" (Gal 3:28), but while we are one in Christ, identities have not been erased and distinctions remain. The apostle Paul is still led to address slaves and free, male and female, and Jew and Gentile (1 Cor. 10:32). Jesus our Lord, in proclaiming the kingdom, told his disciples, "Do not go among the Gentiles or enter into any town of the Samaritans. Go rather to the lost sheep of the house of Israel" (Matt. 10:5–6). In the apostle Paul's schema for the church age the Jew still has a special identity, as evidenced by his "first for the Jew" (Rom. 1:16) and "first for the Jew, then for the Gentile" (Rom. 2:9–10).

The witness of the Great Commission in its several forms was for "all nations" (Matt. 28:19–20) and was to begin in Jerusalem and spread "to the ends of the earth" (Acts 1:8). Certainly the Lord Jesus came to offer salvation from sin to all peoples but especially for "his people" (Matt. 1:21). He himself "as to his human nature was a descendent of David" (Rom. 1:3); the apostles were all Jewish; the composition of the earliest church was Jewish. Paul spoke to Agrippa of "the promise our twelve tribes are hoping to see fulfilled" (Acts 26:7), and James writes to "the twelve tribes scattered among the nations" (James 1:1). Not once in the fifty-four references to Israel in the New Testament is the church called Israel. In each instance the point of reference is ethnic Israel, even in Galatians 6:16, where Paul speaks of "the Israel of God." There is no compelling reason to deny that, like the rest of the New Testament examples, this is a reference to geopolitical Israel.

So the Good Shepherd has "other sheep that are not of this sheep pen. I must bring them also. They too will listen to my voice, and there shall be one flock and one shepherd" (John 10:16). These "other sheep" are the Gentile believers, and the "one flock" is a reference to the new people of God, which will include both Jews and Gentiles. The mystery made known to Paul was not that Gentiles would be saved, but that in the new heavenly people of God, "the Gentiles are heirs together with Israel, members together of one body, and sharers together in the promise of Jesus Christ" (Eph. 3:6–9). Paul's argument in Romans 15:27 is that the Gentiles share "in the Jews' spiritual blessings."

But does the inclusion of the Jews in the body of Christ in this age negate "the covenants of promise" from the Old Testament? Does the church supersede Israel, or do they remain prophetically two distinct streams for the manifestation of God's grace and glory? I believe that the data support two distinct entities as the age draws toward a close. In Matthew 10:23, Jesus makes a remarkable prediction to his disciples: "When you are persecuted in one place, flee to another. I tell you the truth, you will not finish going through the cities of Israel before the Son of Man comes." Is our Lord speaking to the disciples as representatives of a future ministry of the church? Surely the reference to the "cities of Israel" rules that out. Is he speaking of the disciples evangelizing Israel until the A.D. 70 destruction of the cities of Israel? Surely the "coming of the Son of Man" did not occur at that time. No, here Jesus addresses his disciples in a well-known manner of speaking sometimes called "prophetic telescoping," which collapses the near and the far into a single prediction. He speaks prophetically to the disciples as representatives of the ministry of an evangelizing remnant of Jews in the throes of fierce persecution in the tribulation period at the age's end.

Another critical passage analogous to Matthew 10:23 contains the words of our Lord to Jerusalem and the Jews: 'Look, your house is left to you desolate. For I tell you, you will not see me again until you say, 'Blessed is he who comes in the name of the Lord'" (Matt. 23:38–39). Clearly a future generation of Jews is in view here, who will welcome Messiah. There were no postresurrection appearances to other than the disciples of Jesus. Thus, a wonderful and gracious future day of national conversion awaits.

And what about the Elijah prediction? John the Baptist said that he was not Elijah (John 1:21). Yet our Lord, in a clear allusion to the Malachi 4:5–6 prophecy of an Elijahn ministry before the consummation of this age, declares, "If you are willing to accept it [i.e., the proffered kingdom of heaven, the theocratic kingdom], he is Elijah who was to come" (Matt. 11:14). The Savior later adds quite baldly, "To be sure, Elijah comes and will *restore* all things. But I tell you, Elijah has already come, and they did not recognize him, but have done to him everything they wished. In the same way the Son of Man is going to suffer at their hands" (Matt. 17:11–13). In other words, the predicted ministry of Elijah with respect to Israel is as yet unfulfilled. The empty chair at Passover awaits Elijah.

Thus, although Jews who believe in Jesus are incorporated into the church, which is Christ's body now, a distinct and defined role for ethnic Israel yet awaits completion in a deferred time and circumstance. How else can we understand our Lord's reference to "the renewal of all things. when the Son of man sits on his glorious throne, you who have followed me will also sit on twelve thrones, judging the twelve tribes of Israel" (Matt. 19:28)? There is more here than that Jews in this age are, along with Gentiles, beneficiaries of the blood of the new covenant poured out for many for the forgiveness of sins (Matt. 26:28). In the promised renewal of which the New Testament often speaks (picking up the language and thrust of Old Testament promises), Israel is not simply absorbed into the new people of God in the age of the church. Israel is a distinct actor on the world stage at the end as God rings down the curtain on history. Indeed, a later generation of God's ancient people will prove receptive to the Messiah's claims (Matt. 21:43). This will involve the evangelization and conversion of the Jews in "the time of Jacob's trouble," as described by Jeremiah: "How awful that day will be! None will be like it. It will be a time of trouble for Jacob, but he will be saved out of it" (30:7). I believe this prophecy is yet to be fulfilled at the time "they will serve the LORD their God and David their king, whom I will raise up for them" (30:9). This passage comports with the idea of David as a co-regent in the restoration (Ezek. 34:23–24, 37:24–25). Thus, the themes of future suffering, salvation, and service are steady.

Threads of both the destruction of Jerusalem and the return of Christ in power and glory are to be found in the rich tapestry of the Olivet Discourse of our Lord just prior to Calvary. Luke enunciates the defining principle: "Jerusalem will be trampled on by the Gentiles until the times of the Gentiles are fulfilled" (Luke 21:24). While we may be approaching the end of "the times of the Gentiles," we are not there yet. We are still living in the time described by Paul in Romans 11:25b: "Israel has experienced a hardening in part *until* the full number of the Gentiles has come in" (emphasis added). Clearly this is referring to events in the eschaton since the return of Christ in power and glory is so movingly portrayed (21:27–28).

In Matthew's record, our Lord Jesus addresses issues of "the end still to come" (Matt. 24:6, "the beginning of birth pains" [v. 8]). Again, as in 10:23, Jesus speaks to his own as representing his witnesses in a great upsurge of persecution and deception in the final scenario. But the Jewish remnant in the tribulation period will complete the work entrusted to Israel: "And this gospel of the kingdom will be preached in the whole world as a testimony to the nations, and then the end will come" (24:14). In this time-frame, the "abomination that causes desolation" will be set up in the Temple (Dan. 9:24–27), and with the breaking of the seven-year covenant by the anti-Messiah at the midpoint, a worldwide wave of anti-Semitism will threaten the testimony (cf. Rev. 12:13ff.).

Jesus speaks of "great tribulation such as was not since the beginning of the world to this time, no, nor ever shall be" (24:21 AV). The undeniable Jewish cast to the passage with its prescription to those in Judea and to avoid flight on the Sabbath (24:16, 20) are hard to explain other than by understanding a converting and evangelizing Jewish presence in a time of unequaled distress in human history. The time will, in fact, be so arduous that Jesus declaims, "If those days had not been cut short, no one would survive, but for the sake of the elect those days will be shortened," that is, limited to the last three and one half-years of the detached seven-year period called the tribulation or "the time of Jacob's trouble." These elect (saved Israel, I believe) will be gathered when Christ comes "on the clouds of the sky, with power and great glory" (24:30–31). The bridal church will, I contend, be in heaven with her Lord at the time of this inferno of judgment and suffering. But a Jewish presence and Jewish ministry will be active at the time of the end. God is not through with the Jews!

At the judgment of the Gentile nations after Christ's return, a critical issue is the Savior's "brothers." Who are these who have come out of a grueling time of privation, imprisonment, hunger, destitution, and anguish (25:34–35)? The millennial earth will be populated largely by the sheep on Christ's right hand, who graciously ministered to these evangelists because they—the sheep—were receptive to the message that was being promulgated around the world.

Lest anyone be in doubt about the restoration of the nation Israel, when the carefully tutored followers of Jesus in the forty days after the resurrection had learned about the kingdom of God from the Savior's own lips, they asked, "Lord, are you at this time going to restore the kingdom to Israel?" (Acts 1:6). Jesus did not rebuke them or give them a failing grade. He did not challenge the premise of their question. It seemed a logical and natural question, but he says that they are not to know the time or dates but to be prepared for witness (1:7). Further, on the day after the Pentecostal effusion, Peter, in calling for repentance, indicates "the times of refreshing" (3:19) are at hand, but that Christ will be sent (even as the angel foretold, 1:11). But he will remain in heaven "until the time comes for God to restore everything, as he promised long ago through his holy prophets" (3:20–21). The prospect of a full restoration fuses with Matthew 19:28 and Acts 1:6, a reality in which Israel as an ethnic people has a determined destiny and function.

The apostle Paul in Romans 11 sheds much light on this future development, and great care ought to be exercised in its analysis. As background to this chapter, recall that the subject in Romans 9 is the election of Israel from among the nations for unique function and purpose in God's plan. In Romans 10 we read of the failure of Israel as a whole to receive the good news (10:16ff.). Romans 11 shows that God's electing purpose for Israel will not be ultimately thwarted or foiled, but that indeed "the elect," the "remnant chosen by grace," "all Israel" would indeed be "saved," and he quotes from Isaiah 59:20–21; 27:9:

> The deliverer will come from Zion;
> he will turn godlessness away from Jacob.
> And this is my covenant with them
> when I take away their sins.

Some have maintained that the reference here is to the salvation of the church, but the text says *Israel*, and the natural branches cut off are Israel. Then the wild olive branches are grafted in, and these are the Gentiles. "Did God reject his people?" (11:1). The answer is incontestably "No!" "God is able to graft them in again" and he will do so (11:23). Theirs is to be "life from the dead" (11:15). This is because God's call is "irrevocable" (11:29). Now does "irrevocable" mean, in fact, "irrevocable"? Even Augustine and some other amillennialists have conceded that Jews will come to Christ at the end of history, and postmillennialists agree.

But more is set forth here than the enhanced conversion of Jews. There is an ethnic identity described here in which "the natural branches" are not made into "wild olive branches" or vice versa.

National Israel is dealt with on the same principle of "saved by grace through faith," but in a different time and in different circumstances than is the case with the bridal church. Not only the apostle Paul but also James the brother of our Lord, at the Jerusalem Council (Acts 15), relying on the great Amos 9 prophecy, declared that God "at first showed his concern by taking from the Gentiles a people for himself" (15:14). I take this passage to be a description of the church age in which we live, and what Paul as the Apostle to the Gentiles spearheaded in his missionary journeys described in the Book of Acts. Then "after these things," the next step takes place in the working out of the divine purpose. "David's fallen tent" will be rebuilt. "Its ruins" will be rebuilt and restored. I believe this is a reference to the restoration of God's ancient people, and by no means is there meant here any replacement or supersession. And this is done in order that—note the purpose clause—"the remnant of men may seek the Lord, and all the Gentiles who bear my name, says the Lord, who does these things that have been known for ages" (15:16–18).

The purpose of Israel's restoration, then, is a great outcropping of evangelism and conversion during the tribulation period. Evangelization is always uppermost in the mind and heart of our God—in Old Testament times, in the church age, in the tribulation and the millennium. God wants people to come to know him, and the Israelitish nation is a tool and instrument God intends to use mightily toward that end. How all of these Old Testament predictions and New Testament intimations come together in the end, I now propose.

JEWISH EVANGELIZATION AND CONVERSION IN THE TRIBULATION: ACTUALIZATION IN JOHN'S REVELATION

The unveiling of Jesus Christ, or the book of Revelation as we have it, is a fitting end piece for our noncontradictory Holy Scripture. It is the book of outcomes. As one brother confessed in explaining why he loved Revelation so much, "It shows that Jesus is going to win!" Preterists and others have held that it describes the destruction of Jerusalem in A.D. 70 and thus must be dated before that conflagration. The overwhelming evidence is for the authorship of the book by the apostle John at the end of the first century. God gave this remarkable disclosure to John "to show his servants what must soon take place"

(Rev. 1:1 NIV), reflecting the expectancy in the early church of the imminent return of Christ. The contents of the book are laid out as "what you have seen" (the vision of the living Christ in chapter 1), "what is now" (the letters to the seven churches of Asia Minor encompassing the church age), and "what will take place later" (events in connection with the final consummation of history;1:19). Thus a futuristic interpretation is consonant with the representations of the book about the Antichrist, the final political and religious collectivisms, the final battle of Armageddon, the return of Christ in power and glory to set up his millennial kingdom and then the new heaven and the new earth. The events complete the kaleidoscope of the Bible from "paradise lost" in Genesis to "paradise regained" in Revelation. They constitute the fitting and fine capstone, which completes the biblical canon.

Here, too, our continuing inquiry finds "the saints" of God (8:3–4; 11:18; 13:7, 10; 14:12; 16:6; 17:6, etc.)—who, in our understanding, include ethnic Israel—and a description of the further and climactic evangelization and conversion of the Jews in the tribulation. I do not believe the church is found in the tribulation (cf. 1 Thess. 1:10; 5:9) as detailed from Revelation 6 to 19. We have the church age in Revelation 2–3, the twenty-four elders (the brace of the Old Testament saints and the church) in heaven around the throne, and then the marriage supper of the Lamb set forth in Revelation 19:6–9. The church is not in this concatenation of woe and judgment and wrath, but is in heaven, in the place promised and prepared by her divine Savior and Lord (John 14:1–3). She is at the *bema* and then relishing the marriage supper. If Revelation 2–3 describe seven actual local assemblies in Asia Minor in the first century and also cross-sectional analyses of assemblies of believers in any age, I am persuaded there is also at a tertiary level a broad anticipation of different periods and phases of the age-long history of the church. So the Philadelphian church (3:7–13) co-exists with the largely moribund church of the Reformation (3:1-6) and on into the apostate assemblies of the end time (3:14–21), at the barricaded entrance of which stands our Lord Jesus. Philadelphia is the church of missions and revival before whom the risen Christ sets an open door of opportunity and ministry (3:8), and to whom he gives the promise that she will be extricated out of "the hour of trial that is going to come upon the whole world to test those who live on the earth" (3:10)—the latter used eight times in the book as code for those upon whom the "wrath of the Lamb" is legitimately and lethally poured out (cf. Luke 21:36).

This faithful "little flock," which has entered the Lord's open door of ministry opportunity, will also enter "a door standing open in heaven" (4:1-2) to take their places with the cloistered ranks of angels to praise and glorify the Lord around his throne. The bridal church is translated to heaven—as inferred from 1 Thessalonians 4:13–18, the classic paragraph on the rapture—and is a nonfactor in the seven years of penultimate rebellion against God led by the satanic trinity— the Dragon (Satan), the Beast, and the False Prophet. I take it that the Man of Sin cannot be revealed until the restrainer—the Holy Spirit in his dispensational fullness through the church— is removed from this hindering role (2 Thess. 2:7–9). The Spirit's restraining influence being removed is not to say that the ever-present Holy Spirit ceases to fulfill his pre-Pentecostal ministry of conversion and testimony to Christ. I therefore commend the understanding of "the saints" in the book of Revelation to be evangelized and converted Jews as well as those who are won to Christ through their testimony in the tribulation since God purposes salvation in that complex of events at the end of history, as he does in all times and periods.

The stubborn fact remains that ethnic Israel, different from the church, continues to be prime actor and player on the stage of the tribulation trauma as described in Revelation. Israel has not disappeared or been absorbed into the church. Thus, even as early as chapter 1—where "those who pierced him" (1:7) are clearly differentiated from "all the peoples of the earth" who will mourn the returning Son of Man—we have prima facie evidence of the distinct identity of Israel. Like disobedient Jonah, Israel has been cast into the stormy sea, but has been preserved in the belly of the fish to be spit up upon dry land (return to *eretz Israel*) and commanded again to bear their witness and testimony with a glorious Gentile response!

As the worldwide exploits of the Antichrist "bent on conquest" are elaborated in Revelation 6, we meet the 144,000 who are sealed "from all the tribes of Israel' (7:1-8). I do not think the 144,000 are the Seventh-Day Adventists (as they hold), or the elite of the elect of the Jehovah's Witnesses, or even the church. If that were so, from which tribe, then, are the rest of us? No, these 144,000 are Jews, and I believe they are the vanguard of the Jews who will be saved in the tribulation. In my view the "great multitude" coming "out of the great tribulation" having "washed their robes and making them white in the blood of the Lamb" are, in fact, great numbers of Gentiles who will be converted through testimony of the converted Jews (7:9–17). The woman of Revelation 12 is not the church, or the Roman Catholic Church, or Mary Baker Glover Patterson Eddy. She who brings forth the man child is Israel: "For to us a child is born, to us a son is given" (Isa. 9:6). The Dragon is enraged and makes "war against the rest of her offspring"—her spiritual progeny, saved Gentiles—who must in most cases lay down their lives for Christ since they will not take the mark of the Beast (Rev. 12:17).

The 144,000 reappear in Revelation 14 (distinct from the angelic host and the twenty-four elders) as those who are pure, true followers of Christ and seen as firstfruits to God and the Lamb, the first harvest among God's ancient covenant people in the tribulation (14:3–5). Armageddon is a place in the land given to Abraham. The Holy City glowingly portrayed in Revelation 21–22 is called "The New Jerusalem," and would seem to come down from heaven as "the dwelling of God" like a gigantic space capsule as the residence of the church, just as the new earth is the residence of Israel during the millennium and into eternity future. Fascinatingly, the gates of the Holy City Jerusalem never close, and on those gates "were written the names of the twelve tribes of Israel" (21:12).

To the last page of Holy Writ, then, geopolitical Israel survives and thrives as an identifiable entity. No replacement theology or supersessionism surfaces here. And this for one basic reason articulated by the prophet Malachi:

> "I the LORD do not change. So you, O descendants of Jacob, are not destroyed. Ever since the time of your forefathers you have turned away from my decrees and have not kept them. Return to me, and I will return to you," says the LORD Almighty. (3:6–8)

And for sure they will at last return "and all Israel shall be saved"—not every single Jewish person, but that believing remnant in the last time.

A PROPOSAL

So it would seem that Jews will come to Christ during the tribulation, beginning with the 144,000 and then others, since some Jews will come back to the land and are saved there (cf. Ezek. 37), and others are saved in foreign lands and then will make *aliyah* or return to Israel (cf. Deut. 30). But when and how will this turning to the Messiah take place? It is instigated, in my judgment, with the conversion of the 144,000 at the midpoint of the seven years in circumstances outlined in Revelation 11, and then continues through the last three and one-half years and is completed when Christ returns in power and glory when "every eye sees him."

In relation to a rebuilt Temple in Jerusalem in this time frame (Matt; 24:15f.; 2 Thess. 2:4), two rustic witnesses have an extraordinary ministry of three and a half years (Rev. 11:3), the first half of the seven years. God is never without a witness, and here is the promised ministry of Elijah teamed up with Moses. In my view, LaHaye's and Jenkins's depiction of this ministry is among the most powerful portrayals in the very plausible Left Behind series. Like the two olive trees of Zechariah 4, the witnesses are greatly empowered. To the consternation of the Beast, they have an impact, and he can't seem to stop them until "they have finished their testimony" (11:7). We are all immortal until our work is done. When they are martyred, the forces and minions of the Antichrist are ebullient. Their bodies are exposed on the streets of the city of Jerusalem (again, God is not through with the Jews), and through the wonders of communications satellites the whole world gazes at this triumph of evil (11:9–10)! Earlier students of Bible prophecy have found this representation incredible, but in today's technology this kind of instant awareness of phenomena on the other side of the world is mundane. All praise be to God!

Then the two corpses are resuscitated to stand upon their feet, to the great terror of onlookers around the world (imagine this on CNN with Wolf Blitzer reporting!). The revived witnesses are summoned up to heaven (remember the rapture summons of 4:1) and a powerful earthquake ensues. The survivors are awestruck and afraid and "gave glory to the God of heaven" (11:13; note the use of the prophetic past tense, emphasizing the absolute certainty of these events). Giving glory to God indicates repentance and conversion. The followers of the Beast, however, do not give glory to God (cf. 6:15–17; 9:6, 20–21; 16:9, 11). They will not repent. But 144,000 Jews do turn to the Lord, the vanguard of Romans 11:25–27. Yet more will follow, and a beautiful and magnificent testimony to Jesus the Messiah will be honored by God to the winning of uncounted throngs. No wonder the loud voice in heaven declares: "Now have come the salvation and the power and the kingdom of God, and the authority of his Christ" (12:10). All glory be to our God!

In the valiant succession of Jewish witnesses to the Messiah has stood Moishe Rosen and his wife, Ceil. We rise with them to give praise to God for his Revelation, these specimen pages of Jewish evangelization and conversion, which today but anticipate the glorious climax yet to be in the unfolding of God's great purpose of grace in Jesus Christ to both Jew and Gentile. *Ad Gloriam Dei.*

14

JESUS' RETURN, OUR BLESSED HOPE

DAVID BRICKNER

*At that time the sign of the Son of Man will appear in the sky, and
all the nations of the earth will mourn. They will see the Son of
Man coming on the clouds of the sky, with power and great glory.*
—Matthew 24:30 (NIV)

I am not a spin doctor for God. I can't explain why Jesus hasn't come
before now. He has certainly been welcome. But the fact that he has

"tarried" doesn't mean his soon coming is unimportant or irrelevant to us today. Imagination what the return of Christ could mean, and not just to you and me, but to many others.

Think of those who are sick and in pain, and the pain only increases. They are nowhere near death, and maybe they are hoping that Dr. Kevorkian will make a call on them. Yes, pain does get that bad, and so does uncertainty.

Or think of the young person who is having difficulty facing the future. He somehow can't seem to get his life together, didn't study well in school, didn't complete school, is sensitive, and knows what it means to fail and can see no way of succeeding.

Think of the fifty-year-old woman, divorced by her husband. She hasn't worked in many years. Even her own children avoid her because of her profound depression.

What is the hope for these people? What can they anticipate? What does the future promise them? What should we say? "Cheer up, it could be worse"?

If we in Jewish missions can't get excited about God and what he is doing, what he is going to do, we don't stand a chance about exciting anyone else. While I praise God for the scholarship of others, the thing that I am praying for—for myself, for you, for Messianic congregations, for all those who love Israel, both Jew and Gentile—is that we might become *beholders*, those who can envision the coming of Jesus. I pray that as we talk about him and what his return means, people can look into our eyes and see the reflection of an event.

Earnestness can be faked. Unless we are ready to resign from worldliness and invest all of our hope in Y'shua, we will never be convincing even to our own families. Comfortable and contented servants of God may have a hard time cultivating a longing for the blessed hope.

In a scene from *Fiddler on the Roof*, the Jews of the village of Anatevka have just been told they must leave or risk another pogrom. One of the citizens of the village asks the local rabbi, "Rabbi, for so long we have waited for Messiah. Wouldn't this be a good time for him to come?" The rabbi responds, "We will just have to wait for him somewhere else." Maybe too many have become complacent and contented with just that, waiting for him somewhere else. Or maybe many are too uncertain over what his coming will be like. The following poem from the Middle Ages reflects the sense of ambiguity that Judaism expresses toward the coming of the Messiah:

Hurry, Messiah of God. Why do you tarry?
Behold, they wait for you with flowing tears.
Their tears of blood are like mighty streams.
For you, O Prince, yearns every heart and tongue. . . .
Awake, our Messiah, rise and shine,
Mount a galloping horse, hitch up a royal carriage.
Woe, all my bones are broken and are scattered.
But should you ride an ass, my Lord, here's my advice:

Go back to sleep, our prince, and calm your heart.
Let the end wait and the vision be sealed.[1]

This poem reflects Israel's anxious longing, but at the same time the uncertainty as to the manner in which he will come. Jewish history has, in fact, been marked by some severe conflict concerning the messianic hope. In the Middle Ages, many false pretenders claimed to be the Messiah, leading many astray, and the Jewish community witnessed many tragedies as a result.

The rabbis, as early as in the Talmud, concluded that those who await the Messiah are better off not trying to determine when he will come because too many mistakes might be made. "Cursed be they who calculate the end, because they argue that since the end has arrived, and the Messiah has not come, he will never come" (Sanhedrin 97b).

The rabbis understood that failed expectations would inevitably breed skepticism. But such skepticism will always be. We can't prevent skepticism by trying to squelch the speculation. We will only end up robbing ourselves of the hope God intends us to share with the world.

Could it be that, like the rabbis of the Talmud, we ourselves have minimized the preaching of Christ's return? The apostle Peter likewise understood this problem and told us that in the last days scoffers will come. They will say, "Where is this 'coming' he promised?" (2 Peter 3:3–4). God challenged the prophet Ezekiel, "Son of man, what is this

---

1. Immanuel Haromi, "Sonnet on the Messiah," *The Messiah Texts* (1979): 49.

proverb you have in the land of Israel: 'The days go by and every vision comes to nothing'? Say to them, 'This is what the sovereign LORD says: I am going to put an end to this proverb, and they will no longer quote it in Israel.' Say to them, 'the days are near when every vision will be fulfilled'" (12:22–23 NIV [throughout this chapter]). I believe it is time for us to heed these words. Jewish missions, Messianic congregations, all those who love Israel, we have focused all our energies on preaching the first coming of our Messiah. It is time we invest our energies in proclaiming the second coming of Christ to our Jewish people.

Do we have to wait until a great economic depression and people are starving to point out that the coming of Jesus is a blessed hope? Isn't there is enough spiritual emptiness within people during this time of apparent prosperity? I believe that it is the wealthy people who really know that wealth doesn't bring happiness. I believe it is the prosperous people who feel the most unrealized. The hungry man can have for his blessed hope his next meal, if only he can get one. A prosperous man is not so easily satisfied by the prospects of eating. The poor can imagine money will solve their problems. A wealthy man knows it will not. It is for the well-considered person to realize that life is empty as it is, that life without God is folly and life offers nothing but death.

Yes, if we all lived in Anatevka and the tsar arranged for a demonstration—a few more people killed, a few more houses burned—we might look for the coming of the Messiah. But the crisis of our day is not a pogrom, it is the very fact that we are empty and desolate, lacking direction and wandering in the desert of ordinariness. We have to be willing to shake off the ordinary and embrace the difficult thing if we want to reach this generation for Christ.

Bringing the gospel to the Jewish people, when it is done right, can cause misery in ministry. Jews will have to decide whether Jesus is the Messiah, and misery can be brought to us as we see so many not wanting to hear. A big part of that misery is the frustration that we feel because we have been taught to be polite and not to shout, to be reasonable and not to insist, to be relational and not to proclaim.

I don't know about the rest of you, but as a missionary and a mission leader, I am frustrated by our position in life and the world. God has sent us, and I don't doubt that for one moment, either in my life or in yours. We are to tell the people a message that they think they have already heard and to raise an issue they think they have already decided.

Frankly, if we are to be successful we need to be prepared to shock people into awareness. We need to wake them up, and we need to take a stand way out on a limb. The most influential book in bringing Jews for Christ into the Jesus Revolution—in which our ministry was born and through which so many came to faith in Christ—is and was *The Late Great Planet Earth*. I could cite many examples of Jewish people who have come to Christ through reading that book. I interviewed a couple of them for this book so they could tell what happened in their own words:

Tuvya Zaretsky: "The book was given to me by the stepmother of a guy I grew up with and went to high school with. His name was Dave Brandt. When she gave me the book she'd written in the front cover, 'I'm giving this to you because I cherish you.' We'd never spoken about spiritual issues so I was wondering why she gave me this book. It was some time in the summer of 1970. I didn't want to read the thing. And I actually left it in a closet buried under dirty clothes for several weeks. [I don't know how often Tuvya does his laundry.] I can't tell you what prompted me to pull the book out of the closet, but one evening I started to read it. And I read the whole book that night. The very next morning I got up to go to the campus where I was supposed to be, and there was a sign, a big banner over the cafeteria that said, 'Hal Lindsey author of *Late Great Planet Earth* speaking here tonight.' I'd been praying that God would show me who he is and I really felt that was the answer to my prayer or part of the answer to that prayer. It was only days later that I prayed to receive Jesus."

Loren Jacobs: "I was a freshman in philosophy at Northwestern University. I was also interested in future trends, economic trends, socio-political trends . . . and I happened to see a lecture being advertised around campus on Bible prophecy. As it turned out, that lecture was sponsored by AMF [American Messianic Fellowship]. Dr. John Fischer was the one putting up all the posters around campus. So I went to see this lecture and it happened to be Jimmy

Williams, who is the founder of Probe Ministries, and Jimmy gave a great talk that night on end-times Bible prophecy. He recommended *The Late Great Planet Earth* by Hal Lindsey. So the very next day, I think I cut classes and read most of *The Late Great Planet Earth*. Within about a week after reading the book I had a spiritual awakening . . . a born-again experience . . . and I knew that the Bible was a divinely inspired book, a special communiqué from God that the Messiah was returning to planet earth."

I am sure there are many others who came to Christ through Lindsey's book. Yet wherever you go, whomever you talk to, even those unashamed, unadorned fundamentalists, will say of Hal Lindsey and *The Late Great Planet Earth*, "While I don't agree with his teaching . . ."

Why all of the disclaimers and why all of the denial? Even Moishe Rosen, in whose honor this book is compiled, was approached by Hal Lindsey when he was writing *The Late Great Planet Earth*. Hal wanted Moishe's opinion about the value of the book for Jewish evangelism. Moishe told him at the time he didn't think it was a good idea, that Jews weren't interested in end-times prophecy. Moishe enjoys telling that story as evidence that he doesn't always get it right.

I am not saying that you have to dot all of Hal Lindsey's *i*'s or cross all of his *t*'s or even read his book. But just know one thing; he had the courage to proclaim a message that was widely ridiculed. The usual response by theologians to that kind of urgent proclamation was to smirk up their sleeves. What I am saying is that we are either going to be the smirkers or be the proclaimers. I am not an authority on church history and revivals, but I have heard it before—and find no reason not to believe—that the preaching of the blessed hope, the return of Christ, accompanied every single revival. There is nothing wrong with sermons on how to have a better marriage under Christ, how to raise your kids better under Christ, but a hope for better marriage and obedient children are not the blessed hope. If we really are willing to be the shock troops in the army of God, we have got to come out and boldly say, *"He is coming again!"*

Until recently, I have stayed away from articulating a specific position on eschatology, and Jews for Jesus has not promoted one evangelical viewpoint over another. Convinced as I am, though, that we need to be preaching the second coming, I did write a book on end-times prophecy as an evangelistic tool. It is titled *Future Hope: A Jewish Christian Look at the End of the World.* When it first came out, Jews for Jesus offered this book free to unbelievers through full-page gospel ads, radio commercials, and billboard and subway car ads that read, "The end of the world is no time to finally realize Jesus is the Messiah." We received well over twenty thousand requests for the book, and a good number came to Christ as a result.

There is a great deal of interest in the future. We must not be ashamed to proclaim our blessed hope. But in order to be proclaimers we must first become beholders. We first must be willing to imagine it. How will it happen?

Indulge me, or better yet, imagine with me. The world has reached a climax of military conflict. Seven years of tribulation, seven years of Jacob's trouble have come to a roaring crescendo of bloodshed and violence. All of the nations of the earth are now gathered under the leadership of Antichrist to fight against the nation of Israel, and there is a lethal dagger poised over and pointed at the very heart of the Jewish people. The blood of Jews and Gentiles has filled the valley of Jehoshaphat, and the stench of death and the furious screams of the dying fill the ears of all those gathered in this ancient land. God, who promised that Israel would be his people forever, must come through; otherwise the end is at hand. He must show himself in power and in glory. The hour is upon us. At this point all of Israel cries out in the agony of a people who have come to the very end of themselves. There is nowhere left to turn. Hope is nearly gone.

Then he comes. The Bible gives us the sequence. The first thing you notice is the sound. You hear it before you see him. The sound of battle and the smell of blood have been intruding up until now. But those senses disappear in the overwhelming, overpowering sound of the coming King. "The Lord Himself descends with a shout." What must the shout of the Creator of the universe sound like? It begins not in the ears but in the bones. It reverberates throughout the body, and beyond, through the valleys and over the mountaintops. The rocks and the ground are shaking at his voice. All creatures—humans and animals—are stopped short, interrupted, forced to look skyward.

That sound is then joined by a second powerful noise, "the voice of the archangel." What does an archangel sound like? It is certainly otherworldly, not the sound of a human or animal or an instrument. A powerful, unknown sound that weaves itself around the already over-powering shout of the Messiah. Is it beautiful? Melodious? We don't know. But the final sound we hear is the trumpet call of God, the ancient call of the ram's horn, the shofar in all its eerie and penetrating holiness. The Messiah, the archangel, the shofar of God. This trio has overwhelmed all sound, indeed all activity on planet earth. All creatures, man and beast, have stopped moving, their eyes and gaze drawn inexorably skyward. What do they see?

The dark clouds of conflict have been cleared. The smoke of war has rushed away. Light, brighter than the noonday sun, now accompanies the piercing volume of sound to overwhelm human senses. The clouds are rolled back as a scroll. A myriad of angels as well as people fill the sky, but all eyes are fixed on that great hope—the Messiah:

> I saw heaven standing open and there before me was a white horse, whose rider is called Faithful and True. With justice he judges and makes war. His eyes are like blazing fire, and on his head are many crowns. He has a name written on him that no one knows but he himself. He is dressed in a robe dipped in blood, and his name is the Word of God. The armies of heaven were following him, riding on white horses and dressed in fine linen, white and clean. Out of his mouth comes a sharp sword with which to strike down the nations. "He will rule them with an iron scepter." He treads the winepress of the fury of the wrath of God Almighty. On his robe and on his thigh he has this name written: KING OF KINGS AND LORD OF LORDS. (Rev. 19:11–16)

Such a vision with all the blinding light of heaven's glory will do more than stop the conflict. It will bring in an instant the greatest military victory in human history. The war is over before Messiah ever reaches the earth. While he is still descending from the clouds, all foes are vanquished in a single instant. And as the foot of Messiah touches down upon this planet, a total transformation occurs. The very topography of the Middle East is altered. The Mount of Olives east of the city of Jerusalem is his landing zone, and the touch of his foot causes that mountain to split in two.

The desert region to the east and south, known as the Dead Sea region, is transformed into a garden with rivers and flowers and wild-life. The very presence of Messiah begins to transform this tortured, war-torn world into a place of peace and tranquility. But it is not just the planet that is changed. The people are transformed as well. Israel, so long in unbelief, now know who their Messiah is:

> And I will pour out on the house of David and the inhabitants of Jerusalem a spirit of grace and supplication. They will look on me, the one they have pierced, and they will mourn for him as one mourns for an only child, and grieve bitterly for him as one grieves for a firstborn son. . . . On that day a fountain will be opened to the house of David and the inhabitants of Jerusalem, to cleanse them from sin and impurity. (Zech. 12:10; 13:1)

He is the pierced one. His name is Y'shua. He is the one whose birth and death has been the date by which all of human history has been marked. Israel as a nation had turned away from him for two thousand years. There will be no more turning away. He is now acknowledged as the King of Israel and the Savior of the world.

That is our great hope.

Y'shua is coming, and his coming will be personal, physical, visible. We must imagine it. We must let it be the object of our greatest longing. The Associated Press took a poll in the United States on Christian beliefs and the millennium. A surprising 66 percent of Americans polled believe that Jesus will return to the earth at some point in the future, but only 12 percent expect him to come in their lifetimes. Paul in Titus 2 tells us that we should be looking for the blessed hope and glorious appearing of our great God and Savior. What does that mean to be looking?

A large fishing boat was returning to port after several weeks at sea. The men on the boat were gazing eagerly toward the dock, where a group of their loved ones were waiting. The first mate looked through his binoculars and called out, "Sam, I see your wife, Gilda; Ben, your wife, Sue, and your kids are there," and so on. One of the fishermen was anxious because his wife wasn't there to meet him. He left the dock and walked to his home, where he could see the front porch light on. As he opened the door his wife ran to him saying, "I've been waiting for you!" The fisherman replied, "Yes, but the other men's wives were watching for them."

You see, it's not enough for us to leave the front porch light on. We need to watch with expectancy for our Lord. He could come at any time. That doctrine of the immanence of Messiah's return has been neglected, as the Associated Press poll reveals. We miss out on so much by that neglect. There has been so much effort expended among believers in trying to discern the signs of the times and so little effort expended in cultivating a longing for his appearing.

Imagine a woman who works as a flight controller at Kennedy International airport. She is expecting a flight coming in from San Francisco International airport. She knows the details of the flight pattern, the departure time, the arrival time, the approach the plane will take, which runway the plane will land on. Now imagine another woman waiting for the same flight. She isn't in the tower; she is waiting at the gate. She doesn't know the details of the flight pattern or on which runway the plane is landing or even how many passengers are on the plane. But she is eagerly waiting for the flight because on that plane is her fiancé, her beloved, whom she hasn't seen in some time, and she just can't wait for him to walk through that gate and take her in his arms.

Which person would you rather be? We all would like to have more details of our Messiah's return, but much more important is the expectation, the longing, and the joy that hope brings to our hearts. The fact that the glorified, holy Messiah of God could step through the door of heaven at any moment must fill us with an unrelenting and impassioned hope. It is intended by God to be the most pressing, incessant motivation for holy living and aggressive ministry, and the greatest cure for lethargy and apathy.

As we behold his appearing, as we tune our hearts to long for his appearing, our lives and our ministries will be changed by that hope. As Paul said, there is laid up for me a crown of righteousness which the Lord the righteous judge will give to me on that day and not to me only but to all who love his appearing (2 Tim. 4:8). Do we love his appearing? Will we proclaim his appearing with passion and zeal?

Earlier, I mentioned the shofar, the trumpet of God. Stop and think of what good thing you can say about the shriek of a shofar. Can you say it is melodious? Or that it is mellifluous? As a trumpet player, I can tell you that the only virtue of a shofar is that it is loud. There is nothing to commend the tone. But it is loud enough to get the needed attention.

We have to ask ourselves if we have been loud enough in our proclamations. We have to ask ourselves if we have put ourselves in the target of ridicule for earnestly saying and believing that Jesus is coming again. I for one would never attempt to preach on hell unless I could stand with genuine tears in my eyes for those who are going to a Christless eternity. Likewise I would never stand to proclaim the blessed hope unless I could have the trembling excitement of someone who might see him in the next moment.

The early believers in Y'shua coined a unique greeting that reflects this hope. Maranatha . . . "Our Lord, come!" It is time for us to reclaim that first-century greeting. Let us make this to be not only our greeting but also the prayer and conviction of our hearts. Maranatha!